SHATTERED HOPES

SHATTERED
HOPES

A True Crime Story of Marriage,

Murder, Corruption and Cover-up

in the Suburbs

BARBARA SCHAAF

Barricade Books Inc.
NEW YORK

Published by Barricade Books Inc.
61 Fourth Avenue
New York, NY 10003

Distributed by Publishers Group West
4065 Hollis
Emeryville, CA 94608

Printed in the United States of America

Library of Congress Cataloging-in-Publication Data

Schaaf, Barbara C.
    Shattered hopes / by Barbara Schaaf.
        p. cm.
    ISBN 0-9623032-9-1: $18.99
    1. Murder—Illinois—Chicago Metropolitan Area—Case studies. 2. Police corruption—Illinois—Chicago Metropolitan Area—Case studies. 3. Masters, Alan. 4. Masters, Dianne, d. 1982. 5. Trials (Murder)—Illinois—Chicago. I. Title.
HV6534.C4S33 1993
364.1'523'0977311—dc20   93-15904
                                                                 CIP

9 8 7 6 5 4 3 2 1

DEDICATION

In loving memory
of my father
WILLIAM SCHAAF
1906-1990
and of my dear friend
PHILIP DUNNE
1908-1992

When he shall die
Take him and cut him out in little stars
And he will make the face of heaven so fine
That all the world will be in love with night,
And pay no worship to the garish sun.

—SHAKESPEARE

TABLE OF CONTENTS

ACKNOWLEDGMENTS

I crossed paths with Dianne Masters on several occasions in the last few years before her death; our homes were in the same general area, we both were trustees of public boards who attended seminars and good government programs, we had a few friends in common, and there were occasions when we went to the same political fundraisers and cocktail parties. Dianne was at such functions because she was taking a greater interest in political work. I had already decided politics was not the life for me, but it was a good way to get together with old friends.

When I read of her disappearance in March 1982, I could summon up superficial impressions of a bright, attractive, lively woman. We were merely acquaintances who exchanged pleasantries from time to time. To write this book, I felt I had to get to know Dianne in death as I never had in life. The insights of Brigitte Stark, Pat Casey, Mary Nelson, Jim Church, and Gen Capstaff were invaluable in this regard. Also, Dianne revealed much about herself in the many letters which survived her.

I owe a vast debt to the members of the Cook County Sheriff's Police who talked to me both on and off the record, but most especially John and Arlene Reed, and their children, John and Nicole, and Robert and Joan Colby, and their sons, James and Robert. Their patience with my questions about police procedure and how policemen can make family life work was inexhaustible. I do regret that the restrictions placed upon Paul Sabin by the state's attorney's office precluded our discussing anything but Sabin's vital statistics.

Assistant U.S. Attorney Thomas J. Scorza made it clear he would rather do something else, but he wanted the most accurate account possible, so he made himself available, again for what must have seemed interminable questions.

On the defense side, Patrick Tuite was always gracious and forthcoming, as was his aide, Jill Schwartz. William Murphy also extended himself to go over the case with me, and Dennis Berkson was likewise cooperative. I especially appreciate this since all three men knew my book would not depict their clients in a favorable light.

Dr. Robert Stein, Cook County medical examiner, took time from his always heavy workload to give me a delightful interview, and his assistant Joanna Krutulis was an invaluable source. Also in the forensics area, Evidence Technicians Henry Spight and Dan Genty, who covered the crime scene and the autopsy, willingly answered questions about their work. My own doctors, Charles Kratz, D.O., and Mario Irigoyen, M.D., and Don Vaught, former president of the Illinois Pharmacists Association, helped fill in some blanks. Psychologists Marc Boney and Nancy Black were a valuable resource on the battered woman syndrome.

Without the help of Wanda Barnes, Judge James Zagel's court reporter, and Verna Sadock, courtroom artist for WMAQ-TV, I might never have understood the day-to-day mechanics of the federal court system. Donald Walker, Judge Zagel's clerk, was always patient with my queries about hearings and scheduling. Gerri Urbanek, head of the Chicago office of the U.S. Bureau of Prisons, talked me through the complexities of that system. All of this was done without so much as a free lunch—but if these individuals ever find the time, I will be glad to treat them.

My thanks to Sgt. Charles Kitchen for discussing the five-month inquiry he conducted for the Illinois State Police after Dianne's body was found.

Former Sheriff Richard Elrod was gracious and forthcoming, but the same connot be said for his successors, James O'Grady and Michael Sheahan. The latter dispatched his inspector general, Richard Stilling, whose ground rules were unacceptable. He demanded I tell him everything I knew. In return, he could not say he would not lie to me but he would be frank, whatever that means. He also said he did not want his name mentioned in this book, a demand with which I am unable to comply.

Several sources close to the FBI and county investigations wish to go unnamed, but you know who you are and I hope I have kept faith. I also want to acknowledge the trial witnesses who were willing to answer questions about their testimony.

Frank Militello, former mayor of Willow Springs, and his wife, Delores, were a wonderful source of local lore, as was James Ross, who replaced Mikc Corbitt as chief of police. Lee Branham, the incumbent chief in Willow Springs was helpful as well.

I owe many thanks to Janet Bower Masters, Alan Masters' third wife, for her willingness to participate in what was a very difficult experience for her. Her only request was that I do as much as possible to protect the identity of Dianne's daughter, and I hope she will be satisfied with the result.

Ted Nykaza and Kathy Jordan were helpful despite what must have been painful, embarrassing revelations about Ted's life, and I wish them well.

Thanks go to Paul Michael Grieves, retired chief of the Blue Island (Ill.) PD, for meeting with me early on about police procedures and the principal players. Also, to Robert Rosignal and Mark Baldwin of the sheriff's police.

There were some individuals who would rather not have been interviewed but talked to me anyway, including Howard Vanick and Clarke Buckendahl, and I appreciate their doing so.

To the women who spoke to me off the record because of fear they would end up like Dianne, I wish you the strength to get out of your painful situations.

Nietzsche said you cannot look into the abyss without the abyss looking into you, and it is true. I needed a little help from my friends, and they gave it. Sean Arnold, Marc Boney, Elsie Chaitkin, Cris Connor, Amanda Dunne, Elisabeth Dusswald, Jay and Janine Fletcher, Robert Goldsborough, Richard Hunt, Suzy Korytar, Anita and Philip Krapp, Roderick Lane, Lorraine Lorenz, Marian Mizgate, Nancy Ochs, Edward Rosewell, June Seip, Jane Samuelson, Myrna Sasser, Mary Spellman, Bill Stewart, Sam Roberts Stewart, Milo Vasich, Jackie Westcott, and Lora-lee Wike were always ready with support. I also owe my gratitude to members of the Oak Lawn Writers group, of which I am only nominally the leader, and the staff of the Harvey Public Library, especially Jay Kalman, who admirably bore with my computer illiteracy. My lawyer, A. Chandler Warren, Jr., of Los Angeles, was a bulwark as well. And my mother, Mary A. Schaaf, just for being there.

It has been a hard three years, looking into the darkness behind the cheerful facade of suburbia, made more difficult by the loss of dear friends, dead far too soon. But Robert Doig, Lily Hahn, Louis Lerner, Evelyn Nelson, my Aunt Ann Schaaf, Peter Simpson, and Charles Swibel will live on in my mind's eye forever.

July 14, 1993

NOTES ON SOURCES

This book is based on thousands of pages of trial transcripts, legal documents, investigative reports, and countless hours of interviews conducted by the writer with individuals who were involved in the events described. There are no composite characters. Anonymous sources remain anonymous; even though Messrs. Masters, Corbitt, and Keating are confined to prison, there is still great fear in the community. Only four names have been changed: those of Dianne's child, Dianne's lover and his daughter, and a source who resides in an Illinois correctional facility.

It is not possible to know what Dianne actually was thinking on her last ride home; the words that have been put in her head or her mouth are based on her conversations with others or her own writings. Other dialogue is based on trial transcripts and interviews.

In those instances where testimony and recollections conflict or diverge, Occam's razor has been applied to arrive at the most likely explanation, based on the weight of the evidence.

INTRODUCTION

"*It* is worse than a crime; it is a blunder."—JOSEPH FOUCHÉ

*D*ianne Masters turned left onto 123rd Street, driving west toward the building she used to think of as home. The anxiety that was always with her lately increased, although for part of the evening, while she was carrying out her duties as vice chairman of the Moraine Valley Community College (MVCC) Board of Trustees, she had been able to wrestle it down to a small nagging feeling in the pit of her stomach.

Going to the Village Courtyard in Palos after the meeting with a handful of fellow trustees, faculty members, and staff had helped, too, despite the scare when she saw a bar patron who resembled one of the men she was sure had been following her. Another woman in the college party had taken care of that by whisking the man out on the postage-size floor and dancing the pants off him. "He's harmless," she whispered to Dianne when the music stopped, "just a salesman with two left feet."

Dianne smiled at the memory. She was grateful that her friends accepted her fears as legitimate and not just some paranoid female delusion. She felt a premonitory flutter in her stomach. On the other hand, it was frightening that no one seemed to doubt that Alan was capable of almost anything. She did not want to think about the downside right now. It would be best to concentrate only on her hopes for the future.

The woman who checked out the bar patron already lived in the Oak Hills development where Dianne had recently picked out

17

a condo for herself and her four-and-one-half-year-old daughter, Georgianna. They would move later this month, as soon as the divorce process began in the courts.

Georgianna would still be close to her friends, and there would be new playmates as well. The complex was a planned development built around a golf course. Now that the population of the Chicago metropolitan area had exploded away from the city, many of the southwest suburban golf links shared the greens and fairways with residences. Besides the golf course and a well-known restaurant, Oak Hills offered a swimming pool and playground, with horseback riding and tennis nearby. Just perfect for both of them. Fresh and new.

Of course, they'd miss the house. For a while, Dianne had hoped she would be able to keep it. She'd found it, decorated it, loved it, almost as if it were a living thing. Until two years ago, the house had been hers alone on the deed. Then, after ten years of promises, she and Alan were finally married. Within a few days, Alan had her sign a document placing the property in joint tenancy with him.

What a fool she had been to do that. If only she had not...he could still have tried to claim an interest, but she would have been in a stronger position to hold on to the house. Then she would not have to uproot their daughter. She had tried to talk to him about it rationally just a few weeks ago. Despite all that had happened, there was something in her that refused to believe she could not reach him, make him understand that whatever they had between them was long gone and their situation was unhealthy for both of them as well as their daughter.

She had talked about how much she hated to leave her flowers, the garden she had tended so faithfully, the back-breaking work she had put in so that there would be different blooms throughout the growing season. She saw it as a metaphor for their relationship, something that could be salvaged. Alan either could not or would not understand, no matter how hard she tried to explain. When she tried to establish what her therapist called a meaningful dialogue, she found herself conducting a monologue. That is, if she was lucky, she was talking to herself. During a recent attempt, Alan erupted, saying, "Dianne, you are going to need flowers soon. You want this house? You will live in this house until you die." She shivered, even though the Cadillac had a wonderful heater.

She knew she had to be the one to make the move. He would never leave. Back on February 1, Alan promised that if she agreed to his staying just one more month, he would move out permanently. His self-imposed deadline came and and he did not go, and when she confronted him on March 4, he said that if she would just wait until Sunday, March 7, he would leave. That was almost two weeks ago, and he showed no sign of packing his bags or finding another place to live. If it were up to him, they would live together in misery until one of them died.

Dianne winced, remembering all those years when marrying Alan had been her dearest wish, the answer to all her troubles. By the time it finally happened, she already had doubts; "We're probably one of the only couples to see a marriage counselor before the wedding," she thought ruefully. When the wedding day arrived, she had gone through with it mostly for Georgianna's sake, so that the child would have a legal father.

"Let's be honest, Dianne," she said to herself, "two years ago there was still a part of you that clung to the hope that you could somehow make it work." Dianne now saw that for what it was: wishful thinking. By the time the Masters' second wedding anniversary came up next week on March 25, the divorce complaint would be filed, and Dianne and Georgianna would be gone.

Unless something terrible happened... the day before yesterday, Dianne had visited her close friend Pat Casey, and they had discussed the situation. Pat was afraid for her. "Do you know what you are up against?" she asked.

"I know I am taking a calculated risk," Dianne replied. "But I can't survive living with him any longer. I have to take this chance.

For myself. For Georgie." The unspoken question was whether Alan would let her survive leaving him.

Glancing at the dashboard clock, Dianne saw it read a few minutes after l a.m. Three more days till her lawyer returned from vacation and filed the divorce and custody suits. Three more days, then free at last.

Lord, it was dark tonight. The stretch of road between the restaurant and her home was not heavily traveled at the busiest of times. There were few streetlights. The only illumination was provided by the headlights of other cars. Much of the surrounding land was given over to forest preserves, and the few scattered houses were set well back from the road. Given the lateness of the hour, most of them were in darkness and what little light they gave was missing, too.

Usually Dianne took pleasure in the feeling of being out in a forest, away from civilization, especially enjoying the knowledge that such rustication lay just a few miles outside the Chicago city limits. Palos prided itself on large, comfortable homes in secluded, woodsy settings. But tonight the trees seemed to press up to the shoulder of the roadway, and without their leaves, they loomed tall and crooked, spiky and menacing. She had driven this route hundreds of times, but it had never before seemed quite so dark and deserted, even sinister. Without realizing it, she tightened her grip on the wheel.

Suddenly she felt incredibly weary. Chances were good that Alan would be asleep in his own room when she got home, or if he could find a sitter for Georgie, perhaps he might even have gone out. Communication had always been a big problem between them, and these days they led completely separate lives. Whatever the case, she hoped she could get to bed without another confrontation with her soon-to-be ex-husband.

Not that Alan accepted the fact that she was going to go through with the divorce. No matter what she said, he just could not believe that he could not argue or threaten her into staying. In the past, he would have tried to bring about a reconciliation by buying her something. Semiprecious gems, furs, a new car, a cruise, a condo in Florida. None of the above would change her mind this time. Sometimes she felt a little sorry for him; after all, material things had worked so well before. She blamed herself for that, for being so desperate that she mistook possessions for true affection.

Pity for Alan did not last long; just as she began to feel a little warm toward him, he would do something to terrorize her. Although his verbal abuse frightened her, talk was better than physical violence. It had been a while since Alan had struck her, but she could tell by the look in his eyes that he thought of it often.

Cringing, she remembered the time when, pregnant with Georgianna, she had to jump off a balcony to get away from his blows, spraining an ankle in the process.

She had been so relieved when he moved out in January. However, after only a couple of weeks of relative peace, he was back again with his promises of not staying long. Her lawyer said Dianne could not leave until the papers were filed without endangering her case's settlement. She knew she owed it to Georgianna to stick it out and get the best deal possible, but even when Alan wasn't home, Dianne felt trapped and nervous.

Lately she had even tried to avoid eating when he was around. Not long ago, he joined her at breakfast, and his company made it seem almost as nasty as being beaten. "I've been thinking about your parents a lot lately," he smirked. "Maybe you'll be seeing them both soon. I've got a feeling you will." Then he gave her a wink so evil that it still gave her chills just remembering it. She had told friends about it; everyone knew her mother and father were dead.

It had been a little more than a month since he threatened to destroy her rather than let her leave. He had repeated the threat several times subsequently. Most of the time she didn't think he would dare. Then there were the other times when the words would make her weep and tremble with fear...but she couldn't let herself dwell on that. Her friends and her therapist told her to focus on positive things and all the options that the future held for her. They were right, of course, but only someone who had been in the same position could understand how hard it was.

Her grip on the steering wheel tightened. She was not an unsophisticated girl anymore. She was a woman who had accomplished things, an asset to the community. She had made powerful friends, and they would protect her. Her mantra had become "I'll think about that tomorrow." Philosophy courtesy of Scarlett O'Hara. A tiny smile began to curve her lips. It didn't stay there long.

Dianne studied the rearview mirror intently. The nearest car was a block or two behind her. Suddenly it slowed and missed the green light at the intersection. Usually the men she had come to think of as the watchers were right on her tail, either because they wanted her to know they were there or they were incompetent. Alan was always representing cops who had gotten themselves into trouble for that reason.

Perhaps Alan had given the watchers the night off. She smiled at the thought. More likely they had just gotten sloppy and decided to wait for her at Artie G's, the restaurant the Moraine Valley crowd usually frequented after board meetings. Dianne wondered how they'd explain it to Alan. If he asked where she had gone, she'd just say, "Some new place," in an offhand manner, without giving him a name. She didn't see why she should make it easy for him to torment her.

Back to tomorrow—which was already here. So much for Scarlett. The trouble with tomorrow is that eventually it becomes today and things have to be faced. This one-day-at-a-time approach needed more work. In a few short hours, Dianne would have to be up and out because it was her turn to drive to Jerry Cosentino's campaign office, carpooling with Lee Harris, another Moraine Valley trustee. She hoped Georgianna's babysitter would be prompt; otherwise, Dianne would have to drop the little girl off at a friend's home to be sure she got to nursery school.

Dianne smiled when she thought of Georgianna, the brightest spot in her life. She frequently took the little girl with her during the day so they could spend as much time as possible together. But the hours downtown were too long, even for so well-behaved a child. Maybe tonight the two of them could go to one of those silly pizza restaurants the little girl loved so much. It would be worth enduring the noise just to see Georgianna enjoying herself.

Soon they would be together, and the tension she knew the child was feeling because of the trouble between her parents would lessen. Sometimes, Dianne fretted that the girl was too quiet, too much in the company of doting adults. She had read everything she could find on the subject, and knew that Georgianna might need professional help. She would get it. Besides counseling, Dianne renewed her most important promise: Georgianna would have all the things Dianne never had growing up; maybe someday she would even have a kind, loving father figure. Alan would always have a place in his daughter's life, but his example was not a good one in many ways.

Someone like Jim would be good for Georgie. "He certainly has been good for me," Dianne thought. If an economics professor from an ethnic blue-collar suburb could be described as down home, that was Jim Church. He was warm and kind and easygoing, and most important, he had always listened when Dianne talked. Their relationship had progressed slowly from professional acquaintance to friendship to intimacy.

Jim knew a lot about little girls, too. His own daughter was just two years older than Georgianna, and Dianne respected him for the way he continued to be a constant presence in Emily's life even though his ex-wife had custody. Dianne had spent time with Jim and his daughter, and she was impressed with how bright and happy Emily was. Together, the three of them shared a Valentine's Day luncheon celebration. Dianne gave Emily a copy of Shel Silverstein's *Light in the Attic*, and the poems had delighted the little girl.

Dianne and Jim often discussed how he and his ex-wife had worked together to see that their child suffered as little as possible from their split. Dianne could not expect the same cooperation from Alan, but she would just have to increase her efforts to make up for that.

Dianne was sure Georgianna would take to Jim. He didn't have Alan's money—Dianne knew all too well how much associate professors at the college took home—but he could provide a different kind of security, the emotional kind, that Georgianna needed as much as Dianne did.

Even though Dianne missed Jim at the meeting and afterwards, she recognized that her lawyer was right. It was better for them to cool it, even though evidence of their relationship would have no bearing on the outcome of the divorce or custody suits. It shouldn't, Dianne thought, when Alan was trying to lay everything but the Atlantic cable, even if trying was the operative word. At one time, this had hurt her, but no longer. She just did not care anymore, and his flaunting his infidelities only increased her contempt for him.

Still, Dianne always felt better when Jim was around. He had become a sort of security blanket. She'd have to watch that she didn't cling too much. She needed some warmth in her life. She had to remember Jim was out there and that things would change for her. They would just have to be more discreet. Mary Nelson, Moraine's public relations director, had handed her an envelope from Jim before the meeting began. Dianne had only been able to sneak a few peeks at it, so at least she had something to look forward to when she was home and in bed, all alone.

Another look in the rearview; the closest headlights were still pretty far away. This time, she caught a glimpse of herself. Brigitte Lunde, her oldest friend, told her she was down to a bag of bones, and Brigitte was right. Not much in the way of appetite these days; her ulcers had flared up again, and the fear that was her constant companion did not help. Combine all that with almost perpetual motion, and it was no wonder she was beginning to look drawn and pinched. All that would change when she and Georgianna got out of the house. Peace and quiet and a proper diet, maybe a regular facial—thirty-five was a tricky age—and she'd be back to her old self. No, she'd be better than her old self. "Born again at thirty-five," she thought, grateful she'd at least been able to cling to her sense of humor during the ordeal of the last few months.

Time to turn left onto Wolf Road; she was only about twenty seconds away from home now. The Lt. Joseph Kennedy Jr. School was on the right. She had always planned to volunteer there because they did such fine work with the mentally handicapped. But she had Alan, and the house and the baby, besides recording for the blind, and starting up the crisis center for battered women, and studying to become a parliamentarian, and the college board. "There's still time," she reminded herself, "you've got years and years left."

Suddenly she became aware of a basic human need: the call of nature, and it would have to be answered quickly. Damn. The ulcer medication Dr. Schwemer prescribed did not seem to be helping with the stomach pain that had become a constant companion. Lately everything she drank or ate went right through her. Having your husband tell you he was going to kill you was not good for your gut.

She hoped it was just nerves. An ugly thought popped into her head; what if Alan were putting something in her food? She would be very careful about what she ate. "Could he be doing something to the water?" she wondered. The well water in Palos was too brackish to drink, so the Masters' had a standing order for bottled water to be delivered to the house. "No, it couldn't be the water," she soothed herself. "Georgie drinks it and the maid, too. It would be too risky. And I'm letting my imagination run away with me." Dianne gave herself a mental shake. "Just because you're paranoid, it doesn't mean that someone isn't after you," she said to herself.

Tonight Dianne had only a couple of glasses of white wine and a few sips of water which seemed to be passing quickly through her system. She squirmed a little as the griping pain increased.

Increasingly she had become worried about studies on alcoholism which indicated there might be a genetic predisposition to the disease. A few years ago, she had quit drinking completely for a while. Given the number of alcoholics on both sides of her family, she was grateful that cutting back her intake did not seem a problem. There were enough of those already.

There was that pain again. Better hurry. There was no traffic tonight, and if she were stopped for speeding, it probably would be by one of Alan's pals who patrolled the area. Even if she got a ticket, Alan would fix it. Putting the fix in was Alan's specialty. Her yellow-over-white Cadillac was unusual and well-known to Alan's cops. Yellow was Dianne's favorite color. An acquaintance had once told her at a party that Dianne's color choice indicated she was immature. She did not care. Yellow was such a cheerful color, and she had been in need of cheering up all her life. It was the color of sunrise and morning and new beginnings. If that meant Dianne was immature, she could live with it.

Dianne was a fast but capable driver. "A hollow leg and a lead foot, that's me," she thought as she slowed only slightly to turn into the driveway of the sprawling ranch-style home. She pulled up to the front of the garage and turned off the ignition. She almost never put the car away; the garage was full of Alan's '79 Corvette pacecar and food for the dogs and wild birds Dianne loved so much. The driveway was always well lighted by a reflector flood, and tonight especially she was grateful for that.

A few lights were shining inside as well, but they were on timers. It did not necessarily mean that Alan was waiting up to continue the running battle their brief marriage had become. Hurriedly she unlocked the front door, then fastened it behind her. Just inside, she was greeted by her golden retriever. She smiled as Rusty yawned and stretched. With a promissory pat on his head,

Dianne made a sharp left turn down the hall, heading for the bed-room.

Pausing briefly at the door to her daughter's room, she peeked inside. The girl was sleeping soundly, clutching one of the army of stuffed toys people had showered upon her. The present-giving was almost obscene, between Alan and the sycophants trying to curry his favor. It was not good for Georgianna. Dianne renewed her resolve that she would wrestle it down to healthy levels once the move was complete.

Next stop, the bedroom she had long since ceased to share with Alan. There had been no noise from the other end of the house, the short part of an L, where Alan slept. What a relief! The other two dogs rose as she entered, but there was no time for them yet. She kicked off her shoes as she crossed the threshold into the bathroom, making a mental note to be sure to put them away or the doggies would have a field day.

Shucking off her pantyhose and panties, she proceeded to relieve herself. Around her, the house was quiet. As she finished, she unbuttoned her blouse, wishing she could slip into her nightie and slide between the sheets. But it would be an early morning, and if she took just a few minutes now it would save time then. Before she got ready for bed, she wanted to empty her tote bag of the college meeting papers accumulated earlier—when they said it would be a paper-intensive meeting, they weren't kidding—and put them in their proper file. No matter how tired she was, she tried to be organized. Discipline was important to her. It had gotten her through the most depressing experiences of her life. It would help her get through this one.

As she worked with one hand, she absentmindedly scratched between Rusty's ears. Suddenly, she had the feeling she was being watched. At that same moment, the dog emitted a low, sustained growl. "Probably just Caleb looking for some petting," she thought, "and Rusty doesn't want to share." Turning very slightly, she caught a glimpse of *him* standing in the doorway, with the strangest look on his face, as if he had never seen her before. He said nothing. She decided to remain silent, too; they were long past exchanging pleasantries, and she had no desire to fight with him at this hour. Perhaps he would just go away if she ignored him.

Dianne returned to her paper shuffling, feeling that fist in her vitals again. She couldn't stand it. She had to know. She swung round. He was gone. "Good," she sighed, until that moment not realizing she'd been holding her breath. She bent to load the tote bag with some notes she'd made, suggestions for the Cosentino campaign.

Dianne Masters was so intent on finishing her work and going to bed that she never heard the man's stealthy return. The thick carpeting hid his footsteps as he crossed her room, the long object clasped behind him in case Dianne should hear him and turn around. She was startled when Rusty jumped up into his guard position; it gave her a creepy feeling. She could feel the fine hairs on the back of her neck stand up. Then she heard breathing right behind her. She knew that wheezing sound all too well.

Dianne turned to see him standing above her. She recognized the look in his eyes; she had seen it more than once, but somehow tonight it was worse. She tried to rise, to flee, but she was trapped. He was holding something. Was it a poker from the kitchen fireplace? She never knew. Out of the corner of her eye, she could see Rusty make a valiant leap for whatever it was. Before she could cry out, the blow fell, catching her right above the nose. The dogs were frantic now. Her last thought was one of affection for them.

Dianne Masters never felt the second blow to the back of her head, nor the damage it did above Rusty's eye as he made one final attempt to protect his mistress. Her skull shattered front and back, Dianne Masters slumped unconscious into her chair.

The tall man in the silver-tipped cowboy boots fidgeted in the darkest corner of the dimly lit bar at Artie G's restaurant in Palos Heights. He knew the college board meetings dragged on for hours—bunch of self-important motherfuckers who thought they could save the world by educating it—but c'mon. The last time he followed Dianne, the group arrived a little after 10 p.m. Tonight he had been awaiting his quarry for more than three hours. If they didn't show up soon, it meant they weren't coming at all. Alan was going to shit bricks if Dianne didn't "run away" tonight, and the man didn't like being in on the receiving end of one of the lawyer's epic rages.

Masters had been bitching for weeks now because the first two attempts to get rid of his wife had failed. You couldn't blame Alan—it was almost two years now since he actively began planning to dispose of the bitch.

The man shook his head, taking another pull on the straight stuff he was drinking, remembering all Masters' ranting about how, "You just can't get good help these days." Al was treating them as if they were goddamn secretaries or something, for Chrissake. The man tossed down the rest of his drink; not as if *he* had to worry about a drunk driving stop—he had only to flash his badge.

A humorless grin failed to make the homely pockmarked face more pleasant, even to the two women left at the bar, clearly on the prowl and far gone in drink. Ordinarily he'd take advantage of the situation, but tonight he was working. He thought about the plan once again. As soon as Dianne arrived with the group from the college, he'd slip out to the parking lot to find where she and the boyfriend had parked their cars. Dianne's car was easy with that odd yellow-and-white combination (trust her to be different) and the vanity plate, but they had Howie Vanick to thank for passing along lover boy's license number.

It was easy for the guys who had been stalking Dianne to discover a pattern. The couple drove separately to the restaurant, had a few drinks with the group—white wine, of course, what else— and then they'd usually ride in his car to one of several nearby motels that specialized in the hot sheet trade. Dianne and the boyfriend did not always go to the same place; that would have been too easy. The man and his backup, another suburban copper who'd been stuck out in the parking lot all night, would have gone directly there.

If the couple had been on schedule, the man might have waited until after they had their fun before he grabbed them. Hey, at least they'd check out and off the planet with their next-to-last memories happy ones. But by being late, they lost their chance for one final earthly pleasure. The lovers probably would know what hit them. It was hard to whack two people so quickly. Their bodies would go in the trunk of Dianne's car, which would then be driven to the salvage yard where arrangements had been made to compact the vehicle. Too bad about the car, the man mused; 1978 had been a good year for Cadillacs.

There had been other plans. Some of them had been really goofy. Alan's original idea, dating back to 1980, called for a home invasion/robbery where "burglars" would catch Dianne in the house and kill her and her pets. But the man and his associates persuaded Alan that route had the potential for too many problems. Even with an ironclad alibi, like being in court or some public place, suspicions would be aroused that Al was responsible. Then there was the housekeeper. Or maybe one of Dianne's girlfriends would show up unexpectedly. The guys didn't want to have to kill too many people. Not that they were particularly fastidious, but the more bodies, the more attention the whole thing would attract. The home invasion thing could turn very messy, indeed.

An alternative was to have the men in place when Dianne drove home late one night so they could grab her in the driveway, get her away from the house, and then kill her. They were still trying to iron out the bugs of that one—she was a small woman, but she could scream. Another alternative was the automobile accident scenario, but that was even riskier; maybe she would just be badly injured, not dead, and some passerby might see the whole thing.

They'd discussed abandoning the car in nearby suburban Robbins and letting the shines take the blame. By the time the poor black folks there got finished removing everything of value on the car and opened the trunk to find it filled with human cargo, there would be fingerprints all over the place. Times were tough in Robbins and after the locals stripped the bodies and the trunk there'd be an epidemic of amnesia all over the village. Everyone would believe that Dianne and what's-his-name simply made a wrong turn and were killed when they resisted being robbed. It wasn't a bad idea.

But the man was sure they'd finally hit on the right plan. Whack Dianne and the boyfriend, put 'em in the trunk, and crush the car. All Alan had to do was call his pal Jim Keating, a Cook County Sheriff's Police lieutenant, and cry about how the worthless broad hadn't made it home again. Missing persons wasn't Keating's job, but even if the case officer thought the investigation was for real, he'd soon find out that Dianne's boyfriend was gone, too, and that would be the end of it. Just another cheating wife who ran out on her husband and kid, taking her big car and her jewelry along. Al would get sympathy and wouldn't have to worry about a messy divorce. One less case on the calendar.

It was a good plan, except it wasn't working. Again. The man slid off the barstool with a sigh and headed toward the public telephones outside the restrooms. They'd agreed not to use the phone just in case someone checked, but under the circumstances, there was no other choice. He had to tell Masters that the third time hadn't been lucky. Besides, since nothing had happened to Dianne, there would be no investigation.

Someone picked up the phone but didn't say anything. The man could hear heavy breathing, and he knew who it was. "Listen, I just wanted to let you know, Dianne never made it here," he advised in low tones.

"You screwed up! She made it *here*! I did your job, so don't expect the full fee," came the screeched response. "If you want to make any money at all, get over here now. We've got to get rid of her before the kid wakes up."

"Stay calm. I'll be there right away," the man said soothingly, then hung up the phone. What a balls-up, he thought as he hurried to join his cahout in the parking lot. Oh, well, improvising in tough situations was his specialty.

Early on Friday morning, Alan Masters' problem wife became Mike Corbitt's problem body, but not for long. The Willow Springs police chief picked up Dianne's car outside the Blue Front Tavern as arranged, but the timetable was way off, and Corbitt didn't like it. The agreement with the owner of the chop shop was to deliver the Cadillac for crushing as close to midnight as possible so that no workers would be around to see the car compacted. The chop shop owner had not been told there was a body involved, and with any luck, he never would know, not that he would talk. It would not do to make the guy too nervous, though. The car would be reported missing along with Dianne early in the morning, and the fewer people who saw it, the better. It was just possible Corbitt could make it there under the wire.

Maybe now Alan could get over his obsession with Dianne, sometimes trying to get her back and others, wanting to kill her before she went into divorce court. Maybe now they could return to really important matters—bribery, racketeering, case fixing, arranging protection for the whores and bookies, the usual. Sin was wonderfully rewarding for anyone who knew how to make it work. Dianne shouldn't have threatened to blow the whistle on what she knew, not that she knew everything. Really, Dianne had committed suicide.

It wouldn't hurt him to have a little something extra on Al, as insurance for the future. She'd made herself obnoxious. Tried to tell Al you should never get too hung up on one broad when there were so many available... Suddenly the big car lurched to one side with a flapping noise. Shit! Without even getting out to look,

Corbitt knew he had a flat tire. March 19 was the Feast of Saint Joseph, and it obviously was going to be one of those days when absolutely nothing went right.

A glance at the heavens confirmed his worst fears: the sky was getting lighter. Definitely lighter. Morning wasn't far off, and Corbitt couldn't afford to be seen driving the car, much less changing the tire. There was very little traffic, but someone might pass by and remember later that, hey, I saw a big guy fixing a flat on that Caddie, DGM 19, and there was this body in the trunk. Not that Corbitt changed tires anymore. He had other people do that. But in this case, he was on his own. He couldn't call one of his loyal subordinates for the same reason.

Lucky it wasn't a blowout, because if Corbitt drove carefully, he could make it to a private garage where he sometimes stashed things that needed to be hidden for a while. He was on injury leave from the Willow Springs PD, so he'd have all day to plan how to get rid of it after dark. No need to tell Masters or Keating about it. They weren't supposed to talk anyway; Al would be too busy playing the worried husband, and Keating, the concerned friend. What they didn't know wouldn't hurt Corbitt.

SATURDAY, DECEMBER 11, 1982

*T*he two scuba divers suited up on the bank of the Chicago Sanitary and Ship Canal under the watchful eyes of James Ross, chief of police of Willow Springs, and a few members of his tiny force which served the suburb southwest of Chicago.

As they prepared for their first dive that Saturday morning, the men joked that a better name would be the Unsanitary and Shit

Canal. The man-made waterway was 160 feet wide and 25 feet deep, and as its official name implies, it served two purposes. It was built to connect Lake Michigan with the Mississippi River for shipping, and it allowed Chicago to send its effluent downriver leaving Lake Michigan relatively pure. The canal accommodated flat-bottomed barges with a shallow draught and was so polluted that any one luckless enough to topple in without protective clothing had to submit to a series of shots for health reasons.

An early traveler declared the topography around Chicago fatiguing in its monotony, and aside from the sometimes dazzling lake on the east, there is little to catch the eye, with the exception of a series of ridges just outside the city limits. These ridges, or moraines, together with stone formations, ponds, sloughs, and riverbeds, are the leavings of the glaciers which once covered the area.

The Village of Willow Springs, like Chicago, was established because of its location on a waterway. Weary boatmen traveling the Des Plaines River took their drinking water from a spring that ran nearby, finding shelter from the sun under a tall leafy willow tree as they did so. The tree perished long ago but gave its name to the town.

The village's first land boom began with the construction of the Illinois and Michigan Canal in 1822, when workers tired of traveling back to the city. When the canal was completed, many stayed. Today Willow Springs is home to about forty-one hundred people. It still carries some of the flavor of the nineteenth-century Indian trading center and settlement it once was. As traffic roars through the nearby spaghetti junction formed by highways and interstates, knowledgeable locals feed deer and watch badgers in sylvan settings provided by surrounding forest preserves which afford an escape from metropolitan gridlock.

For all its potential charm, Willow Springs has been a hard-luck town with a shady reputation, plagued by tragedies and scandals. Some residents think it might have something to do with the fact that the village was built on land used for burials and holy rituals by the original inhabitants. A large plot of land on the Des Plaines River was sacred from prehistory to the Pottawatomi Indians. Known as the Land of the Healing Waters, it was surrounded by a half-moon circle. The Indians believed that the numerous springs inside this crescent had special healing powers and that the land itself gave out vibrations, which when combined were responsible for many cures. It was regarded as a sanctuary, and any Indian en route to the Healing Waters was given food, clothing, and lodging, even by hostile tribes.

Sacred fires burned like eternal flames in multiples of seven, tended by members of the Moscution Society, a highly religious group of medicine men supported by the Pottawatomis in their work, which was believed to be inspired by the Great Spirit. Before they were forced to leave when the land was ceded by treaty in 1816, the Moscution priests doused all the sacred fires.

Not long after the holy men left, trouble began. In the nineteenth century, fire destroyed most of the higher priced homes. Throughout Prohibition, Willow Springs had a notorious red-light district which attracted gangsters from Chicago on the east and Joliet on the west. During periods of intramural gang warfare in the next twenty years, such gentry occasionally used the local woods and waters as informal burial grounds.

In 1943, Willow Springs became the first nuclear dump in the world. The previous year, the Manhattan Project created the first sustained nuclear reaction on the campus of the University of Chicago. Because it was deemed too dangerous to build a reactor large enough to be useful in creating war materiel in the city, the U. S. Army Corps of Engineers leased one thousand acres in Red Gate Woods, just outside the village boundary. By the end of May 1943, the world's second nuclear reactor, dubbed CP-2, was up and operating. It was soon followed by a nuclear waste disposal site named Plot M.

In 1956, the Red Gate Woods reactor was shut down. The site was returned to the Cook County Forest Preserve District, supposedly restored to its prelease condition. More than three decades later, tritium, a radioactive isotope of hydrogen, was found in three water wells. A uranium fuel cylinder was also located above ground. Until this happened, Willow Springs residents were unaware of possible radiation danger.

Another threat to the environment is posed by another kind of dump site, a huge sewage plant and sludge farm just across the village boundary. The fumes and smell have been known to bring tears to the eyes of the strongest men.

For those who believe in it or have seen too many movies, the disruption of burial grounds and the contamination of sacred land is enough to explain the strange events that plague Willow Springs. Ghost tours regularly visit the area because of sightings, not just of Indians, but of people who died or disappeared under mysterious circumstances.

Those who regard this theory as nonsense have to admit that since the Ice Age, Mother Nature and man have used Willow Springs as a place to dispose of unwanted debris.

The diving operation had been going on for almost three months. It began one September morning when Willow Springs Police Officer Charles "Sonny" Fisher was making one of his frequent patrols of the canal bank. Fisher's affinity for the canal was well known to fellow officers. He spent so much time hanging about under the bridge that they liked to joke that he was actually a troll in cop's clothing.

During one of his frequent excursions, Fisher noticed tire tracks that led right down to the water and then disappeared. Concerned that someone might have accidentally driven into the canal during the night, Fisher claimed, he radioed a report back to the station.

Willow Springs could not afford the luxury of sending any of its public safety officers through police divers' training. As a result,

Chief Ross reached out to a more affluent nearby suburb for men with the right credentials.

Once in the water, the police divers found more than Ross expected. Instead of locating one submerged vehicle, they discovered an underwater parking lot. Visibility was close to zero, so it was impossible to estimate how many cars were down there. In some spots the cars were stacked on top of each other, prompting a local wag to observe that this was one place where it was possible for anyone to walk on water.

Before the recovery effort was halted in 1983, more than seventy automobiles, a number of vans, and several motorcycles were recovered from a three-mile stretch of the waterway running through Willow Springs. There were at least a couple of launching sites. Fisher's find, right under the Wentworth Avenue Bridge, was one. Another seemed to be around the Ashland Chemical plant dock.

The canal and the banks on either side belonged to the Metropolitan Sanitary District of Greater Chicago, which had its own police force. For the most part, they were retired cops supplementing their pensions by patrolling various sanitary district properties, including the nearby sludge farm. Technically, the diving should have been their job, but if there was one common characteristic among them, it seemed to be a deathly fear of any encounter with the fluid in the canal. Handling of real crime on district property—anything more serious than enforcing the curfew and trespassing rules—was left to local or county cops.

The borrowed divers had other duties, and when it became clear that operations could continue indefinitely, Chief Ross knew he would have to hire some civilians. WSPD Sgt. Lee Branham recalled seeing diving tackle in the rear of a local home while he was waiting in the alley to catch drivers speeding through a nearby intersection. The equipment belonged to Tom Skrobot, who had become hooked on diving while taking an adult education course at Moraine Valley Community College.

When Branham asked Skrobot about helping with a salvage operation in the canal, Tom was eager to oblige. Skrobot enlisted the assistance of his friend Jerry Los, presented a proposal to Chief Ross, and they were off.

On this typically grey Saturday morning, Skrobot and Los followed the established routine. In addition to the regulation diving gear made necessary by the chilly eighteen-degree weather and the pollution, the divers wore heavy denim overalls over their wet suits. While this made them feel better, the fabric afforded little actual protection from possible cuts and gouges they might sustain from the rusty metal, which could slice right through to the skin. The overalls did make it easier to clean off the muck that quickly covered anything submerged, however briefly, in the canal. It took a little longer to get rid of the smell of raw sewage that accompanied it.

The sanitary district called the canal the eighth wonder of the modern world because digging the channel twenty-eight miles through solid rock in the 1890s had been a major engineering feat. After developing new equipment and techniques to move fifty million cubic yards of solid rock and earth, the S&S builders were the natural choice to dig the Panama Canal.

Wonder No. 8 1/2 was how the barges were able to navigate past the vehicle-strewn stretch of the waterway. As the barges passed through, churning the water with their powerful screws, the buried autos bounced around. In fact, as more and more vehicles were winched ashore, some of them bore marks of having been hit by the barges. No reports of these encounters had been filed by the barge captains or owners, however.

Years later, a barge captain was asked how it could have passed notice that something unusual was down there. He shrugged, saying, "You see a lot of strange things on the canals and channels around Chicago. But even if you see a floater [a dead body], you don't report it unless it drifts right into your screws. Too much paper work."

This may sound callous, but it is only practical. The 1970s were a time of great upheaval in the Chicago Mafia; as a result, so many bodies drifted into suburban jurisdictions along the canal that some members of the county police suggested placing submarine nets at the city border. And they were only half joking. The canal meanders through Will and Du Page Counties, and during this same period, their law enforcement officials complained that Cook County was pike-poling floaters into neighboring jurisdictions.

People familiar with the canal knew that it was a popular place to get rid of other unwanted objects, some of which posed a danger to shipping. When it got too bad, the U.S. Corps of Engineers would come through with a sand dredge and smash a path.

Almost immediately, even before the dimensions were clear, Chief Ross realized he had a major scandal on his hands. As he began to run license plates and serial numbers through the police computer, he found that the vehicles had been reported as stolen and insurance money collected. After only three months as chief, he had stumbled on an insurance scam of considerable proportions.

Making matters worse, a number of the cars belonged to policemen from Willow Springs, Chicago, and surrounding towns, or to members of their immediate families. All this naturally attracted the attention of other law enforcement agencies, and Ross was concerned. Because some policemen were involved, he could not be sure who could be trusted.

Ross himself had been brought in to clean up the Willow Springs Police Department by Mayor Frank Militello. Elected in April 1981, Militello had run on a platform of ridding Willow Springs of police corruption, especially as personified by longtime chief Michael Corbitt.

Militello, owner of a local graphics and printing business, knew his town was a notorious speed trap where policemen did business "on the street," collecting fines on the spot. Also, he knew that for a price, Chief Corbitt was willing to satisfy the longing of some people for a police badge and the right to carry a gun. Even worse, Corbitt was rumored to be involved in gambling, burglaries, prostitution, and drugs.

Corbitt had been the defendant in at least one civil rights case, where he had shot a man in the groin for allegedly attacking the chief. The man in question was in the Willow Springs lockup with an alcohol level seven times the presumptive level for intoxication under Illinois law. It was argued that with so much liquor in his system, the man would be incapable of standing up, much less attacking the burly Corbitt.

There were questions about Corbitt's shooting of a peeping tom, and there were accusations of intimidating individuals for the sheer fun of it. In one instance, he had drawn his gun and fired through his girlfriend's beehive hairdo. Although Corbitt had his admirers in the town—the revenue from traffic tickets was incredible and kept down the local tax burden—Corbitt's corruption was too much for Militello and his supporters.

Shortly after being sworn in, Militello announced he was replacing Corbitt with James Ross, a longtime sheriff's deputy and judge's bailiff. Corbitt's response was swift; he took the mayor to court, claiming his firing was political. Judge Joseph Wosik, sitting in the Fifth District courthouse in nearby Chicago Ridge, issued a restraining order. Militello protested that he was acting within Illinois law by dismissing appointees when their terms expired on April 30, 1981.

In June 1982, the Illinois Supreme Court refused to hear Corbitt's appeal of the Illinois Appellate Court ruling that Militello's action was legal. It took fourteen months of expensive litigation, but the mayor was able to make good on his campaign promise. Corbitt's lawyer went to the U.S. Court of Appeals, but was denied a stay, and the longtime chief handed in his credentials and cleared out his desk. When Jim Ross took possession of the office, it was stripped clean, especially of any evidence of Corbitt's misdeeds.

Corbitt boasted he would be named chief of his hometown of Summit next to Willow Springs, but that fell through. As usual, he landed on his feet, with a badge and a gun, working as a deputy to Circuit Court Clerk Morgan Finley. Although frozen out in Willow Springs, along with fifteen policemen who were parties to his suit, Corbitt was still able to wheel and deal in the southwest suburbs.

Militello and Ross believed they were rid of all the dirty cops, but they could not be sure. In fact, they had no way of knowing how many Willow Springs police stars were out there or who had them. At no time did the number of full- and part-time officers ever total more than twenty, yet some wore badges with numbers well over one hundred. Before the courts ruled him out, Corbitt had ordered another three hundred stars, although Willow Springs had neither the funds nor the need for such growth on the police force. There was simply no way of knowing how many people were strutting about, waving Willow Springs' credentials.

The mayor and the new chief were aware that "everybody knew" that policemen outside Willow Springs were willing participants in Corbitt's corrupt activities, and Militello and Ross agreed to be extra cautious with other law enforcement officials, including those with the Cook County Sheriff's Police Department (CCSPD).

Militello and Ross were prepared to clean up the town. What they did not expect was having to clean up the canal as well. Today the schedule called for the work to continue under the bridge. According to Militello, Ross asked the mayor to be available that day because Ross had received a tip about finding something especially interesting in the canal.

After a quick cup of coffee provided by the chief, the divers lit the little pile of brush they had gathered from around the bank to provide some warmth. Even on the sunniest day, no natural light penetrated more than a few inches below the canal surface, and the Willow Springs budget did not stretch to the rental of underwater lighting. Over their years of diving together, Skrobot and Los had perfected a system of communicating with each other underwater by tugging on ropes. It came in handy during the Willow Springs operation.

Once the divers located a car, they would signal the crane operator to drop the hook near them so they could attach it to the front or rear axle on the underside of the vehicle. Then the divers got out of the water while the car was being winched to dry land.

The police would photograph the car, take down the model, license plate, and VIN (vehicle identification number), and the car would be towed or placed on a flatbed truck to be taken to the yard owned by District Auto, the company which provided the crane and towing services.

For the divers, the waiting periods seemed longer than they were. They would certainly never get rich on the fifty dollars they split for each car they found. Luckily, it was the diving that counted.

The men slid into the murky water. They found one car, then another, getting out of the water for safety's sake while each was lifted ashore, as well as for coffee and a snack to keep up their blood sugar. They also took advantage of the opportunity to skim off the worst of the mud and muck that covered them, peeling off the sludge in long, disgusting strips.

At 2 p.m. they located a third car, which was to become the last of the day. Like all the others, it emerged upside down, covered with slime, its roof badly dented. It was still recognizable as a Cadillac, probably yellow over white. The license plates were still on it. At first, Ross read the plates as DGW 6l. When Bruce Gipp, the tow truck operator, turned the car over, the chief saw them correctly: DGM l9.

There was a flash of recognition; for the past nine months, there had been a missing persons bulletin out on Dianne Georgia Masters, last seen driving a car of the same make and model, bearing the same plates as the filthy vehicle before him. Her disappearance had received county-wide coverage in the newspapers and on TV, and the gossip surrounding it had taken on a life of its own.

Every woman in every beauty shop in south and southwestern Cook County had a theory about what had happened to Dianne, who had come to be identified, as "the attractive civic-minded thirty-five-year-old wife of a prominent suburban attorney." The ladies in the beauty shops had no corner on the gossip market in this case; the occupants of the local courthouses and cop shops also speculated about it. Since the days of Al Capone, placing bodies in the trunks of luxury automobiles had become something of a tradition in Chicagoland.

Once an auto was upright, it was standard operating procedure for Gipp to use the hook of his tow truck to pull open the trunk to see if there was anything—or anyone—in it. To him, it was ironic that out of all the cars he dealt with in this way, Dianne's Cadillac was the only vehicle where this maneuver did not work. The outer trunk lid popped open, but the inner lid remained down, although it did come away at the edges, revealing what was left of a human body inside.

Accustomed as Gipp was to seeing the effects of what two thousand pounds of metal can have on the human body when he was sent to tow cars involved in accidents, the discovery of decomposed human remains left a lasting impression on him. As the outer boundaries of the inner trunk lid separated, a stomach-churning odor escaped, the sickly sweet, musty, rotting smell that signaled death to experienced police. Gipp could see that the body was naked from the waist down; he never looked any further, nor did he want to do so. It looked more like styrofoam left out in the weather than human flesh. Gipp was happy to step aside and let the cops take over.

After designating one of his men to guard the Cadillac, Ross left for his office to make some phone calls. He was reluctant to use his car radio; there were too many policemen involved in the dumpings, to say nothing of the buffs who took pleasure in just monitoring police transmissions and the media who listened for possible leads. The last thing Ross needed was a crowd at the site.

It took only a few minutes to reach the police station on Archer Avenue. There Ross called Mayor Militello. Because of the increasingly sensitive nature of the canal discoveries, the men had agreed not to discuss them over the phone, although they were reasonably sure that Militello's was not bugged. The conversation was accordingly terse. "There's something I think you should see," Ross said, without identifying himself. "I'll be right there," the mayor replied.

Next, Ross called the office of Robert Stein, the medical examiner (M.E.) of Cook County, to request that a team trained in forensic pathology be dispatched. Finally, almost against his will, Ross called the Cook County Sheriff's Police at their Sixth District office in south suburban Markham. The Willow Springs PD was not large enough to have the highly trained evidence technicians (E.T.'s) required to handle any death from suspicious causes, and they routinely called on the sheriff's staff to provide such support. Ross and Militello had reasons to distrust the sheriff's men because of Corbitt's close ties to many of the higher ups, but they hoped the Corbitt virus had not spread to the E.T.'s. Calls finished, Ross returned to what had now become the crime scene. Realizing they were done for the day, the divers had changed into dry civilian clothes and were preparing to leave. Ross told them they would have to stay until the area was cleared, so Skrobot and Los relit their fire and settled in.

Soon officers began to arrive, first from Willow Springs, where the shift was changing and the word had gone out about the find, then from the Sheriff's South Suburban Criminal Investigation Unit, known as South Dicks. Among these were Lt. Howard Vanick, head of the South Dicks squad, Sgt. Clarke Buckendahl, assigned to Vanick's unit, and less explicably, Lt. James Keating, commander of vice operations. A number of routine photos were taken, and then the police began their examination of the car. The windows were down; the keys were in the ignition, the gearshift left in drive. This fit the pattern of the other dumped autos.

The sun goes down early in metropolitan Chicago in December, and once all the necessary on-site work was completed, it was clear that the M.E.'s team and most of the sheriff's E.T.'s would not arrive until after dark. Ross made arrangements with the tow truck operator to lift the Cadillac onto a flatbed truck. The truck was driven to the fire department garage, which shared the Willow Springs public safety building with the police department. He also ordered that all the men at the site, including the divers, report immediately to the firehouse. If the missing person's bulletin had attracted attention last March, the recovery of the car with a body in it was likely to generate even more. Ross wanted to keep the press away until there was more to go on.

Once the car was safely inside the firehouse, cardboard was placed in all the windows of the firehouse to shield from the curious whatever grisly secrets Ross and Militello expected to be revealed when the trunk was finally opened. Additional photos were taken of the car as more men began to gather, just milling around, waiting for the medical examiner.

Shortly before 6 p.m., Robert Stein, his support crew, and the sheriff's evidence technicians were in place. The team donned protective garments and white latex gloves and began their work. First, Stein ordered that the trunk lid be removed by Willow Springs firemen. This done, Stein stepped up to the car to study the remains so that he could make the legal pronouncement of dead on arrival at exactly 6 p.m.

The body was very decomposed, but it was obviously that of a once shapely woman. Whoever had stuffed her in the trunk had left her little dignity. She lay on her back, with her head turned toward the passenger side of the car and her right arm covering her face. Her clothes had been pushed up above her navel, so that she was naked from waist down. From the knees down her legs were jackknifed under her. What had once been appealing flesh had turned mostly into adipocere, a waxy substance which develops as the result of moist burials. It has a consistency similar to that of a bar of soap left too long in the tub.

Like almost everybody present, Frank Militello assumed the body, unrecognizable as it was, would turn out to be that of Dianne Masters. He had dealt with her in a business capacity, handling graphics and printing for her various civic activities. There was little left of the woman he knew.

As Dr. Stein proceeded with his preliminary examination, he found the head to be almost completely skeletalized, with a few bits of scalp attached here and there, and a wisp or two of blonde hair. The distinctive green eyes were gone; so were the ears and nose, the fingertips and toes. The teeth were bared in a hideous parody of a smile. Definite identification would have to come from the dental records.

Militello had grown up on some of Chicago's meanest streets, where an occasional corpse was no particular shock. The body in the trunk had an unreal quality, almost like that of a department store mannequin. Except for the skull. No store display would include a skull like that; it was even too rough for Halloween. Militello could only shake his head in pity.

Search as they might in the cluttered trunk, the technicians could find no trace of the woman's shoes, panties, panty hose, or handbag. The corpse bore jewelry that matched the description of what Dianne Masters had been wearing when she vanished in March. So did her clothing, so far as anyone could tell after so long in the canal.

As the forensic men worked, the others talked among themselves. There was some joking—"sure doesn't look like suicide to me," and so on. They meant no particular disrespect. Most of the men in the firehouse had spent years in public safety work, where learning to distance themselves from almost daily tragedy was a necessity.

A gurney and body bag were moved near the trunk. Dr. Stein had done all he could outside his morgue. Almost all the soft tissue around the woman's neck had dissolved or turned into adipocere. When Stein directed that the body be moved, the head rolled away and a bullet casing feel out of a sleeve. Both were retrieved and placed inside the body bag to be taken by ambulance to the morgue on Chicago's West Side. The cause of death would have to await the autopsy findings, but it looked as if Dianne Masters had been shot before her car was launched into the canal.

After Stein left with the body, the E.T.'s began their search of the car, especially the trunk. Every item located had to be logged on inventory forms, dried out, and placed in an evidence container. The container was then marked with a description of the contents, the date, and the name of the technician. When the time came for a trial, this would be important in proving the chain of custody of everything found at the scene.

Because the Cadillac was still wet and muddy, the technicians decided to complete their search after it had dried out. Chief Ross made special arrangements to prevent tampering with any evidence that remained. A police officer was detailed to stand watch, and later Ross ordered Officer Robert Olson to set up a security camera that could be monitored by the dispatcher in the radio room.

It had been a long day for Chief Ross, but he still had one last duty to perform, the one policemen dread most: telling the next of kin. In this case, that meant Alan Masters, a widely-known, even notorious, lawyer whose Palos home was a few miles south of Willow Springs. Sgt. Clarke Buckendahl of the sheriff's contingent was a friend of Masters and offered to go with Ross. Both men had known the lawyer for years; his office was located in Summit, a working class suburb between Willow Springs and the Chicago city limits, and the majority of his cases were heard in the Fifth District Circuit Court, which then sat in southwest suburban Chicago Ridge.

The question of notifying Alan Masters had come up earlier in the day. While the car was still on the bank of the canal, CCSPD Sgt. Don DesRemaux, the officer in charge of the evidence technicians, asked of nobody in particular, "Has anyone talked to Masters yet?" At first, there was no reply. It was understood that none of the investigators had any wish to deal with the husband of the missing woman. Finally, one officer wisecracked, "We don't want to alert him."

Lt. James Keating had been taking a lively interest in the proceedings ever since his arrival at the canal, shortly after the sheriff's office was notified, even though he had no official responsibility for conducting the investigation. He seemed amused by the proceedings, laughing and smiling as the investigators continued with their grim work. At one point, when Alan Masters' name was mentioned, several policemen heard Keating remark, "The poor man will be upset enough when he learns his wife has been found." The men within earshot considered this strange, and their reaction must have shown on their faces, because after a long pause Keating added, "dead."

Ross phoned Masters, telling him that the car had been found with an as yet unidentified body in the trunk and that he and Buckendahl were on the way to Masters' home. The call was a departure from standard practice. It is axiomatic among policemen that when a person is murdered, other family members are the primary suspects, and the element of surprise is always helpful. Statistics have borne this out, especially in the case of spouses.

Besides, it was well known that Alan and Dianne had been having marital problems. Immediately following her disappearance, Alan had denied this in the press accounts. When Dianne's close friends protested, Alan admitted that a divorce had been in the works, resulting in increased buzzing in the beauty parlors.

Alan Masters had nine months to prepare himself for this moment, but the telephone call gave him a little extra warning. Ross told Militello that Masters gave "an Academy Award performance" as a grief-stricken husband on receiving the news. Buckendahl recalled it differently. According to Buckendahl, when he and Ross arrived at the Masters' home, Alan seemed calm and not at all surprised. Given Ross' earlier phone call, he had no reason to be. But Diane Economou, one of the lawyers in Masters' firm, was at Alan's side, and she seemed very distressed indeed.

The formal identification would not take place until the M.E. could compare dental records, but no one who was privy to the discovery doubted that Dianne Masters had been found, that she had been murdered and her body disposed of in a way that apparently was supposed to suggest mob activity.

From the start, nobody swallowed this. While Alan had long been rumored to have connections with the syndicate, the Mafia, the outfit, the boys, whatever they were being called, it was well-known in police circles that the mob did not make war on women. Not unless a woman family member turned government witness or went public, and sometimes not even then. Overlord Moe Giancana's daughter had written a book about her life as a Mafia "princess" which sold well and was made into a movie, and she was still alive and well. Trying to disguise the murder as a mob-style hit just didn't make sense.

When the Sunday papers hit suburban driveways the next morning, the ladies in the beauty parlor knew they had been right all along.

PART I
Diane

When lovely woman stoops to folly
And finds too late that men betray,
What charm can soothe her melancholy?
What art can wash her guilt away?

The only art her guilt to cover,
To hide her shame from every eye,
To give repentance to her lover,
And wring his bosom, is—to die.

—Oliver Goldsmith

CHAPTER 1

*T*he people who loved Dianne Masters expressed their grief over her murder as "tragic" and "a terrible waste." More than ten years later, her friends are easily moved to tears and laughter when remembering Dianne. She had an enormous capacity to inspire affection; even after her death she was able to draw people to her.

John Reed, Paul Sabin, and Bob Colby, the three detectives who solved the case, and Thomas Scorza, the assistant U. S. attorney who took it to court, never knew Dianne Masters in life. They probed into the most intimate details about her, a kind of scrutiny that the average person is fortunate to be spared. Despite this and having been trained to distance themselves from victims and tragedies so as to preserve objectivity and sanity, they found themselves developing positive feelings for her. "I grew to like Dianne," Scorza reflected, "even though I only knew her as a corpse and a grotesque one at that."

"Attractive, civic-minded suburban wife and mother," the capsule catchphrase the media used to describe Dianne Masters after her disappearance, was accurate in a superficial way. At thirty-five, she had entered the phase where the fresh prettiness of youth frequently fades, but Dianne had tended her looks. Her friends say she would have been pleased with the posthumous descriptions of herself as drop-dead gorgeous, but in private with them would have had a good laugh over it. She knew all her imperfections.

53

This is not to say she was self-absorbed, although she wanted to please others, and she believed appearances were important. Experience had taught her that if she looked successful, prosperous, confident, and well put together, most people would accept her as such.

She had green eyes, fair skin and blonde hair, with a well-proportioned, slender figure on a five-foot, four-inch frame. Because she had grown up wearing hand-me-downs, she was particular about her clothes because people often made snap judgments of others based on their wearing apparel. Over the years she had worked hard at developing clothes sense and opted to dress in a classic, understated way.

Like many attractive women, when Dianne looked in the mirror, the first things she saw were flaws she would like to correct. The pale blonde hair that caught the eye was a terrible trial to her. Mary Nelson, the MVCC public relations director during Dianne's tenure on the board, remembers that Dianne's hair often gave her a pre-Raphaelite, even ethereal, quality. Dianne saw it as baby-fine, wispy, and flyaway, and she was forever consulting her hairdresser on how to improve it. She tried to augment it with hairpieces; she tried permanent waves; she tried other hair colors. She found the early grey unattractive and had it tinted close to the blonde of her youth.

In his opening statement to the jury, federal prosecutor Tom Scorza characterized Dianne as a "kept" woman, a term her friends disliked and one which seems rather quaint today. It conjures up the image of a sexy floozy draped across a chaise lounge, eating bonbons, without a thought in her head but seedy pleasures. That was not the cultivated, intelligent, witty, and kind Dianne they knew, the person Dianne had worked so hard to become. Even harder to take was the defense depiction of Dianne as a feckless woman, an irresponsible mother, and an unfaithful wife who was unkind to the man who had supported her for twelve years.

In death, Dianne Masters became the object of many a male fantasy about loose women. Even the fact that her panties were missing when her body was found added to the locker room-type gossip. A political public relations man, who had never met her, chortled that the absence of undies meant, "She was always ready for action." Sworn testimony that Dianne always wore undergarments by women friends who traveled with her and the last man who loved her had no effect on dispelling this particular slur, nor did the fact that not even a dedicated nymphomaniac would go about bare bottomed in a Chicago winter.

Men who met her in passing later recalled even such innocent exchanges as "hello" and "that was an interesting speech" as evidence that Dianne had been after their bodies. Whatever they may want to believe, they flatter themselves. For a person who came of age during an era of relative sexual freedom, Dianne's track record was unremarkable. As Tom Scorza put it, "I knew people in college who did more in one semester than Dianne Masters did in her whole life."

Reporters who covered the story over the years passed along salacious tidbits that were equally unfounded in fact. Even her sometimes erratic spelling, in personal letters she had no reason to expect would ever be seen by anyone but their recipients, was criticized and held up as evidence of her generally poor character. This reached ridiculous heights when after the verdict, one less-than-well-turned-out suburban reporter who had met Dianne when she ran for the MVCC board wrote that at the time she was "frumpy."

All of this combined to trivialize what had been done to Dianne Masters and to obscure one simple fact: that no one deserves to be murdered, not even if the individual is unfaithful, promiscuous, a bad speller, and frumpy to boot. Not even if they are male.

Who was the real Dianne Masters? She was a late bloomer who struggled for years to find out who she was and what she wanted to do with her life. Like Fitzgerald's Great Gatsby, Dianne had carefully set about inventing herself, although without Gatsby's need to completely hide her background.

Just as she had summoned up the strength to act on her self-discovery, she was murdered. The notion that he was losing control over one of his most prized possessions was too much for the husband she had waited so long to marry and tried so hard to please.

As she wrote shortly before her death:

I have floundered with my emotions, tragedies, grief, and identity for many years. Yet all the while I realize today, I have been moving toward this moment. For time did not simply pass me by. All the while, I was learning, assimilating, replying, projecting, experimenting and to cut it short—growing.... But, inspite [sic] of our emotionally torn situation, I have grown. And it is this growth that excites me.

She was born on June 25, 1946, to George Turner and the former Anne Strzalka. Tragedy was no stranger in Dianne Turner's life; long before Dianne's birth, her mother had been the victim of a terrible crime, and its aftermath had a significant influence, especially during Dianne's formative years. At the age of fifteen, Annie Strzalka was raped by a young man she had been dating. Fully intending to leave no living witness, the youth then shot her in the head.

Astonishingly, her wounds, while grievous, were not mortal. The sight in one eye was completely destroyed, and she was left with partial vision in the other. This was lost due to medical inattention during her hospitalization, and she was given glass eyes. According to Dianne, her mother had just received a scholarship to study at Chicago's Art Institute and was a promising dancer. All of that was now lost to Annie, and in her despair, the understandably depressed teenager tried to jump from her hospital window.

A year before she was slain, Dianne wrote about her mother in a letter to a friend's teenage daughter.

She [Annie] was sent to a school for blind students. She never fit in. She wasn't handicapped in her opinion...Most of the students had never seen. It is much less painful when you don't know what you're missing.

Her mother was Catholic, but following the rape, Annie's experiences with what Dianne termed "the iridescent statuesque Catholicism of her day" were not pleasant.

Annie was told repeatedly that the rape and blinding were punishment for her willfulness or her sins, something the newly blind teenager could not accept.

The question "why me?" plagued her...On a visit home from school she went with one of her sisters to the neighborhood Church for Confession [sic]. Perhaps to seek comfort. Perhaps to have that resounding question answered. Or perhaps to receive forgiveness for those sins that caused her condition. Clumsily making her way through the church she stumbled on a pew. An old, grouchy priest came by and in Polish said, "What's wrong with you, stupid girl? Are you blind?" And she said, "Yes, Father, I am." And that was the last time my Mother entered the church, other than for a few funerals and her children's christinings [sic].Wow, that's anger. Yet let me tell you this: She NEVER lost her faith...She refused to be HANDICAPPED. She accepted each phase in her life graciously. Truly an incredible woman. One I miss each day since she died.

Her mother's experience in church following the rape had an effect on Dianne's attitude toward religion as well; even as a child, Dianne sensed her mother's antipathy toward the Catholic Church. "I was Alice looking through the stained glass," she wrote. "I had to walk two miles to church on Sundays, alone. My Dad was an alcoholic and Lutheran. (Please don't make any permanent associations here.) I went to catechism alone. My Dad went to my Communion and Confirmation. (It was an occasion for a party.) My Mom stayed home." Dianne left the Roman Catholic church during her adolescence because, "It wasn't personally easy for me to meet the requirements necessary for a religious commitment."

Indeed, feelings of abandonment and isolation from such institutions as the church and from her family were among Dianne's earliest memories. Dianne adored her mother, and friends who knew Annie Turner marveled at how wonderfully she coped with her handicap. She was able to orient herself after just one visit to a friend's home or even a public place like a restaurant. The casual observer would not even notice she was blind. But while Dianne was growing up, having a blind mother made her different, something no child enjoys.

While her love and admiration for her mother was boundless, Dianne had very little to say about George Turner. She felt she owed him a measure of filial devotion, but it was hard to maintain respect for a man who was increasingly drunk and abusive and could not provide adequately for his family. His alcohol-enhanced rages placed additional pressure on the youngster, who was fearful about bringing other children home to play and who worried that something in her behavior was responsible for Turner's drinking. This established a pattern she would follow in her relationships with men given to extreme rages; she would shoulder the blame and accept punishment, anything to restore harmony. Her desolation and pain over her relationship with her father was all the more obvious when compared with her devotion to her mother.

George Turner knew Annie in high school, but they began to date only after the rape. Turner felt sorry for the pretty girl whose promising future had been cut off, and he offered to marry her. The union was not a particularly happy one, and it grew less so as time went on. Turner was a truck driver, but his earnings became increasingly erratic as his drinking problem progressed into alcoholism. Eventually, no cartage companies would employ him, and he could find work only as a part-time bartender, not the best solution for a man with a formidable thirst.

The children of alcoholics often have special problems, and Dianne's were compounded because George Turner also beat his blind wife. It is also believed by some of her friends that he abused Dianne, verbally and probably physically and sexually, as well. She talked about his drinking, but seldom about his battering Annie; she felt great shame about both situations. In front of others, she treated her father gingerly, as one would a ticking time bomb.

All in all, the atmosphere in the Turners' poky little house in Franklin Park, a blue-collar suburb due west of Chicago, was emotionally as well as economically impoverished. Increasingly, Dianne found her hiding place in books. "A young girl, embarrassed by her home life, can find great comfort in words," she wrote.

Dianne did not like to talk about her unhappy childhood. However, her family's predilection for booze troubled Dianne. An aunt and uncle died of related diseases. She wrote to Jim Church on the subject in the weeks before her death:

> I worry about drinking because my parents, family etc. were alcoholics. Do you drink every day? Do you, or anyone who has been close to you, perceive this to be a problem? What I'm getting at is I don't want our girls (Georgianna and Church's daughter, Emily) to grow up thinking that adults only have a good time when alcohol or drugs are present. Would there be a need for us to drink daily if living together?

Dianne was relieved when Jim assured her that he felt no such need.

Although the Turners lived in the suburbs, the family also spent a good deal of time in the city neighborhood where Dianne's mother grew up. Milwaukee Avenue is main street of one of many ethnic enclaves in Chicago, the kind of area that every immigrant resident hopes will be a temporary stopping place on the way to achieving the good things of the American way of life.

When Dianne Turner was a child, the community was predominantly Polish, predominantly poor. Dianne loved her mother's family, particularly her grandmother, but she hated the family home, a tall, narrow, ramshackle frame dwelling that lacked central heating and other modern conveniences. It reeked of poverty and depression, and its miasma affected Dianne deeply. All around her was evidence that hard work and good intentions did not always bring the simplest of rewards: a clean, comfortable home, adequate nutrition, or even warmth for old bones, let alone financial security. Early on, Dianne knew that the American dream could turn into a nightmare, that even the brightest and bravest sometimes were unable to escape such surroundings. It was frightening to young Dianne, but it strengthened her resolve. She was determined that this wound not happen to her. Somehow she would make it up and away.

The Turner home in Franklin Park was only a slight notch above the old neighborhood, and their way of life was only nominally suburban. There was no money for the improvements that might have turned their tiny house into a pleasant home. For years, every time there was a major downpour, the sewers backed up into the basement, and George Turner would order Annie downstairs to clean up the nasty mess.

Given the many problems that beset their union, and the fact that they belonged to a pre-Dr. Spock school of parenting, it is not surprising that George and Annie were not particularly affectionate or warm with Dianne. In later life, people who did not know Dianne well pronounced her to be spoiled and pampered, blaming her upbringing. The truth was quite a different matter. Far from being the doted upon only daughter, Dianne had no sense of worth in the family unit, especially after her brother, Randall, was born when she was five years old.

It is not unusual for children to feel jealous about the arrival of a sibling. Dianne definitely felt a chill in terms of her parents' attitude toward her, which may have reflected their limited capacity to cope with two small children rather than any change in their feelings for their daughter. Because of her mother's blindness, Dianne also had to shoulder more than the usual big sister's responsibility for the brother to whom she always referred as "the kid." Whatever the case, very early in life Dianne picked up the idea that girls were just not as important as boys, and she struggled against her second-rate status throughout her life.

As Dianne grew, the Turners' domestic situation worsened. Her father's drinking problem increased, and the household's economic and emotional climate deteriorated. Dianne especially resented having to share a room with Randy. When she was sixteen, she decided to take what steps she could to correct the matter. She cleared a space near the furnace in the damp, depressing basement and moved her bed and other teen-age treasures down there. There was no door she could slam to keep the world out, but having some measure of privacy was well worth a flood or two.

Dianne attended grammar school in Franklin Park and finished at Leyden Township High School. School friends remember Dianne as bright, outgoing, pretty, ambitious, and popular. Her grades were good, and she participated in many high school activities, especially those centered around music and writing.

But Dianne had a different recollection of herself growing up. In the letter to her friend's daughter, she described this painful time.

> Aside from my personal problems, I learned to function from my forehead up. Being a little stranger/odder than your usual questioning adolescent, I was having a very hard time growing up. I had started reading Freud and began looking into existentialism and Zen. Undoubtedly wierd! [sic]...I have seen and experienced aspects of this life we live that I pray you and your siblings never see. I know about alco-

holism, syrousis [sic] of the liver, cancer, death, suicide, son beating mother, degeneration and on and on and on. I am a survivor and have always attributed this to inheriting my mother's Polish fortitude. It wasn't until recently that I have looked at myself, my strength, my fight for causes, my love of life, family and friends with a different slant.... Through all of the R-rated viewing of life, I have always felt sustained. And though I attributed my fighting spirit to my heritage, it could have better been called Faith.

Like many young girls, Dianne became fond of poetry and enjoyed reading it. But writing it became a form of release for all those difficult emotions she was feeling and could not discuss with anyone. Gwendolyn Brooks, who would become Illinois' poet laureate, visited Dianne's class and made a great impression on the girl. Unlike most young women, who leave their poetry writing behind with other teenage souvenirs, Dianne continued hers up to her death. It filled a need for her.

In the Leyden Township High School yearbook, Dianne appears as a typical high school senior of the time. Under her graduation photo is a caption listing her activities and her goal: college. It was an objective Dianne fulfilled, but it was not the type of experience she wanted. She wanted to go away from home, to live on campus, to enter a different world than she had ever known, a world where she could become the Dianne she wanted to be. Instead, she remained in the midst of the depressing situation at her parents' home. This led to what she told friends was her first big mistake as an adult.

On August 17, 1967, Dianne was married to a young man she met at college. Although fond of her young husband, the couple were not well matched. Playing house on a shoestring was fun at first, but the times worked against the newlyweds. The Vietnam War was in high gear. Dianne's husband had neither the resources nor the inclination to avoid military duty. Within a year of their wedding, the army claimed him. For all intents and purposes, the couple stopped living together as man and wife on September 1, 1968.

Dianne quickly realized she had married for the wrong reason: to get away from home. Many people do this, and the marriage either thrives, or the couples make the best of a bad situation. Once her husband left for the army, any hope of putting in the effort necessary to make a go of the marriage was lost. Snapshots of Dianne in Hawaii during her husband's rest and recreation leave in December 1969 show a tense, sad young woman who was obviously not enjoying the tropical splendor around her. Her divorce complaint stated that her husband attempted a reconciliation for one day during that time, but it was unsuccessful.

There were other disappointments. If marriage was not her ticket to a different world, neither was higher education. In June 1968, Dianne received the bachelor of arts degree in English literature, with a minor in high hopes. These were soon dashed. She quickly found out that there was little she could do with the degree in terms of a job that would pay enough to get her out of her emotionally and economically deprived environment.

By 1969, she had tried to work her way up out of a number of low level jobs, with no success. There was bad news at home, too; she was intent upon obtaining a divorce. Her husband was due for his army discharge in March 1970 and would be coming home. Dianne felt it was the right time to make a fresh start.

The lawyer she retained to handle her divorce was named Alan Masters.

CHAPTER 2

*B*y the time he met the former Dianne Turner around the end of 1969, Alan Masters was operating like a medieval baron in the suburban fiefdom he had carved out of an area just outside Chicago. His law office was located in southwest suburban Summit, but he had serfs and vassals ready to do his bidding in local police stations and courthouses throughout western and southern Cook County.

Masters established himself as king of the small Summit heap. Sometimes called Summit-Argo, after Argo Corn Products Company, which owned 350 acres and was the single largest area employer, Summit has always been a working-class town full of boardinghouses and bars catering to immigrants and other new arrivals drawn by the availability of jobs for the unskilled. Cutbacks and closings have taken their toll, and the housing and commercial buildings are showing their age. But then Summit has had a somewhat scruffy air ever since its founding in the nineteenth century to facilitate the building of the I&M Canal.

Masters also maintained an office in Chicago's Loop, but he remained in the legal bush leagues as compared to the highly respected, distinguished law firms inhabiting whole floors of skyscrapers with fashionable addresses. Such firms represented important corporations and wealthy families. In contrast, Masters' clients were unaccustomed to strolling through the corridors of power. For them, he drafted wills, filed personal injury suits, appeared in traffic court, negotiated divorces, support, and child custody cases, and defended them in the sort of criminal cases that seldom made the headlines in Chicago's daily newspapers.

To the extent that Alan Masters was known at all to the big firms, it was as a fixer, a sweeper up of small, untidy messes. To be sure, they sometimes had a need for lawyers who could perform such services; even clients with the best pedigrees and resumes sometimes required the kind of assistance that the old-line firms prefer to farm out. Some attorneys who met these needs gained the respect and the referrals of their more gentlemanly brethren. Alan Masters was not one of them.

Some say it was his personality; others, that it was his personality and the fact that his sphere of operations was in an unfashionable section of the county. No matter. When a valued client faced drunk driving charges, a scandalous divorce, or criminal liability, Alan Masters was on no one's Rolodex. The snubs were unsettling, to say the least. It was particularly galling because not all these men were born to the inner circle of the legal establishment; many had come from even more humble circumstances than Alan. Even worse, some hailed from Alan's old neighborhood.

Until the 1950s, Chicago's near west side was home to a thriving community of Jewish immigrants from central and eastern Europe. Throughout the 1930s, the havoc wrought by the Depression was everywhere, but so was an atmosphere of hope. The streets were lined with run-down apartment buildings teeming with vibrant life. However limited money may have been, there was an abundance of respect for customs, tradition, and religious heritage. Hope and ambition were as omnipresent in the atmosphere as oxygen. What the parents did not have, their children were sure to get, and the key to this was education.

Alan Masters was born on March 9, 1935, the second son of the former Esther Bulmash and Samuel Masters. As a child, Esther Bulmash Masters had left Poland with her parents. Like many West Siders, back in the Old Country, the Bulmashes lived in an area known as the Pale, near the Russian border. Over the centuries, countless invading armies had tramped through the Pale. As one immigrant from the same vicinity put it, "You could be Russian one day, Polish the next, with Germany always waiting in the wings."

When World War II came, there was scarcely a single family on the West Side that did not lose relatives to the death camps. As one refugee who arrived in Chicago as a teenager said, "If I had stayed there, they'd have turned me into a bar of soap." The impact of this knowledge on the community, especially on young people, is incalculable.

Sam Masters was American-born to immigrant parents from a similar background whose name had been Americanized. Sam never talked much about his parents' roots, possibly because there was not a lot to tell. Further, he was reared during a time when newcomers wanted their children to be as American as possible as quickly as possible. Still, among the Bulmash-Masters clan, there is a curious reticence to talk about their roots, especially puzzling because ethnic neighborhoods and ethnic backgrounds are prized in Chicago. Indeed, it is often difficult to stop people from the old Jewish West Side from talking about their immigrant backgrounds.

Like the vast majority of their neighbors, the Masters were observant Jews who sent their sons to Hebrew school. Also like most of their neighbors, theirs was a multi-generation household. Esther Masters' parents lived with her and Sam, and her five siblings were accustomed to weekly gatherings in the Masters' home. It was a warm, close-knit family; Alan was one of sixteen cousins who played together as children and kept up with each other over the years. As an adult, Alan liked to refer to his home as a tenement, and the community as a slum, but others who lived there thought of it as a crowded apartment building in a working-class neighborhood.

Sam and Esther Masters are remembered by their neighbors as lovely people who ran a hardware store on nearby Roosevelt Road.

As the neighborhood changed and the store's business fell off, Sam Masters opened a currency exchange in southwest suburban Summit, where he acquired a reputation for being helpful, kindly, and honest in his dealings.

A few neighbor kids went on to fame and fortune, but most grew up to be solid citizens and a credit to their upbringing. On the face of things, Alan Masters' childhood and youth were unremarkable. As a boy, after he finished his day at the local public school, he helped out in the family store. Scholastically, he did well. Personally, he is remembered as always being anxious to curry favor with those who were in a position to help him, a pattern that was established for life.

Alan liked to recall how during the hot summers he would sleep in the grassy median strip in the boulevard outside his home along with other details that would indicate he had further to rise than was actually the case. Embarking on flights of fancy that put him in a good light also became part of a lifelong pattern. He keenly felt his short stature and nondescript looks. He was born with a harelip, which, while not severe, set him apart from others, and not in a positive way. Children can be cruel, and Alan sometimes responded to their questions by denying that it was a birth defect, attributing it to accidental causes.

He attended Farragut High School on Chicago's near southwest side where he made both the wrestling and football teams. Many find the latter difficult to believe because of his height, but Farragut did not have much of a team or much of a chance competing against some of the local powerhouses in high school football. Off the record, neighbors and classmates describe him as average in every way, except for his loud mouth and occasional flashes of temper.

Early on, Alan decided to become a lawyer. He was the first in his family to get a college degree, from Roosevelt University, an institution of higher learning founded after World War II and located in the landmark Auditorium Building on Chicago's South

Michigan Avenue. On graduation, he entered DePaul University's School of Law. Alan supported his undergraduate and graduate studies by working as a janitor. The choice of DePaul, a Catholic-run university, was somewhat surprising; it is much favored by Irish-Americans and other ethnics who seek a career in local politics, while John Marshall is known as the "Jewish" law school. In appearance, even as a young adult, Alan was something less than a matinee idol. His face was plain, and when he gained weight, his features tended to lose definition and take on a porcine cast. Even the best suits could not hide the fact that he was short (around five feet, six inches) and tended toward overweight. No matter how he combed it, it was obvious he was losing his brown hair.

He was self-conscious about how he looked, and this made him more determined to get attention in other ways. Masters often told people that on leaving college, he had served in the Marine Corps and/or had worked for the FBI for three or four months. Neither story was true. After completing law school, he joined a law firm, leaving after six months to go out on his own.

By the time he met Dianne, Alan was in his middle thirties and had established a thriving practice in Summit, near his father's currency exchange. The locals respected Sam Masters, and it was natural to go to his son with their legal problems. It became easy to characterize Alan as a "brilliant" lawyer, but there is little evidence of this. Perhaps the potential was there in the beginning, but it shriveled and died from lack of use.

Early in his career, Alan developed a reputation as a fixer on the legal scene. He did this by cultivating policemen in the surrounding area and judges in the local district courts, as well as downtown. He made no bones about his "motions to fix" and loved to boast about how many people in the law enforcement and justice business he owned. Why try a case when you could fix it and be sure of its outcome?

If Alan had restricted himself to sharp business practices and sailing a little close to the legal wind, well, there was room for that kind of lawyer in the Chicago area. But as in everything else, Alan Masters went to extremes. As one acquaintance put it, "if you bought a cow, Alan would buy two, or maybe a whole herd." He was not satisfied with just keeping up with the Joneses, he had to surpass them, even if this meant telling whopping great lies or breaking the law.

He did not always bribe with money; it was known to the police that if they needed some free legal assistance, Alan Masters was the man to see. He had other ways of collecting.

In retrospect, it is easy to view Alan Masters as a sort of human monster and the people he used and abused as having no worth or value. While this is true of some, the description does not fit all.

Alan Masters was first and foremost a collector of people. His antennae were acutely sensitive to men and women who were down on their luck or in some sort of trouble, finding it impossible to cope, or feeling isolated from the rest of the community. He would sit that person down and say, "Let me do your thinking for you. Everything will be OK." To people living in despair, for whatever reason and no matter how temporary, this approach was irresistible. How could they not feel loyalty and affection for such a man? How could they refuse him any small favor he might request later on? After all, Al was their pal. He was there when it counted.

Masters performed favors for these people on spec. It was known among the police that if a copper was having marital problems, needed representation in a divorce or custody suit, Alan Masters was there—and he never sent a bill. At least fifty such cases were uncovered during the investigation, and that number is thought to be the tip of the iceberg.

If there are no free lunches, there are no free lawyers, either. Eventually the bill would come due. Sometimes grateful officers would suggest Masters as legal counsel to people they had arrested. There is nothing wrong with this; who better to ask for a referral than a cop who sees lawyers in court every day? But Masters, who wanted to keep the benefactor/suppliant relationship in place, would up his fee and share the difference with the referring officer, leaving that man still in Masters' debt. This is against police regulations and legal ethics, but in the atmosphere in which Masters operated, that was of no consequence. If some of the recipients of Alan Masters' largesse escaped without being called upon to make good on the *quid pro quo* arrangement, it is simply because Masters did not get around to them before he was caught.

For example, in 1968, Herman Pastori, who would serve as chief of police in several suburban jurisdictions, was working as a patrolman in the town of Hodgkins. One day the chief there announced that he was meeting an attorney named Alan Masters to go shopping and that Pastori was invited. Masters picked up the two policemen at the station and took them to a shopping center in Oakbrook, Illinois. Once inside a store, Pastori's eye was caught by a display of sweaters. "These are nice," he observed to Masters, who was standing beside him. "Do you want one?" Masters asked. "You're kidding," Pastori replied. "Go ahead and take it," Masters urged. "Don't worry about it. I'll pay for it." Which he did, to the tune of twenty dollars. There was nothing illegal about Masters buying a present for Pastori; that part would come later.

Soon after the shopping expedition, the chief of the Hodgkins PD told Pastori that if Pastori referred cases to Alan Masters, Masters would "take care" of him. Pastori understood this to mean that Alan would pay him, and his understanding was correct. As Pastori moved up the promotion ladder from patrolman to sergeant to lieutenant to chief, he had increasing access to records in his department, and he referred all types of cases from other jurisdictions, as well.

Beginning approximately in 1968 and going through 1983, Pastori regularly referred cases to Masters, sometimes as many as nine a year, and Masters paid him a finder's fee in cash ranging from $50 to $300 each. The financial transaction usually took place at Masters' Summit office, although once the money changed hands right inside the Hodgkins police department. Pastori never declared these cash payments on his income tax.

In return for a twenty-dollar sweater and an unknown amount of referral fees (no point adding them up if the IRS was going to be kept in the dark), Pastori forfeited his reputation and personal integrity, got his wife involved in one of Alan's schemes, and lied to the IRS. If he was not exactly a major menace to society in general, Pastori certainly was not a model of rectitude, either. His story is typical of many law enforcement officers who fell into Alan's clutches.

Pastori was aware that other policemen had similar involvements with Alan Masters. One of them was Willow Springs Chief Michael Corbitt. Pastori, who then headed the Hodgkins PD, had a conversation with Corbitt during a meeting of police chiefs. "I've been having some problems with Alan Masters," Pastori said. "What kind?" Corbitt asked. "Well, I referred a case to him, and he told me that he had to take care of other people so there wasn't any money left. On another occasion, I referred someone to him and when I called Alan, he says the guy never showed up. When, in fact, I know he did. He said, 'I never handled the case,' when I know he did." Corbitt replied that he had been referring cases to Masters and he had similar problems, but it was no big deal, nothing serious.

That Masters was assured of his hold over men like Pastori, despite the relatively small amounts of money involved, is demonstrated in a conversation that took place between him and Pastori outside a Fifth District courtroom when the court was meeting in Worth. Earlier, Masters told Pastori he had to take care of the state's attorney in several cases that were coming up. When the two men met again, Pastori asked, "Did you get everything arranged?" "Absolutely," Masters replied, adding, "I have most of the judges in my back pocket except for one."

Masters went on to tell Pastori, "It's easy to get to a police officer."

"Well, what do you mean?" Pastori asked. "How is it easy?"

"All you have to do is when a police officer's handling a case...when the case was over [I'd] just put ten dollars in his hand, and say, 'Thanks for treating me all right.' And if he took the ten dollars, then I had him."

To assure the right decision from the bench, Masters passed money to judges and entertained them lavishly. He liked to throw stag parties where pornographic movies and later videos were shown. If a judge expressed a fondness for a particular feature, Alan would hand him the cassette. Sometimes he would give him the VCR as well. Over the holidays, rivers of Scotch flowed to his coterie. "We have the best judicial system money can buy," he liked to say, even in front of members of the judiciary. By concentrating his attentions on the needy and the greedy, Alan Masters made a handsome living, although probably not as much as he liked to pretend.

Masters needed all the money he could lay his hands upon, legally or illegally, and not just to maintain his corrupt entourage. His personal life was not uncomplicated. Alan Masters was first married on March 22, 1958, when he was twenty-three and his bride almost twenty-one. Their son Steven was born in 1959, and a second son, Douglas, came along in 1963. The family lived in Lincolnwood, a comfortable middle-class suburb northwest of Chicago. Unlike Alan, who increasingly gave only lip service to religion, his wife was a devout Jew, highly thought of in the community. People who knew the couple well say that Alan seemed to be almost in awe of his first wife, who is described as a worthy individual who raised their sons virtually by herself. To Alan, being married to such an admirable woman could sometimes be a burden.

Alan's infidelities began almost immediately after the wedding. Not all were brief encounters, though he enjoyed those, too. A long-term extramarital relationship had broken up just before he met Dianne because the woman tired of waiting for him to obtain his freedom and she decided to marry someone else. Masters seemed to thrive on the challenge of juggling two separate private lives.

When she met Alan Masters, Dianne Turner was emotionally and financially vulnerable. Her job hunting had turned up nothing in which she could find either financial or personal satisfaction. She had very little money and was afraid of continuing an existence bordering on poverty. Her parents were in no position to provide her with either emotional or financial aid; George's alcoholism was making life increasingly difficult, and Annie was drinking heavily, as well. Dianne was, as always, on her own.

To Masters, Dianne must have seemed like a shiksa dream. Young, blonde, pretty, gentile with a good figure, she was feminine and more than a little lost. She could be brash, caustic, a bit rough around the edges, and her personality was not completely formed. When she consulted Alan about her divorce, Dianne was barely making the rent on her small, shabby apartment and could not afford a decent meal. Her clothes were shabby; even the head scarf she wore babushka-style to her first appointment with Alan was of inferior quality. Despite her obvious physical assets, she was lacking in confidence and her self-esteem was a statistical trace. Just the ornamental, malleable type Masters liked for diversion.

With Dianne, it all started with a nice scarf, some food, and a few kind words. At first, Dianne resisted. But Alan knew how to manipulate and even dazzle basically unsophisticated young women. In February 1970, he wrote Dianne to tell her he had talked to friends in the fields of marketing and promotion about her, and that these people seemed interested. He suggested they get together so that he could help her prepare a resume, a variation of the old "would you like to see my etchings" routine. The wooing continued. There were flowers, especially her favorite gardenias. There were expensive gifts. The necessities of life for which she had to scrimp arrived unexpectedly. There were lunches and dinners at expensive restaurants. There were promises of trips to exciting places she could never afford to visit at the rate she was going. And there was Alan. By the time she found out he was married—in her naivete, she believed that he was single because he wore no wedding ring and seemed to be always available except when working—she was hooked. By April 1970, the two shared an intimate relationship. In a note to her on his law office letterhead, he wrote, "As I must have told you a hundred times, my love, feelings, desires and thoughts of you and for you are more magnanimous than words can express...I, as much as you do, want to marry you and be with you forever. I do not cheat on you in any manner, shape or form." It is the sort of thing married men have always said to their single lovers, but Dianne desperately needed to believe him.

In the beginning, he seemed a considerate lover as compared with her previous experiences, which were limited to young men who rushed through the act intent only on their own satisfaction. She found herself enjoying sex more, especially cunnilingus, which was new to her.

As time went on, Alan would describe his first encounter with Dianne to friends and acquaintances, depicting her increasingly as The Little Match Girl. Again, it was as if the contrast between what she had been and what she had become would reflect credit on him, rather than on Dianne. It was true that she was down on her luck, depressed by her past and frightened by her prospects for the future. As for the present, she was simply trying to get from day to day. However, she was not exactly a bag lady.

In her youthful enthusiasm, Dianne thought she could help Alan change, especially his gluttony and vulgar manners. She was not turned off by Alan's harelip, which he sometimes tried to hide with a moustache. When Dianne asked him about it, he claimed it was the result of a childhood injury rather than a birth defect. Later, when she was pregnant and concerned that their child should have the best possible start, she pressed him about it. Following his established practice of never telling the truth when a lie would be more comfortable, Alan created a legend about his so-called injury: When he was small, his older brother had hit him in the face with a swing. What remained was a scar, not a harelip. When Dianne finally met the brother not long before her death, she remonstrated with him. "What you did to Alan's mouth with the swing was terrible," she complained. "Don't be silly," he replied. "Alan was born that way."

Alan spent years overcompensating for his limited physical appeal by buying friends and lovers, although when he wanted to, he could turn on what passed for charm among people who did not look too closely. To Dianne, it was flattering that an authority figure like a lawyer would extend himself to make her feel comfortable in a difficult situation. That he was obviously interested in her as a woman was rewarding, too, but she was wary about men. Over the years, she had become convinced that sex was all men ever wanted from her. What's more, once the hunt was over, they seemed to lose interest. She was determined to avoid being an easy mark.

The more Dianne hung back, the more intrigued Alan became. He showered her with gifts and invitations. The difference between the life he seemed to be offering her and the life she was living widened. The age difference of just more than eleven years was a plus in her eyes. Alan seemed knowledgeable on so many subjects and could discourse on them for hours. It was not until later that she realized how superficial this knowledge was, and that like many lawyers, Alan was trained rather than educated or cultivated.

It seems impossible that she was not more suspicious about his marital state from the outset. Initially, she was determined not to be interested, and so it was not an issue. Later, as she began to take the bait, she may not have wanted to know. Finally, by the time she discovered the truth, she was committed to him. He swore he would marry her, and quickly, too. He even wrote her a promissory note: "By January 1971, we will be married! We will be successful! We will have everything! [sic] we both want."

Alan complained about his wife and marriage in the usual terms used by straying husbands. At twenty-three, he was too young to be married, he told Dianne. His wife was too inexperienced. Gradually it had become a marriage in name only, for the sake of their sons. His wife did not understand him.

As evidence of this, he related details of his homelife that portrayed him in the best possible light. His wife had a cleanliness fetish; there was even a rope, of the type used to hold back the line at movie theaters, across the entrance to the living room. He was relegated to a life in the basement. His wife was well aware of his previous affairs. He claimed that she tolerated the situation so long as appearances were maintained. As soon as both boys were grown, there would be a divorce. In short, he fed Dianne the usual line right out of the original edition of the philanderer's manual.

In a 1975 letter Alan hoped would win over Dianne's psychotherapist, Alan betrayed some truths about himself, writing in the third person. "Alan is a person who has all of his life sought happiness and then when he really found it, failed to realize it...I equate money with happiness." Masters admitted trying to "compensate" for his mistreatment of Dianne by "buying, buying, buying...her." "I am insecure," he whined. "I know that I cannot compete in the social world with another man. I am not physically the man that wins and gets the woman in our world." Realizing he may have been too blatant, Masters admitted that there was no reason for this attitude with Dianne as she did love him.

It was clear Alan realized that somewhere along the line, the tables had been turned on him. When he met Dianne, he did not feel he could take her anywhere. As the relationship progressed and Dianne grew as a person, the reverse was true.

The one fact that stands out in the midst of all this "honesty," is that Alan Masters had to blame other people for his faults. He did not make a clean break from his wife because of his parents, who would not accept "the concept that I would 'give' up my children and family. They would not understand that I could be unhappy with what they see as a good mother of my children and a woman who does not exhibit to the world that thinks it knows her, any overt major faults." Yet he was such a staunch family man that it was unthinkable to him that he would put "my happiness over my family."

For his parents' sake, he claimed, he married the wrong woman, one who "fit into the stereotype of the Jewish mother's indoctrination of the Jewish son..." He had come to realize that he never "knew" his wife and even prior to the birth of his second son in 1963, did not want to be with her "socially, physically or in any way." Not only did he never love his wife, he did not like her, either, and he stayed married for "foolish" reasons, including sparing his sons the problems of children of divorced parents. "This is now also a false concept and I realize that Dianne and I are more important than anyone else in the world and kids do survive and the scars if any will heal."

The scales had fallen from his eyes, and he realized that his relationship with Dianne was the most important thing in his life. "The rage and anger and physical abuse I gave her is totally without cause, reason or justification. There can never be and there will never be again, ever, under any situation or circumstance, any outbreak or even the thought of it again. *Never!*"

Dianne was never introduced to her predecessor, nor did the Mesdames Masters ever speak. However, as the years went by and she began to lose her illusions about Alan, Dianne also came to believe that the first Mrs. Masters had understood Alan all too well. On the outside there was the dutiful son, the prize student, the able lawyer, the concerned friend, the loving husband, and doting father who cared deeply about his extended family. On the inside, there was the grasping opportunist who never did anything without an eye to what was in it for him, the cheating husband and absentee parent, the crooked lawyer who corrupted others, the brutal philanderer, a man who broke all promises and squandered his honor and that of others without a backward glance.

CHAPTER 3

Soon after she succumbed to Alan Masters' full courtship press, he rented an apartment for Dianne at Four Lakes Village in Lisle, a complex much favored by young singles in a far southwestern suburb outside Cook County. Alan paid her almost daily visits, but seldom, if ever, stayed the night. Then he figured out a way to explain such an absence to his wife.

Suddenly he was spending a lot of time with a new client located in Indiana, who could only see him on Friday night or Saturday morning. Since the family home was in far north Lincolnwood, it seemed logical for Alan to remain in "Indiana." In fact, he stayed with Dianne, sometimes until midnight Saturday. He would return to the family home to sleep, and on Sunday, he would be back at Dianne's, having told his wife he needed to make use of the quiet time at the office.

During the early days of her liaison with Alan, Dianne met Brigitte Lunde when both were bridesmaids for a mutual friend. They took to each other immediately. A native of Germany, Brigitte was pretty and self-confident, a natural charmer, a few years older than Dianne. Despite differences in personal circumstances and background, both women felt they had at last found the sister they had always wanted. Dianne was particularly interested in Brigitte's stories about growing up in Germany, where her family still lived.

Dianne's judgment about men may have left something to be desired, but she had good instincts about people in general and picked her friends carefully rather than impulsively. When she knew Brigitte well enough to be confident Brigitte would not judge her, Dianne made no secret of the nature of her relationship with Alan.

Despite the fact that he was still very much married, Dianne began to use Alan's last name. He obtained a driver's license and credit cards for her as Dianne Masters. In Illinois, this is not illegal; a person may assume any alias, so long as there is no intention to defraud.

Her name was not the only thing that changed in Dianne's life circa 1970. Before Alan, Dianne's clothes came from such discount department stores as KMart. Now she wore designer labels, furs, and a diamond. It was a sign of her immaturity that one night Dianne decided to flaunt her finery at a bar in her mother's old Chicago neighborhood. She fancied the owner, but he ignored her. She thought her new trappings might make a difference, but they did not. However, there was another man at the bar who was very interested indeed, and Dianne turned to him. As Dianne was to learn, Alan was extremely jealous and had almost a sixth sense about such things. For some reason, that evening he phoned her all night long. Receiving no answer, he went to her apartment early the next morning in a jealous rage. By that time Dianne was home, with no intention of telling him about her one-night stand with a gas station attendant. But Masters was trained at cross- examination and could obtain information from more experienced and better-prepared individuals than Dianne. When she finally confessed, saying she had no intention of seeing the man again, it made no difference. Alan went berserk.

A terrific struggle ensued, during which Dianne ducked once and Alan put his fist right through the wall of her apartment. Most of his punches landed on target, however, and she was badly beaten. Alan also threatened that he would have the man castrated. It never happened, but in ensuing years, Masters liked to repeat the details of the nonevent, sometimes substituting Dianne's ex-husband as the victim.

The morning after, Alan sent Dianne a special delivery letter apologizing. "Please, Please forgive me for this shameful, terible [sic] thing I did to you! Please do not leave! I love you so very much. Please give me the chance and opportunity to show you my love!! I am ashamed and sorry!!" Being contrite after bashing Dianne around was one of Alan's specialties. On July 4, 1970, he wrote her asking that "you forgive me for the display of temper last evening...you are my whole life and existence."

Dianne was distraught after the beating, for more than the obvious reason that she was physically hurt. All her life, she had worked toward escaping her background, and all her life she had failed. Alan had his faults, but he was an educated man and only a social drinker, unlike her father. She never anticipated that Masters would abuse her physically, and when he did, Dianne blamed herself. The relationship with Alan was a mistake, and it was her fault. In front of Alan, she berated herself, prompting him to write her about the "terrible things you said about yourself...You are not a loser! You are the biggest winner in the whole [world]. The love we have for each other will live forever." Unfortunately, Dianne's life would last less than twelve years.

As is the pattern in abusive relationships, gifts and special attention followed the beatings. On one occasion, an indication of the volatility of their life together, Masters gave her a gold charm that read "angel/devil." Dianne always forgave him, just as her mother had forgiven her father. Each time he beat her, she was sure they had worked things out, and it would be the last. She believed that Alan loved her; the hot and cold running presents, the constant phone calls, the efforts to stretch time to be with her, all proved that. Marriage was in the not too distant future, when Alan's sons would be better able to cope with a divorce.

In the meantime, however, the novelty of having everything provided and nothing to do but prepare herself for Alan's visits began to wear off. Dianne wanted some sort of a career. Alan picked up on her restlessness and became concerned that it could lead to a rupture between then. After weeks of discussions, it was decided that Dianne would obtain a real estate broker's license. Dianne felt it would make use of her ability to get along well with others. Alan approved because it was the kind of job where the hours were flexible enough to permit her to join him whenever he was available.

To give their relationship the outer trappings of marriage to further consolidate his hold on her, and to distance her from the singles scene at the apartment complex, Alan purchased a house for Dianne in Naperville, a suburb in the collar county of Du Page much favored by the upwardly mobile with children. Decorating it and taking care of it would give Dianne another interest.

"Buying" Dianne a license became one of Alan's boasts, but she was certainly bright enough to pass the state exam, which is not known to be intellectually taxing. In 1971, not long after receiving her license, Dianne obtained a broker's job with First United Realtors in Naperville.

In 1973, Dianne became friendly with another broker from the company's Hinsdale office. Dianne invited Pat Barna to a party at her new home at which Pat met Alan. At this point, Pat believed the pair were married; after all, they had the same last name and lived together, she thought. A few months later, Pat made some reference to Dianne's "husband." Dianne just giggled a little, and said, "Pat, you are so dumb. We're not married." Dianne explained that Alan was waiting for his two sons to leave for college before getting a divorce. Pat had known other women who fell for this line, and she wondered if Dianne was not living on false hope but kept her doubts to herself.

On the subject of her attitude toward marriage at this time, Dianne reflected:

I was a 20th Century woman and a piece of paper meant
little to me as long as I finally had the man I loved. And I
was assured that when the time was right, the situation
would be legalized.

Pat began to see more of both Masters after they introduced her to
Bob Casey, a friend and client of Alan's, who built dome-shaped
houses. They became a foursome, sometimes going out with
Brigitte and her escort.

Because Dianne was left alone so much on nights and week-
ends, she saw as much as possible of her female friends, including
Pat, Brigitte, and Helene Maignon, a native of France who dated a
married lawyer who was one of Alan's friends. During this time
Dianne worked hard at learning how to dress and use makeup to
her best advantage, and she constantly embarked on self-improve-
ment projects.

Dianne was generous by nature, a caring and thoughtful friend,
who tried desperately to rise above her insecurities and lack of self-
esteem. She was a quick study, acquiring social graces beyond anything that she had experienced. Despite this emphasis on training
and educating herself, she never lost her highly developed, slightly
wacky sense of fun and her love of silly pranks.

Dianne tried to make the best out of difficult situations. Alan
was notorious for his snoring, and once on a cruise, she could bear
no more in the close quarters, choosing to sleep in the closet or
bathtub for the duration.

Sometimes there was a sharp edge in Dianne's reaction to
Alan's behavior. On one occasion, they went to Florida on holiday,
but Alan told his wife he was trying a case in Boston. While deep
sea fishing off the coast, Alan hooked a big one. Dianne and the
other guests hid below so he would have to reel it in by himself,
sustaining a brutal sunburn in the process. How he explained why
the sun beat down so fiercely in a Boston courtroom to his wife

was unknown. The subject was not discussed in front of Dianne's friends.

Initially, the pair was sexually compatible, but Alan began to demand as a preliminary that Dianne perform complicated cleansing rituals, involving bathing and showering, and then anointing herself with oils and lotions. By the time she had finished all this, Alan usually had fallen asleep. She did not make a practice of discussing the details of her sex life, but she thought this bordered on the ludicrous, and she had to tell Brigitte. "I am certainly not going to wake up any man in order to have sex," she laughed. She also tired of his requirement that she ask for intercourse in writing. "Weird," she observed to a friend.

Ordinary mishaps did not seem to get her down, perhaps because she was aware of the nature of real tragedy from an early age or possibly because she had become an expert at covering up. Dianne knew that other people are drawn to individuals who seem able to handle anything, so she was an expert at coping with life's daily disasters, at least in public. Behind the delicate facade, there was determination and toughness.

Brigitte remembered staying one weekend in Naperville shortly after a dishwasher had been installed. She was watching television with Dianne and another woman in the downstairs family room. Suddenly they heard a loud crashing sound, followed by a cascade of water, which put out the fire in the fireplace. The installers had neglected to connect some essential tubing which caused a flood upstairs and downstairs. After the three women dragged out the sopping wet kitchen carpet, Dianne found three umbrellas, and they sat watching TV and sipping wine as the water dripped on them.

Dianne loved animals and had acquired a calico cat when she lived in Lisle. In the Naperville house, she added a Persian cat and Baron, a Labrador retriever she obtained from a shelter. Not to be outdone, Alan arrived one day with a fish tank, which he filled with piranhas. He liked to bring live goldfish to feed his pets and tried to persuade Dianne to give them raw meat. She put her foot down, fearing for the safety of her cats who played around the tank, and the piranhas were removed to his office, replaced by tropical fish.

During this period, Dianne's ex-husband contacted her because he was about to marry again, and his fiancee wanted a Catholic wedding. To make this possible, a church annulment would have to be obtained, and there was paperwork that Dianne had to sign. She was upset when she saw that she would have to swear that she did not want children.

Angrily she phoned Brigitte, who reminded Dianne that her ex was not asking her to tell a lie; Dianne had not wanted a child out of that union, which in retrospect seemed doomed before it even began. After some tears and temper, Dianne agreed that a good person, a big person, the kind of person Dianne wanted so desperately to be, would sign the documents. She obliged. She could not help but feel a twinge of envy that her former husband had found happiness so quickly without her and that he was proceeding to build the kind of "normal" family approved by society. Despite all her talk of being a "20th century woman," she craved the same conventional type of marital situation.

Shortly afterward, Dianne found that she was pregnant by Alan. She wanted to have his baby, but when she told him, he was furious. "I will not have a bastard of mine running around," he shouted. Then he issued an ultimatum: if she did not have an abortion, they were finished. The timing of this pregnancy, so soon after the news about her former husband and his new wife, prompted some friends to question whether the pregnancy was truly an accident; perhaps, they suggested, it was an attempt on Dianne's part, however unconscious, to speed up Alan's divorce plans and bring him to the altar. Dianne firmly denied any connection, saying she would never risk a baby's well-being in this way. In her despair, she was utterly believable.

She agonized over the situation, desperately trying to find an alternative, hoping to the last that he would change his mind. If he loved her as he said he did, how could he not love their child? As far as the child's legitimacy, if he meant his promises to her about being married, their union would be legalized long before the situation could prove embarrassing to their offspring. His flat refusal to even consider her having the baby, let alone keeping it, hit Dianne in the middle of her efforts to bolster her self-esteem and self-confidence. The rejection was enormous.

She felt trapped; the walls were closing in on her. She knew that if Alan left her, she could not possibly support the child on her own. After all, she had not been able to support herself. What kind of a future would the two outcasts face? Her family could offer neither financial nor emotional support. Besides, she did not want to return to the impoverished life of her childhood, especially as the ultimate female failure, an unwed mother. It would be too shaming.

Time was running out; she was almost at the end of the first trimester. Alan stepped up the pressure; the procedure became more risky as the pregnancy advanced, but more important, once Dianne had felt life, her willingness to go through it would have decreased. Finally, in despair, she agreed to follow orders. Alan dispatched her to New York City, where it was easier to get an abortion. Dianne was accompanied by her mother, who thought they were going on a shopping trip, and a friend. The abortion was over quickly, and physically there were no ill affects. Emotionally, however, it was a tragedy which haunted her for the rest of her life.

After she returned from New York, her relationship with Alan became increasingly strained. His sons would soon be off to college, but he showed no sign of preparing his family for a divorce. She met with indifferent success as a broker, not because she did not take it seriously or was not willing to work hard, but because Alan's demands on her time kept her from developing contacts and following through on leads. She was approaching thirty, and felt she was throwing her life away.

At this point, a man who owned a landscaping business came to Dianne for help in finding a house. He was single and attracted to her, and she began to go out with him. When Alan became aware of the situation, he was enraged. One weekend while Helene Maignon was staying with Dianne, she heard shouting upstairs. Helene hurried out of the kitchen to see Alan hitting Dianne at the top of the stairs as he accused her of being unfaithful. As Alan began to drag Dianne by her hair, Helene rushed to her friend's assistance. Alan shoved both women down the stairs, then stood looking at them, holding a fistful of Dianne's hair, which he had pulled out by the roots. On other occasions, her friends observed Dianne with bruises and other signs of physical abuse.

In addition to the beatings and the abortion, Dianne's health was not robust. In 1969 and again in 1970, she was diagnosed with infectious mononucleosis. In 1971, she developed ulcers. In 1972, she was treated for a spasm of the heart muscle, unusual in so young a person. It also was discovered that her lymph and thyroid glands were enlarged.

That same year she began to see a psychiatrist, Dr. Cullen Schwemer. He treated her for severe depression and low self-esteem over a three-year period. On one occasion, Alan called Dr. Schwemer, asking him a series of questions about Dianne's condition, rather like a parent discussing a child with a teacher. At first the questions were innocuous enough, but suddenly Alan posed an ambush question. "Has Dianne been with another man?"

Taken aback, Schwemer paused to collect his thoughts, inadvertently confirming Masters' suspicions. Before he could reply, Alan warned, "Someone's going to get hurt, Doc." Schwemer was obviously shaken, for he added a note to Dianne's file which read, "Now I know how Napoleon felt at Waterloo." When Dianne came in for her next appointment the following week, she had bruises on her arms and around her head.

Dianne was still trying everything possible to please Alan.

Sometimes in her frustration, she would do something frivolous, such as dying her hair red. Another time, she seriously considered converting to Judaism, although Alan was something less than religious. She did not find a warm welcome at the temple and abandoned the plan. Eventually she returned to the Roman Catholicism she had rejected as a teenager.

Increasingly, Dianne doubted that Alan would ever make a clean break from his family. He could not understand her attitude; he gave her everything that money could buy, but she wanted more. What WAS all this crap about stopping to smell the roses? He was satisfied with his life the way it was. Dianne's efforts to discuss their failure to communicate ended in shouting matches, so she began composing letters that she hoped would get her point across. This gambit was unsuccessful, as well. The missives were too long and Alan's attention span too short.

In 1974, pressed beyond endurance, having reached the limit of her seemingly inexhaustible tolerance for the situation, Dianne and Alan split up. Dianne was hoping to make it an amiable separation. Instead, "I was threatened, beaten, forced to sign the house over to him, cut off from credit cards, money, etc. Not the kind of thing you want to attribute to a man you've called the best kisser ever. Instead, you should have seen my 'kisser'!" The beatings continued.

Dianne's hopes of keeping the Naperville house were dashed when Alan insisted on selling it to his policeman friend Jim Keating. Dianne was given $23,000 from the proceeds of the sale and moved into a condo in nearby Woodridge. She was unhappy with her new place, and it was not simply that the condo was much smaller and in a less desirable location. It was another loss, both of the illusion that she and Alan were building a home and a life together and of the atmosphere she had tried to create. She felt that the house was an extension and an expression of her personality. It was very hard to let go.

Dianne reminded herself that she was a survivor and resolved to look to the future, hoping to find happiness with the landscaper. Things did not work out, however, and the pair decided to go their separate ways. She did not turn to Alan, but once again, his antennae seemed to pick up on the change in her circumstances, or he may have had her under surveillance. Whatever the case, he called, offering to take her back. It was an offer she could and did refuse. For a while.

That she could leave him for another man was a blow to his male pride, but this was a reason he could understand. It was an even greater blow that given a choice between him and no man at all, she opted for the latter. All his friends knew he had lavished money and gifts on Dianne, and he felt they were laughing at him behind his back for not realizing a return on his investment in Dianne. What's more, he was now in his forties, and pretty, vulnerable young blondes were not easy to come by. All of these feelings would be assuaged if he got her back. Obviously, it was going to take more than a new bauble or two—she was surprisingly resistant to his old techniques—but he knew the right buttons to push. This time he would give her the commitment she had always wanted.

Early one morning I found him on my doorstep with his possessions in black plastic garbage bags. That alone should have been an omen. He finally left his wife. Before I could digest that awesome fact he moved back without a flick of the wrist. Before anyone could say abracadabra he had left [his wife] for good and we were going to be married... 'We were together,' as they say in the movie mags. 'At last.'

Despite her doubts, Dianne made only a token resistance to Alan's return. She had not made as much progress as she thought on her journey to self-reliance and self-esteem, she was lonely, and she really had loved him. But the reunion was nothing like the movies. It did not take long for her to realize that behind all his promises of a new beginning were the same old attitudes.

Once again, she found she could not get him to discuss their situation, and once again, she resorted to putting her feelings in writing.

You don't seem interested in participating in our daily lives. I would like to go grocery shopping together...I would like to walk the dog together. I need a companion. You have seemed indifferent to the ideas I have for my future. When I tried to discuss appraisal courses you didn't get involved...I miss work...I feel like I am in limbo. I may not be as successful as you, but I need to be productive...I also need some financial independence...I don't like to have to ask you for money....I would like to see you get involved in a hobby. Something I can share with you.

Dianne continued to write that Alan's biggest interests, in her opinion, were his work and his children. "As for work, I am a good listener and feel that is important to you. I'm sure I resent a little the fact that I cannot relate on the same level because I am not working.

"As for your children, I am completely out of the picture. I feel you are missing them more than ever and at times wonder if you would not be happier moving back...It is not something I am hoping for."

Dianne hated inactivity, especially watching Alan fall asleep in front of the TV set every night. She wanted them to join the YMCA. In addition to togetherness, "I have visions of you becoming physically active, loosing [sic] weight, having more energy and becoming the Alan I used to know. Wouldn't you like this?" she asked plaintively. She feared they were slipping into what she called the old married couple syndrome even before the wedding he assured her was imminent.

"Please don't flippantly skim this letter," she begged. "You have been known to do that. I am on the verge of explosion...There have been many occasions lately when I felt I could live happier by myself."

She discussed her plight with her psychiatrist and this made Alan very agitated. He had to try to win the doctor over to his side, first by telephone, then in writing. His need for dominance and control and inability to accept fault was due to his insecurity, he wrote Dr. Schwemer. "The rage and anger and physical abuse I gave her is totally without cause," but then "I am a man, my pride, my ego, etc. was [sic] hurt and broken!" As usual, there was the promise that no such thing would ever happen again because Masters was now mature and knew what he wanted.

"She doesn't think I am what I say I am nor does she believe that *now* I can do and act as I say I can because I never did before. She refuses to believe that, yes, a bolt of lightening [sic] can strike a person...make him realize what it's all about," In this, Dianne's instincts were correct.

CHAPTER 4

$\mathcal{D}$ianne's determination to change her life, with or without him, got through to Alan Masters. In 1975, he purchased a home for her in unincorporated Palos Township, an upscale area southwest of Chicago. They would live together as husband and wife until his divorce came through and they could make it legal. The memory of Alan forcing her out of the Naperville house caused Dianne to have screaming nightmares, so she insisted that the new place be in her name only, as evidence of his good intentions. She truly believed that this would be her last home. It was, but not because she was going to grow old there.

The property was on Wolf Road, just outside the village of Palos Park, which has some pretensions toward being a town with old money and a touch of class. It was a few minutes and several tax brackets away from Alan's Summit office. Pricey homes sit on large, wooded lots. There is no Junior League, but membership in the garden or women's clubs is sought after. Dianne was determined that no one would ever know from her behavior that she had not been born to all this.

The house, a single-story ranch with a basement, needed some work, as did the grounds. Dianne did not mind; quite the contrary. She saw it as a challenge and an opportunity, a last chance for a fresh start with Alan.

She loved the rustic setting so close to the big city. Her new home was set well back from the road but was not screened from

93

view by trees as were so many neighboring dwellings. A driveway angled to the right towards a garage, and a path took the visitor past the kitchen/dining area windows to the front door. An addition had been built behind the garage, giving the interior an L-shape. A fireplace separated the kitchen from the living room where windows looked out on a backyard that stretched way to the rear, around an in-ground swimming pool and a cabana, into more trees. To the right of the entry hall was the kitchen; to the left, a long corridor broken by two doorways, one leading to a bedroom, the other to a bath, and ending in the master bedroom with its own private bath. The addition on the other side of the house held a third bedroom and an enclosed porch. The rooms were on the small side considering the neighborhood, and the interior was comfortable rather than lavish.

Dianne plunged into creating the kind of atmosphere that would foster the stability and warm sense of family she so desperately craved. She pored over paint chips and wallpaper samples until patterns and colors danced before her eyes. Anxious that everything be just right, she enlisted the help of a decorator friend to put her own stamp on the house, choosing earth tones with liberal dashes of her favorite yellow.

She worked hard outside, too, spending days on her knees to plant the flower beds, designing gardens around the pool and whirlpool, keeping the poolhouse and barbecue area attractive and inviting.

No animal was ever turned away from Dianne's door. Pat Casey used to tease Dianne that there was an invisible symbol there that alerted stray animals to the fact that an easy mark lived inside. She added two more cats and two more dogs to her menagerie and loved to feed the wild birds. Soon the garage had room for only one car because of the space given over to the dog, cat, and bird food, plus the peanuts for Dianne's squirrels. She even constructed a squirrel run for them, with galvanized buckets filled with their favorite nuts. "Welcome to my zoo," she would giggle as friends tried to steer a path through what seemed like all God's creatures, great and small.

No one who witnessed it ever doubted the depth of Dianne's devotion to animals, but there was something sad about it. Dianne possessed an enormous capacity for love. Her parents and Alan did not seem to need the boundless affection she so wanted to bestow, and she transferred it to pets. There was no risk of rejection from the domestic and wild creatures upon which she lavished her attentions; rather than ignoring, criticizing, or berating her, they returned her love unconditionally.

Dianne realized that it was not enough just to have the perfect setting for the model family she was determined to build; she needed more human companionship. She set out to build new friendships and to be a part of the community. For years, she had studied how the "right" kind of people acted, dressed, and did things, and she was determined to come across as a lady. She went slowly, did not push too hard, and fairly quickly, her efforts paid off. Her natural warmth helped her to fit in.

Alan was a different proposition. He was not quite acceptable even to those who did not know his reputation. The neighbors usually met Dianne first, and they were surprised when they eventually encountered Alan. He simply did not fit their expectations of the kind of man Dianne would choose. Instead of the prosperous, athletic, interesting, tweedy, and gracious "husband" they anticipated, here was a short, fat, loudmouthed braggart. The fact that he had plenty of money to throw around did not impress the Masters' new neighbors. It was expected that anyone who lived in Palos would be comfortable financially. It did not do to boast about it, however, and that was one thing Alan could not seem to learn.

As it turned out, the impression Alan made did not matter much. For all Dianne's dreams of togetherness, they continued to lead basically separate lives. Alan rose early, went to work, came home, ate dinner, and went to bed. "Time went on and there wasn't a marriage for the primary guilt reason that it would harm his sons," Dianne wrote.

That was not the only source of friction. Alan was having sexual problems, which he blamed on Dianne because of her involvement with the landscaper, and because "...we didn't sleep in the same bed [which hadn't mattered for the previous five years]. A number of attempts were made on both our parts to correct the sleeping situation....A solution was never found."

It was clear to Dianne that although physically he had left his wife, children, and home, Alan was still trying to lead a double life. His family was not aware of his liaison with Dianne, and there were no signs that he had any intention of changing this. He told his sons he was living in an apartment on Chicago's north side, and to maintain the myth, he installed a private telephone line in his bedroom so that his sons could call him. No one else was ever to answer it. "There were letters from his son in college pleading with dad to become a part of his life. [Both sons] wanted to know where he lived. They were growing up and dad had grown even further from reach."

To Dianne, who so longed for a big "normal" family, the situation was terribly sad, even though she missed Alan when he left her "to be with his other, and what began to appear his real, family...The only hope I had was that time was passing swiftly. Soon [Alan's sons] would be grown and we would be left with each other." Increasingly, Dianne began to doubt that this would ever happen.

Once Alan's separation was official, Dianne believed that after a suitable period of time, Alan would introduce her to his family and old friends, and that by demonstrating how much she loved him, she could win their acceptance. This did not materialize. Alan continued to hide her existence from his family, including his sons, his parents, and his brother. Dianne never got to meet any of Alan's boyhood pals from the old neighborhood, his college friends, or fellow lawyers outside his own shady circle. It may not have occurred to her until the end of her life that he had either lost these associations on the way or that perhaps they had never existed.

With a couple of exceptions, such as Pat and Bob Casey, the normal friendships were those Dianne had made on her own with women like Brigitte. When the Masters entertained, it was usually because it was payback time: judges, cops, and regular clients. Dianne learned to hate these parties, and gradually Alan began to hold them when she was out of town or visiting friends. The Masters' household help characterized the relationship between Alan and Dianne as distant during the best of times. They were on different tracks and different schedules. At the worst of times, there were arguments, with Alan threatening to "get" Dianne or "make her pay." New Year's 1976 must have been especially rough, because on January 2, 1976, Alan wrote Dianne a promissory note for $200,000, apparently to make up for whatever he had done to her. The preprinted form bore the likeness of George Washington and promised to pay interest at a rate of seven percent. Despite the image of the most honest of U.S. presidents, the promise was never kept.

While she waited for marriage, Dianne began to take an interest in joining community groups, such as the local chapter of the American Association of University Women. Working with several other women, Dianne became an activist against domestic violence to the extent of helping establish a twenty-four-hour hot line for victims, which she ran out of her kitchen. Only a carefully chosen handful of her new friends were aware that Dianne was a victim of such abuse. Even so, the assumption was that it had occurred in her first marriage. It was just impossible to believe that a woman so vocal and knowledgeable on the subject was living in the same situation she was trying to help others escape. Her old friends, Brigitte and Pat, knew better.

So did Mary Nelson. Mary was interested in the crisis center and first met Dianne when they worked together to set up a meeting at the college. Mary found herself caught up in the arrangements to the extent that she became one of the original board members of the Crisis Center for South Suburbia along with Dianne.

A sharp judge of character, Mary liked Dianne from the beginning. Some people thought Dianne aloof or standoffish, but Mary recognized that the younger woman was more cautious and careful about letting new people into her life. The older woman became one of Dianne's mentors, and within a few months, Dianne confided in Mary about her unmarried status. Dianne sensed that Mary Nelson was not going to judge her. She was grateful for that acceptance, because try as she might, she felt both shame and guilt over her irregular situation.

Dianne spent so much time at the college (sometimes called "Moron Valley" by locals) that she became aware of a chapter of registered parliamentarians which sometimes offered training workshops there. She began to attend classes and seminars, hoping to pass the examination. Once certified, parliamentarians were in demand to advise on procedural questions at conventions and meetings all over the country. The pay was good, as much as $300 to $400 per day, there was some flexibility in accepting assignments, and Dianne felt it was a baby step toward some degree of financial independence. What she did not foresee was Alan viewing it as a threat to his all-important control.

By the end of 1976, Dianne had good reasons to be pleased with her personal progress in almost every area, except with Alan. It had been more than six years since they met, and more than a year since he separated from his wife, but there was still no sign of a divorce. But Dianne had a secret that brought her real joy: in the fall of 1976, she discovered she was pregnant.

To Dianne, this was the greatest achievement of all, and one she was not going to share with Alan until it was too late for him to force her into another abortion. She wanted this child, and all her new accomplishments had given her confidence that she had the power to make him want the baby, too. He was always talking about how much he loved her. He finally had left his wife. Their marriage was just a question of timing. Everything was going to be all right.

CHAPTER 5

*B*rigitte and Pat knew what the termination of Dianne's first pregnancy still was costing her, and they were sure she could not go through another abortion. They did not share Dianne's optimism about Alan's positive reaction. They were right. When Dianne was well into her second trimester, she broke the news to Alan, and he was not pleased. That was about all she would say, though later she sometimes tried to give the impression he was as delighted as she. As far as anyone could see, he pretty much ignored the fact that she was pregnant.

Later, Dianne would write about Georgianna, calling her "the purest thing that ever came from our [Dianne's and Alan's] abnormal, destructive type of love. I was guaranteed that prior to the baby being born, we would be married. I really believed him for I knew how much he cared for the welfare of children? For hadn't my welfare suffered many years in order to give his boys a normal childhood?"

Neither Annie nor George Turner had particularly liked Alan in the first place, but Dianne was so determined to make the relationship work that there was little they could say or do. Alan knew how much Dianne loved her mother, and he worked overtime to make himself agreeable to her. As time went on, this had its effect on Annie Turner, and she made it her business to get along with Alan, who in turn was generous to Annie. He arranged to have the basement flooding problem corrected, for example, and paid for Annie to accompany Dianne on trips and shopping excursions. Dianne's father never altered his attitude toward Alan. George Turner did not like his daughter's lover at all, and he paid the couple very few visits, increasing his emotional distance from Dianne.

Despite her acceptance of the relationship between Dianne and Alan, Annie Turner was distressed at the prospect of her first grandchild being born out of wedlock. Because Dianne hated to see her mother upset, she told her parents that Alan and she had married quietly. Still, Annie had her doubts.

At the end of March 1977, Brigitte invited Annie and Dianne to her home. During the visit, Annie caught Brigitte alone in the kitchen. She was concerned about her grandchild, she said, and she wanted Brigitte to swear that Brigitte would be around to watch the child grow up as a sort of substitute for Annie. "Oh, you're young yet," Brigitte scolded her gently. "You'll be around when Dianne's baby has babies." "No," Annie replied, "I'll never see Dianne's baby," and it was clear that she was not referring to her blindness. Brigitte tried to jolly Annie out of her mood but was to remember Mrs. Turner's premonition a couple of weeks later.

Easter fell on Sunday, April 10, 1977, and Brigitte joined Annie Turner in celebrating it with Dianne and Alan at their Palos home. Annie was in a strange mood that day. Out of Dianne's hearing, Annie asked if Brigitte knew whether Dianne and Alan were really married. The question made Brigitte uncomfortable. "Of course, she is. They're having a baby, aren't they?" Annie seemed to hear a doubt in Brigitte's voice.

"But are they really?" Annie asked again. "If she says she is, I have to believe her," Brigitte said uneasily. But Annie pressed Brigitte further. "Have you seen the marriage certificate?" she inquired. "No," Brigitte replied. "Would you ask to see it for me?" Annie pleaded. By now Brigitte was wringing her hands. "Oh, Annie, I couldn't do that. Dianne is my friend, and she would think I didn't trust her." Mrs. Turner seemed to accept that.

Later when they were helping Dianne with slicing the ham, Annie startled Dianne by placing her head down on Dianne's stomach and cooing to the baby. Then she told Dianne she was sorry that she had not hugged and kissed her more and that she had always loved her daughter very much. Neither Annie nor George Turner came from a touchy/feelie family, and they thought they should raise their children as they had been reared, Annie explained. As they were leaving the kitchen, Annie extracted a promise from Dianne that she would not hold back such attentions from her baby, an easy request for Dianne to grant. To Dianne, the assurance of her mother's devotion and the acknowledgement that Dianne had been a lovable child was a special gift, made all the more poignant by subsequent events that day.

After dinner, before Brigitte left, Annie asked her to help her in the bathroom. Brigitte was surprised, because despite her handicap, Annie was very independent. In addition, the relentlessly cheerful Annie seemed on the verge of tears. Hugging Brigitte, she asked her to promise to always be there to help Dianne with the baby. The older woman seemed fearful for some reason. "Oh, Annie," Brigitte said, "you know I will, but you are going to be here, too, to see us all get old and your grandchild grow up." "Just promise me," Annie insisted. "Of course," Brigitte said. "Dianne is like my sister, and now I'm going to be an aunt."

Not long after, Brigitte departed for her home in the northwest suburbs. She felt highly anxious throughout the forty-minute drive. After letting herself in, she went straight to the phone. It was 10:45 p.m., usually too late to call Dianne, but she wanted to make sure everything was all right.

Instead of reaching Dianne or Alan, the answering service cut in, telling her Dianne was not home. "What do you mean?" Brigitte asked. "When I left less than an hour ago Dianne was in her pj's, ready for bed." The operator told her that the Masters' had taken Mrs. Turner to Palos Community Hospital. On calling the hospital, Brigitte discovered that Annie had fallen down the basement stairs and was in critical condition.

Annie Turner's skull had been fractured in the "accident." She lost consciousness, and gradually her head became so swollen that visitors could not even see her neck. Brigitte wanted to visit Annie, but Dianne said, "I'm doing you a favor. She looks awful, and it's better that you remember her as she was." The prognosis was not good, and on April 19, 1977, at fifty-seven years of age, Annie Turner died.

The law is a little hazy on such matters, but in general, much less serious incidents are examined by the police. If an investigation of Annie Turner's fall or subsequent death was carried out by the Cook County Sheriff's Police, who had jurisdiction, the records have disappeared.

However, because the attending physician would not sign the death certificate, the Cook County Medical Examiner's Office assigned an investigator. The inquiry was conducted by telephone with Alan Masters, who identified himself incorrectly as Annie's son-in-law. He explained that after eating dinner, Annie got up from the table, and while Alan watched, she walked through a hallway and opened a door, which she thought led into another room, and fell down the basement stairs. This was inaccurate on two counts: dinner had long been over when the fall took place at 10:30 p.m., and there was no door to the basement. The investigator was told that Annie had been blind for years, and the file was marked "no signs of foul play." Case closed.

Dianne took her beloved mother's death very hard. It was even more difficult because George Turner was firm and vocal in his belief that Alan had something to do with Annie's fall, that he had pushed her down the stairs in one of his rages. Dianne's father thought he knew why the police showed no interest; the cops were in Alan's pocket.

Dianne and her friends believed Alan was responsible as well; they believed that Annie had confronted Alan on the marriage question, and in response, he had struck out at her. If so, he got away with manslaughter so easily that it was a simple matter to progress to premeditated murder.

What neither Dianne nor her friends knew was that for some time before Easter, Alan had been complaining around the office that he was tired of having Dianne's mother at the house all the time and that "the old lady" was getting to be a "real pain in the ass." After the "accident," Masters told associates he had to apologize to Dianne repeatedly for leaving the nonexistent basement door open. Alan told one man, who knew the layout of the house, that he "could not convince Dianne" that he had not been responsible in some way for Annie Turner's death. To people who knew Alan well, this was as good as a confession of some measure of culpability.

The last months of Dianne's pregnancy were haunted by her fears about the truth behind her mother's death. Annie Turner had been dealing with her handicap for more than forty years. She was found lying face up, with her head on the basement floor and her legs on the stairs. If indeed she had tripped and fallen, the reasoning went, she would have landed face down. Dianne was puzzled because the police did not step in, she told one friend, unless it was because of Alan's power.

Dianne's dreams were turning into nightmares. She struggled with her grief, not wanting it to affect the baby she was carrying. Dianne's friends rallied to help her through this time. She ate carefully, took her vitamins, and drank no alcohol at all. She tried to think pleasant thoughts, and when seamy topics would come up on television talk shows, she would pat her stomach and say to the baby, "You mustn't listen to this now." In her mother's memory, she became a dependable volunteer at Recording for the Blind.

Dianne wrote of this bleak time, "Five months pregnant, living with an often conspicuously absent and late man, my mother died. Another story. Previous to my grief we had grown so far apart that I had no one to hold me as I sobbed myself to sleep alone at night."

On July 20, 1977, Dianne was delivered of a healthy baby girl at Hinsdale Hospital. Dianne wanted to name the child after her mother, but knew she had hated being called Annie. Instead Dianne called her daughter Georgianna, which was shortened to Georgie by family and friends.

The baby changed Dianne's life. Georgie helped to alleviate Dianne's grief over Annie's death and to come to terms with her mental anguish over the abortion. However, there was still no marriage planned any time soon, and she worried about protecting Georgie. In a handwritten document headed "Acknowledgement of Paternity" and dated July 29, 1977, Alan Masters affirmed that he was the father of "a female child born to Dianne G. Turner a/k/a Dianne Masters." As he was not at that time a practicing Jew, he agreed with Dianne that Georgie should be raised a Roman Catholic and attended the baby's baptism.

On a par with her concern over Georgie's illegitimate status, Dianne was troubled by Alan's attitude toward the baby. Now that the child was born, she hoped he would take an interest in the little girl and share Dianne's joy, but he showed no signs of wavering. She discussed this at length with Pat and Brigitte. She resorted to stratagems that would force Alan to pay attention to the child. Dianne would put Georgie down for her nap and then announce she had an errand that had to be completed, promising to be back before the baby woke. Instead, on occasion she stayed out late on purpose, knowing Alan could not stand to hear the infant crying and would pick her up. To some extent, this worked. Dianne came home to find him changing the child's diaper.

Still, Alan ignored Georgie for long periods. Just as he had done with Dianne, in lieu of more homely demonstrations of affection and caring, he showered his daughter with big, expensive presents. Like Dianne, in public he treated Georgie as an ornament, something to be displayed and then shelved in private. He even used Georgie's July birthday party as a way of repaying social obligations. Instead of the simple family and children's party Dianne wanted, it turned into a political and police bash, with tents and clowns and ponies and carrousels. As Georgie grew, she was required to stand at a microphone as she opened the presents, thanking her benefactor in a manner too adult for her years. Dianne tried to reason with Alan about this but got nowhere.

Dianne continued her outside interests in recording for the blind and in the battered women's hot line, and there were outings and trips with friends. She studied baby books to find the best advice for raising a child and heeded her mother's admonition to demonstrate her love for Georgie at every possible chance.

Friends sometimes got a glimpse of what life with Alan could be like. One night the Caseys arrived for a barbecue to find that the Masters' had been quarreling. This had happened with other friends, and it was just part of married life. But when it came time to eat, Alan prepared three steaks, leaving Dianne out. When Pat told Alan she thought this was terrible and certainly would not lead to increased harmony, Alan turned on her, saying "Don't YOU ever tell ME what to do." The words themselves are not horrifying; it was his tone and the way he looked at her that made Pat shiver. Later, she would remember his voice and appearance when Dianne would mention the increasing ferocity and mercurial aspects of Alan's temper.

CHAPTER 6

$\mathcal{I}$n 1979, Dianne marked her fourth year in Palos. She and Alan had been together for almost ten years, more or less. Their daughter was growing and thriving, and Dianne told everyone who would listen that there was no such thing as the "terrible twos" when it came to Georgie. Her home was under control, at least in terms of refurbishing, but her relationship with Alan was deteriorating. Four years after he officially separated from his wife, Dianne was still unwed.

She compensated for her disappointments by redoubling her efforts in other areas. The abuse hot line had evolved into the Crisis Center of South Suburbia (CCSS), a shelter for abused women and their children. It was housed in an unused building on the Moraine Valley campus.

During the course of establishing the shelter, which allegedly had been built as a honeymoon cottage, Dianne came in contact with many members of the MVCC staff. There was a vacancy on the board that year, and Dianne decided to run for it.

She put a tremendous amount of energy into the race for what was a low profile, unpaid position. On election night, she awaited the returns in her family room with friends. When her campaign manager called to say she was over the top, Dianne clapped her hands and said, "Yippee." Pat Casey remembers being terribly pleased to see her friend so joyous.

109

Her mood did not last long. "You should have won after I bought it for you," Alan said. "And by the way, you still owe me $350 for your divorce."

A crushed Dianne fled upstairs. Pat waited a short time, then followed, finding Dianne in tears in her bedroom. "Never mind," Pat soothed. "You know what you did and how hard you worked. Don't let him take that away from you." Tearfully Dianne replied, "I know. What hurts most is that he just cannot ever let anyone believe that I am capable of doing anything on my own. Everything has to belong to him, be under his control." She splashed water on her face, brushed her hair, and returned to the gathering, which had lost its celebratory atmosphere.

Through her campaign and during the years that followed, Alan would brag that it had cost him $20,000 to "purchase" Dianne's seat on the board. On several of these occasions, Alan added that, "At least Dianne has a decent insurance policy now" (referring to a policy that the college took out for all board members). "Yes," Dianne interjected, "I'm worth $100,000 to him now but only if I'm dead."

No one realized how prophetic this remark would be.

Despite everything—another home she had come to love, meaningful work to do, financial security, beautiful clothes and jewelry, an adored child—the Masters' personal situation kept going downhill. They tried seeing a psychiatrist for marriage counseling, but to Dianne he seemed to be completely on Alan's side. "Do you suppose we're the only people who've gone to a marriage counselor without being married?" she asked Brigitte ruefully.

Alan was letting himself go even further. Dianne tried to help him stay with his various diets, preparing healthy foods, none of which he liked, urging him to slow down when ingesting meals. But Alan's body type, sluggish metabolism, and sedentary life-style all worked against him. Bob Casey told Alan he needed someone to work out with, and so Masters finally joined the Y. According to Pat

Casey, "If Alan did something, he did it 300 percent. He showed up at the gym in an expensive exercise outfit, with sweatbands everywhere, and then proceeded to sit and watch while Bob jogged and exercised." Casey tried to persuade Alan to join him, but Masters soon left, and Casey found him watching television in the locker room.

His baldness was another problem. Like many men who try to disguise a seriously receding hairline, Masters grew his hair very long on one side and tried combing it over the ever-increasing bald spot. Caught in a breeze, this long strand would blow across his face, causing even his best friends to collapse with laughter. After one such incident, Dianne said, "Remember Samson? Well, some night, when he is asleep, I'm going to slip into his room with the scissors..." He tried expensive hairpieces but could not seem to get a decent fit.

Understandably, Alan did not enjoy being reminded of his faults. It was not as if he could actually DO anything about being bald, fat, and middle-aged. He went on periodic diets and lost hundreds of pounds during his years with Dianne, but the loss never held. He would accuse Dianne of nagging, and then the battle would be joined.

No matter how it looked to outsiders, the only source of delight which never failed was Georgianna. Having a daughter made Dianne take stock of herself and her life. She added up her pluses and her minuses and redoubled her efforts to be a good mother and a better person.

She was determined to attend a convention of parliamentarians in Washington, D.C., but worried about leaving Georgianna. She knew Alan would be gone most of the time, and the usual babysitters they employed would not give the child the care Dianne wanted for her daughter. Because she knew how important the long weekend was to her friend, Brigitte volunteered to stay at the house and look after Georgie, including taking the little girl to Saint Michael's Catholic Church on Sunday.

Dianne called every day, but to make sure the baby did not feel abandoned, Brigitte had strict instructions to read Georgie letters Dianne had written, one for each day she would be gone. Upon rising, Georgie would run to Brigitte and ask, "What does my mommy say today?" Each missive started with, "Good morning, darling, mommy loves you. Just wait till you hear what fun you and Auntie Brigitte will have today." And then Dianne would go on to describe plans she had made for the little girl, adding little poems and funny stories for her.

Inevitably, it was Georgianna's well-being that made her re-evaluate her situation with Alan. She did believe that he had grown to love the girl in his own way but that it was a destructive kind of love. He seemed disinterested in the simpler aspects of parenthood, such as just getting down on the floor and roughhousing with the girl. Some of it she attributed to his age. He was forty-five when the baby was born, grossly overweight and out of condition. Most worrying of all, he showed signs of treating Georgie the way he treated Dianne: as a sort of windup doll, a toy which performed when he felt like it and could be ignored when he did not. The one exception was shopping trips where he indulged Georgie's every whim. Dianne felt this was unhealthy, too. Dianne returned to Dr. Schwemer, her psychiatrist, for help. She knew she had to become stronger.

With all the signals Dianne was transmitting, it was predictable that Alan would sense that she was moving toward some sort of epiphany. If he did not head her off, it could mean the end of their relationship, troubled as it was. She was making new friends and developing her skills. The house was in her name, and he had admitted that Georgie was his child, so he would have to support her. Dianne was young and beautiful and had every expectation of finding other men. She was making excellent contacts in Democratic politics and could expect to move in circles where Alan, despite his money, would never be welcome. None of this sat well with his pride or his sense of ownership.

Their always troubled relationship escalated once again into violence. Dianne took Georgie and her jewelry and fled to the home of a friend. She was prepared once again to cut him off, and Alan seemed to sense this. He left pathetic notes for Dianne. "I'm going crazy without you, Please come home, please." Another said, "After you read this note Destroy it...I am going to see Steve [his son] and I shall arrange to die so you and all others can collect the insurance." The breakup was further complicated when Dianne's jewelry and seven thousand dollars in cash she was holding for her father disappeared during a weekend out of town. She suspected Alan was behind the theft, and he was stung by the accusation. "I had no knowledge of your dad's money...to call me a thief is the worst thing anyone has ever called me...Please consider how these weeks have messed up our family and please return with the baby. I am trying and have been on Stillman [one of many fad diets Masters tried] for a week and will stay until I weight [sic] 200 pounds." The house where Dianne was staying was just across the Cook County line. Alan told Dianne that he arranged with the sheriff in neighboring Will County to take a lie detector test, which he passed.

Not long after, Dianne and Alan reconciled. He made all the usual promises about losing weight, improving their communications, stopping the physical abuse, and marriage. Dianne had good reason to doubt him, but finally he did begin to move toward obtaining a divorce. The arrangement was that his wife would file, using desertion for more than one year without cause or provocation as the grounds. The petition was granted on March 24, 1980.

The property settlement and child support agreement was extremely generous. Alan's first family would continue to live in their home in Lincolnwood. The elder boy was already of age, and full custody of their sixteen-year-old son was granted to the former Mrs. Masters, with Alan retaining visitation rights. Alan would be responsible for seeing his sons through college. In return for dropping her claim to any rights to other properties Masters owned, his ex-wife accepted a property settlement of $300,000, to be paid in 300 installments of $1,000 per month. These monthly payments were not to be altered by any change in Alan Masters' circumstances, including his death.

CHAPTER 7

March 25, 1980, started just like any other Tuesday for Dianne. Alan had left the house before she rose for breakfast. Increasingly, he came home just to eat dinner and was in bed, asleep, by 8 p.m. In the morning he would be gone by 5 a.m., supposedly to the office to catch up on his work. From time to time, she would call there, to find he had not yet come in. Dianne assumed he was being unfaithful to her. She tried not to think about it much for Georgie's sake, and she certainly refused to give Alan the satisfaction that she knew he was up to his old tricks and that it bothered her. Basically, Dianne did not want her suspicions confirmed.

Even though she had nothing special planned, as always, Dianne took pains with her appearance, applying her makeup carefully and dressing in her at-home uniform of pants and a silk blouse. Nice, but nothing out of the ordinary. She took care of board-related paperwork, talked to the housekeeper, and played with Georgie.

Late in the morning the phone rang. It was Alan, asking her to jump in the car and meet him in the Loop for a late lunch. Dianne was surprised and rather pleased. This had not happened for a long time. "I'll have to change clothes," Dianne told him. "There's not enough time for that," Alan said. "I have to be back in court. You'll have to leave right away."

Dianne made arrangements for Georgie's lunch and nap, grabbed a coat and was out the door. On the drive into the city, she looked forward to the unexpected outing. Maybe there was some hope for them yet.

On the way home later that afternoon, her mood of happy anticipation was gone. "For ten years, I wanted to marry that man in the worst way," Dianne fumed, "and that's exactly how I did marry him. I can't believe he did this to me, without warning, with no chance to prepare, without being able to ask Brigitte or Pat to be there. Damn him anyway!"

A trucker cut in front of her, and she barely was able to brake. "I've got to calm down, or I'll have an accident. On my wedding day. All these years together and through all the trouble, and this man hasn't got a clue about me. He knew yesterday his divorce had come through...he could have told me last night...I could have made some plans...bought something new to wear or at least worn a really good dress...made this into a special day. Instead he rushes me into driving downtown in any old thing...and I was so pleased to be asked!"

Her mind raced on as she sped down the expressway. "It's not as if I expected a full-dress wedding...I've done all that already...and for Georgie's sake we've got to pretend this happened years ago anyway...but it could have been *nice*. He owns all these judges...he could have arranged for one of them to marry us at home or in chambers...anywhere but that dreary courtroom in the county building filled with pregnant teenagers and crying parents. All we needed was a father with a shotgun to make the farce complete. Then he couldn't even be bothered to come home with me...press of business again...I'll just *bet* he had to go back to the office..."

The newly official Mrs. Masters arrived in her driveway in record time, with a terrific headache. The first thing she did, after checking on Georgie, was call Brigitte to tell her the news. Brigitte would understand how Dianne felt. Brigitte did, but she also tried to calm her friend. "You know how men are," she reasoned. "They just don't understand these things. And Alan is less sensitive than most. I do wish I could have been there with you to throw rice...."

Dianne could not help but snort at that. "Rice! It would take more than some antique fertility symbol for me to get pregnant...if I wanted to. It would take a man with a stiff...you know what I mean. If Alan can do it anymore, he's doing it with someone else."

"Dianne, you don't know that," Brigitte soothed. If nothing else, she wanted Dianne to have some peace of mind today. "He's getting older, he's so overweight, he's probably just losing interest in general, not in you." It would be best if she could distract Dianne. "We can still get together to celebrate. We'll plan it together, we'll all get something new to wear, and we'll make it a time to remember."

"We'll have to leave Alan home if we want to do that," Dianne snapped. "Oh, Brigitte, I'm so sorry. I'm being a bitch when none of this is your fault. It's just that I always thought this day would mean so much to me, but now that it is here, it's just like everything else with Alan...empty. Everything else but Georgie, that is. I suppose he's trying, within his limits. He's promised me a 'honeymoon'—try not to laugh—and he did buy me a new ring. It's a cluster of diamonds that looks like a flower. Now I can take off the band that spells 'love' in diamonds." She laughed but not merrily.

Brigitte seized the opportunity. "There, you see? He did plan for it but just not the way you wanted. It could have been more romantic, but that's not Alan. Try to be glad that you have what you wanted: protection for Georgie. She'll never have to know that you weren't married when she was born." To herself, Brigitte thought, "And if and when you two split up, Alan will have to take care of his daughter in the same way he took care of his sons." The two women had discussed Dianne's worries about the security of Georgie's future, but Brigitte did not want to bring up the specter of a possible divorce on an already tarnished wedding day.

Dianne thought for a minute and then replied, "You're right. I have what I wanted. So why do I feel so sad?" Before hanging up, Dianne added, "I keep thinking of something. Isn't there an old saying about be careful what you wish for because you might get it?"

After the wedding, the couple saw increasingly less of each other. In the beginning, they at least shared dinner and discussed their day's activities. That some came to a full stop. Alan rose early and left the house promptly. He was gone all day, and even if he was home for dinner, it was a silent meal, and then he went to his separate bedroom. Dianne recognized the pattern from the days when Alan was cheating on his first wife. Throughout their years together, she was aware there had been a procession of other women in Alan's life. For the time being, she chose to ignore his philandering.

Behind Dianne's back, Alan boasted that he had sexual intercourse with his receptionist on the day he married Dianne. Most of Alan's other women were passing fancies, but this one seemed particularly adhesive. Dianne took a trip to Florida with Pat Casey one summer, and she came back to find charge slips belonging to this woman and some female underwear not Dianne's under the seat of her car. Dianne confronted Alan, insisting the woman would have to go. Alan procured another job for her but continued to see her and other women on occasion.

On April 3, 1980, George Turner died a painful death from cancer. Dianne had not been close to her father, but still she grieved. Now her brother was the only member left of her immediate family. Except for Georgie, she felt terribly alone.

Dianne did not know that Alan's undermining of their marital relationship did not stop with infidelity. He was contemplating murder.

CHAPTER 8

$\mathcal{E}$arly in the fall of 1980, Charlie Bates was lunching at the L&N Restaurant in Summit. The L&N is the type of eatery which serves solid meatloaf-and-potatoes cuisine at a reasonable price and is popular with local business people. Bates needed the best buy he could get for a buck; he was in big trouble. His problems with the law, beginning when he swiped the class field-trip money in the fifth grade, now were of epic proportions. He was in violation of the terms of his parole in a neighboring state and faced many outstanding warrants in several local jurisdictions. He had no visible means of support.

As Bates was contemplating his many woes, Alan Masters sat down opposite him. As a little boy, Bates met Masters when the attorney represented Bates' mother in a divorce case. Bates was aware of Masters' reputation as a fixer *par excellence*. He had first-hand experience; in December 1979, Bates was present after hours at Al's Fox and Hounds tavern in Willow Springs, where Alan Masters and Michael Corbitt were assisting a Bridgeview official in disposing of a car used in a murder. The body had already been dumped in neighboring Will County, but Corbitt and Masters advised that the auto in which a young woman had been slain by the official's son be taken to an auto wrecking yard and compacted. Masters also insisted that the clothing worn by the men involved be placed inside the car previous to its demolition so that it would not be possible to match up any fibers should the body be found.

119

No doubt about it; Masters was good, but the chubby little lawyer was way out of Bates' price range.

"What's new?" Masters asked, and Bates told him. The two men discussed the outstanding warrants against Bates. Masters appeared to take an interest in Bates' situation and invited the young man to his nearby office that evening.

When Bates arrived, he was surprised to find also present two corrupt policemen of his acquaintance. Bates had worked with Michael Corbitt, chief of police of Willow Springs, on a number of occasions. One memorable night, Bates helped loot a semitrailer full of Canon cameras right in the middle of Willow Springs while Corbitt stood guard.

The other man was a cop from west suburban Berwyn, a close associate of Alan Masters who was notorious for his willingness to stop at nothing when profit was involved.

Bates was accustomed to committing crimes with the assistance of local cops; in addition to Corbitt, he sometimes worked with officers from several southwestern suburbs, and he had a lucrative arrangement with a sheriff's lieutenant who would set up a score and act as lookout while Bates and two confederates burgled drug stores, offices, and homes.

Bates quickly discovered that the meeting had been convened not so much to help with his problems, but to assist Alan in a little difficulty he was having with his new wife. Masters explained that Dianne was unfaithful, although this was not true at the time. It may have been a ploy to get Bates' sympathy; Alan knew that Bates' young wife recently had left him.

More important to the two policemen, Masters admitted that during what he called "pillow talk" with Dianne, he revealed information about their combined illegal activities that could be damaging should she decide to use the details in a divorce action. Alan mentioned how much his first divorce had cost him, and he made it clear he was not going to sit still for another expensive settlement.

As the three men listened, an increasingly enraged Alan revealed his plan to have Dianne murdered in a home invasion while he had an alibi elsewhere. When the men poked holes in the scenario, saying that the situation could easily get out of control and that Alan would be the first suspect after such an event, Masters swore that his sheriff's police friends would take care of everything. He was willing to pay twenty-five thousand dollars, which would be split three ways. In addition, he would provide Bates with free legal representation. When Masters was finished, Corbitt spoke in behalf of the two other men, promising that they would be in touch.

"I have to be nuts to be even talking about this with a couple of cops," Bates thought to himself as he was leaving. Burglary and hijacking were one thing; murder was another. The idea that he might be set up flashed through his mind, but Alan's plan was so crazy that Bates gave it no serious consideration.

In early 1981, Bates once again was summoned to meet with Masters, Corbitt, and the third man about getting rid of Dianne. Alan had been convinced by the two cops that his original plan was not workable, so he came up with a viable alternative. Masters would tip the men off when Dianne would be at a restaurant she frequented on a regular basis. If an abduction in the parking lot was not possible, they would intercept her before she could get out of her car at home. Corbitt and the third man would drive her in her Cadillac to the canal in Willow Springs, while Bates followed in his own car. Once at the canal, the third man would shoot her, and she would be left in the trunk of the Cadillac. Bates would leave his car for the other two men to use and would drive Dianne's Cadillac to a local wrecking yard to be crushed and shipped to a scrap metal collection location.

Besides driving and providing a getaway vehicle for the two cops, Bates' role was to use a contact who worked at the wreckers, which was just a block from the home of Bates' girlfriend. The day after Dianne was whacked, Corbitt would return Bates' car and pay him his share.

During the discussion, Masters joked about Dianne's insurance policy, saying that in effect she would be paying for her own murder. Even better, Alan said, he would realize a seventy-five thousand dollar profit. As a show of good faith, Masters would represent Bates in his next court case.

Bates went along with the planning session but had no intention of participating any further for two reasons. First, his concern that he was being set up escalated, and second, he would not involve his friend at the wrecking yard. He would have to extricate himself from the deal somehow.

Shortly after Alan Masters, as promised, got one charge against Bates thrown out of court in Oak Lawn, the young man was arrested, tried and convicted in another case in another county. He was given a long sentence in the Illinois prison system.

This caused no small amount of consternation among the conspirators. They feared Bates might give them away in exchange for a sentence reduction. As a result, Alan Masters wrote the imprisoned Bates a letter urging him to be a "stand-up guy," a term Bates understood to mean he should keep his mouth shut. Bates had no intention of becoming a snitch.

By the early summer of 1981, Masters was sufficiently sure of Bates' silence to resume his planning, returning to his original home invasion plan. He inquired of his friend CCSPD Sgt. Clarke Buckendahl, "If something happens at my house, who would handle it?" "The Cook County Sheriff's Police," Buckendahl told him. "No, no," Alan replied, "I mean who, specifically."

"That would depend on what beat car happened to be working at what shift..." But Masters interrupted Buckendahl before he could finish. "No, what investigators...would Lieutenant Vanick handle it?"

"Yes," Buckendahl replied. But Masters was not satisfied. "Well, wouldn't Keating handle it?" "No," Buckendahl explained, "that's not Keating's function. Anything out in this area is Lieutenant Vanick."

Alan was nothing if not persistent. "Keating could order Vanick," he asserted. Buckendahl disagreed. "No, Keating is not Vanick's superior officer." Clearly disappointed, Masters let the matter drop.

Dianne was aware that her communications problem with Alan had become even more pronounced, and during this same period, she again wrote in an attempt to get through to Alan, even though such efforts angered him. She still clung to the idea that they were both rational people who could work something out. Besides, for Dianne, writing was a way of letting off steam and avoiding an emotional explosion.

Dianne admitted that in the past she had refused to accept the fact that Alan would never change. "I'm not saying that the way you are is bad, etc. I'm just saying that the way you are is not good for us... I'm not saying you don't care for me, love me, think of me, support me. You can't, won't, get inside of me. Learn who I am, where I'm going, what I need. And because of this inability to relate to others, those who love you suffer. Think about this and I'm certain you will agree. Your relationships are superficial and you are comfortable with this." The first portion of the letter continues in this vein, and the complaints are not unusual in a union of more than ten years where one partner feels she is being taken for granted. For instance, Alan no longer seemed interested in hearing about her work with the crisis center. "I thought you liked to hear about it. This was one thing we shared. You have come to me at the end of the day with your experiences and I to you with mine...CCSS came at a time when I needed to fill my life with something to help me forget all of the death and dying." Dianne felt she had done as much as possible in this area and she wanted to move on, but she did not know to what. "I will still need something to fill my time. To fill the hole that should be filled with our relationship."

She felt she had made every effort to comply with Alan's complaints. In the fall of 1980, he criticized her for being involved in so many activities that kept her out evenings, so she cut down. She even began cooking more to please him. But while Dianne was bending over backwards, she felt Alan was doing nothing. "If there is a promise heaven, it must be overflowing with your vacant promises. All of the things you said you realized about my feelings and needs when we were seeing Dr. M. [the marriage counselor] was a guise."

Up to this point, the letter dealt with gripes that arise in most marriages, and would probably have provoked Alan only to accuse Dianne of more nagging. But suddenly the tone changed from plaintive to ominous. "You thrive while I drown. Quietly. Well, I'm tired of being quiet...This letter is my shouting. My crying quietly at night is my shouting. I know that raising my voice has never made you hear..."

She knew how Alan would respond. "I have a beautiful life because of you. Not WITH you. I should be eternally grateful....And what good is all of your work if we don't enjoy life...A walk in the woods, a cool swim at night, a breathtaking sunset...Our life is to be what you want. If you don't want me to get involved with local politics, then I should not...I'm tired of you making decisions.

"Aside from your business you are the laziest person I have ever met. You don't work at anything...Perhaps you don't see how hard I have worked to create the kind of environment you like to live in. I vowed to myself that I would maintain this as long as I could. If you were content, then you would be able to give me what I need...You have had your peace and I...what? Laziness! You don't even help at the house. You have made so many promises of exercising that I don't even listen...You are a lazy lover. Passive. You are lazy with Georgianna."

Masters had handled many divorces, and to him this letter read not just like a checklist of grounds for a permanent breakup; it read like a threat. Although Dianne had suffered brutality at Alan's hands, she was not yet aware of just how far he would go, or she might have been more careful. Her words continued to spiral downhill.

"I can't give any more. I'm not saying I will change drastically. I will continue to be pleasant, converse, make meals, organize our family and social lives. I refuse to raise my only child in a climet [sic] of turmoil. So it will continue to be peaceful on Wolf Road. But you must know, and should keep in mind that there is a volcano brewing beneath."

> Then Dianne listed a series of positive steps she would take:
>
> I intend to go back to see a counselor...
>
> I intend to seek comfort and direction from religion/the church/my faith.
>
> I plan on confiding my turmoil in a friend or two....
>
> I need some space. If you are begging to say some negative things to me than do so as I have, in writing. I don't want hostility rampant in this house.
>
> I intend to remain sexually faithful. You know that this will be impossible indefinitely.

Any of the above would be enough to send Alan into one of his epic rages, and Dianne sensed that it was necessary to soften the impact these words might have. She reassured Alan that she still loved and cared for him, writing, "You have been my world and life."

But her desperation was such that she could not let it rest there. "I don't know what else I can do for us that will make things better. Other than become a different person. This last year I have been more at peace with myself than in my entire life. I like me. I am proud of me. I am a basically good person...I stand by my commitments, as I have stood by you through some very trying times. I am not saying I intend to leave you. I just know that what we have is not enough..."

That Dianne had indeed become a different person was to Alan the greatest threat of all. In the past, he had always been able to get her back, even while abusing her mentally and physically, because she was terribly insecure and could only define herself in terms of a man. Now, suddenly, the trophy wife was behaving in an independent fashion, and he could sense he was losing his hold on her.

If Dianne hoped that it would provoke Alan to take some positive action, she was tragically mistaken. Instead, it alerted her husband to what he had already sensed: that if he did not change, something he was extremely unlikely to do given his level of self-satisfaction, Dianne was readying herself to bolt.

During this same period, Dianne began telling friends and associates that she had collected enough information on Alan's corrupt activities to guarantee at least one indictment or the interest of the IRS. When they expressed concern, she assured them that she was keeping the data, which she called her "life insurance policy," in a safe deposit box where Alan would never find it.

Word of this inevitably reached Alan, either through his spies or the bugs placed in his home, or both, further inflaming the situation. It was bad enough that she would not stay bought, that she had become socially acceptable in circles where he met with nothing but contempt, that she was young enough and pretty enough and accomplished enough to undoubtedly attract other well-to-do men. But now she was endangering not just his livelihood but his freedom as well. He enjoyed boasting to her about his corrupt and illegal activities, how he owned cops and judges and fixed cases, and how he cheated the tax men by taking some fees and bribes in cash, which he did not declare as income. If Dianne went to the authorities, he could lose his license to practice law or might even go to jail. Should it come to a divorce, it was always possible that the case might not be assigned to one of Alan's tame judges, and he would lose control of the situation. It was now abundantly clear that at long last Dianne felt she could be responsible for her own life. She did not require validation any longer, especially from a man. She could not have posed a more serious threat if she had confronted Alan with an automatic weapon.

CHAPTER 9

*J*im Church had been attracted to Dianne Masters from the first day he saw her. She was running for election to the MVCC board and had come before the faculty to ask for their support in her campaign. The big question was would she be proadministration and antifaculty. Dianne answered by saying that she would be procollege and would vote whatever way would bring about the best for administration, faculty, and students.

Jim thought it was a good answer, but Dianne did not win the backing of the faculty association. As a member of that body's executive board, it was Jim's responsibility to call the candidates and advise the winners and the losers. He told Dianne that she had lost in a very close vote and that he liked her presentation.

After she won the 1979 election, he began seeing her around the campus and at the monthly board meetings, which he attended as a faculty observer, and at school functions. They slowly became friends; Dianne was learning as she went but obviously was feeling good about the job she was doing. She was elected vice chairman of the board; she probably had the votes to become chairman, but she wanted to take it slowly.

In the middle of 1981, the number of special meetings of the board increased because they would soon be hiring a new president to run the college on a day-to-day basis. Dianne was named to head the search committee, and since the college presidency was

129

very important to the faculty, she and Jim were thrown together even more frequently. The board members had no offices on the campus, so in the interests of privacy, Dianne would go to Jim's office to use his phone. By that time, they were at ease in each others' company and found they had many interests in common.

Under the previous administration, the policies at Moraine had acted to keep the board and faculty at a distance. Most of the board members, especially Dianne, wanted to bridge that gap. The board began going out after meetings, inviting whatever members of the staff and faculty were present to join them. It was purely voluntary but a good way to get to know each other as well as to relax after the often tedious meetings.

Jim and Dianne drew closer, and they began communicating in several ways. The telephone was difficult because Jim was usually in the classroom, and leaving messages for Dianne at home would fuel Alan's suspicions even before there was any basis for them. Because the faculty did not as yet have enclosed mailboxes, they began to leave letters and notes for each other in the office of Mary Nelson, a mutual friend. These missives not only are a source of insight into Dianne's feelings and attitudes in her last months of life but ultimately would help to direct the serious investigation of her murder.

There was a time when Dianne would have plunged impulsively into an intimate relationship, but she had learned a lot, mostly the hard way. She thought she knew Jim, that they were kindred spirits, but she wanted to be sure there was more than just physical attraction, for both their sakes. She had no intention of taking this lightly.

As the fall of 1981 wore on, Dianne confided in Jim more and more about personal matters, especially her problems at home and the decision she was reaching to file for a divorce. She wanted a lawyer who had no connections with Alan, someone he could not fix. She was given the name of Maureen McGann-Ryan by another MVCC board member and decided to hire her to handle divorce proceedings.   Jim Church seems an unlikely player in the tragedy about to take place, especially to Dianne's detractors. If she really was a money-hungry adventuress, out for all she could get, the Dianne-Jim thing made no sense. He was not rich, he was not powerful, he was not famous. And he probably would never be any of those things.

The person Dianne had become valued a kind heart above all other appearances or qualities. Jim Church is a cozy sort of person, affable and immediately sympathetic. Stockily built and a little over average height, with a pleasant rather than handsome face, Church seemed solid. He brought an element of safety and security into Dianne's life.

Sometime in December 1981 or early January 1982, Dianne and Jim progressed from being friends to being lovers. Dianne felt the bond between them was all the stronger because they had grown to like and admire each other first. She was not trying to get back at Alan or teach him a lesson, and while in the past she had felt empty without a man in her life, she knew this was no longer a necessity. Her attachment to Jim was based on genuine feelings, and she was proud of that. She was not without guilt over the situation, however. She discussed it with the priest who was counseling her because, as she wrote to Jim, "I know that my relationship with you had hurt the man I was married to. It didn't matter...what he had done to me for that is what he has to live with. I did feel bad that I had caused him pain. He was hurting. I was sorry."

She was reassured when the priest told her that her value systems were "in place and true to form." Still, she fretted about what other people would think. "I know that I am a good person," she would tell Jim. "Realistically speaking, to other than intimate friends, I am going to look like a leper rejecting the medical doctor sent to heal them. I am internally gearing up to be portrayed in that light."

Jim had become her sounding board, her rock. She drew on his calm nature and his willingness to wait for her. She was rediscovering the pleasures of sex with him, but to Dianne, that was a bonus. Both of them had previously failed in matters of the heart, and they could scarcely believe their good fortune in finding each other.

Born in 1947, James Church was brought up in Calumet City, Illinois, a suburb right on the Indiana line that was trying to live down its reputation as a sin city. Away from the honky-tonk strip, pleasant homes were inhabited by house-proud members of the lower middle classes who worked in the nearby steel mills and automotive plants. Cal City had several ethnic flavors, but Polish was a dominant one.

Jim attended St. Joseph's College in Indiana, receiving a bachelor's degree in economics. He went on for his master's at Northern Illinois University in De Kalb. After finishing in 1973, he joined the Moraine faculty as an instructor. At the time he met Dianne, Jim had risen to the level of assistant professor. He also taught part time at Morton and Thornton Colleges, both two-year community institutions similar to MVCC. The extra money came in handy because Jim had child support to pay. His marriage ended in divorce in 1979, and his ex-wife had custody of Emily, but he saw the little girl regularly. Emily was two years older than Georgianna, another bond between Jim and Dianne.

Their common Polish heritage was another link. For years Dianne had largely ignored it, was even ashamed of it, but since the deaths of both parents she had felt its tug. She wrote Jim, "Walking into your parents' home was like going back to my child-hood-heritage. I was as comfortable there as I am with you and Emily. As though I knew (the fact) for so long. What? That shifting ethnics is hard: that basics beget basics, that familiarity is comfortable; that Mom would have liked you; that real existence [sic] is more than status..."

Their liaison grew more intense and important to her, and Dianne made no attempt to hide it from friends or colleagues. She seemed to believe that there was some safety in public disclosure. As head of the committee that was seeking a new president for Moraine Valley, Dianne met with the successful candidate several times before he actually took up the reins. On one of these occasions she told him she was filing for divorce and was having an affair with a member of the business college faculty. "I might not get through this alive," she added. As did many people who were on the receiving end of such confidences, the man assured her that "such things usually work themselves out."

For some time, Dianne had been involved in such partisan political activity as precinct work for Jerry Cosentino, the democratic committeeman of Palos Township. When Cosentino decided to run for secretary of state in 1982, Dianne volunteered for his campaign staff. She was very excited about this for several reasons.

After lunch with the statewide campaign manager, she was so excited that she could not wait to reach Jim by phone to discuss it. Instead she wrote to him, her enthusiasm bubbling off the paper. She would start out as a part-time volunteer, but if all went well, by fall she would join the full-time staff, possibly even running the office. It was pretty heady stuff, but Dianne was realistic. She knew such jobs did not pay well, but she looked on it as "a great experience, an opportunity to work with some fascinating people and a beginning. I know I can do the job, for it is exactly what I do so well: Dealing with people, phone work, fund solicitation, research, organization. IF Jerry is elected there will be 4,000 jobs in the sec. of state's office. Surely there will be one for a proven worker." As an added bonus, working downtown would give her more opportunities to be with Jim.

Dianne was making orderly plans for a life away from Alan. After her death, much was made of her alleged ambition to run for political office, but there is no hint of this in her writings nor did she confide it to those who knew her best. She was hoping for a political patronage job to supplement whatever alimony and child support she would receive from Alan. She was a bright woman, and she knew that if she aimed much higher than the MVCC board, there would be people—reporters and the opposition—probing into her background. It would take no great effort to discover that she had married Alan after being his mistress for ten years and that their daughter was born out of wedlock. Alan's reputation as a fixer would be used against her, as well. The chances of winning any public office in Illinois after that came out were nil. But there was no reason why she could not expect a career in the administrative and/or campaign end of politics.

She worried about Alan bringing his influence to bear to keep her from getting the job. After meeting with the campaign's managers, she wrote Jim, "I posed a hypothetical question: What if Charlie N. [Alan's crony Charles Nicosia, a shadowy political and organized crime figure tied to Chicago's notorious West Side Bloc and First (downtown) Ward] from the first ward calls and says that (my working for Cosentino) is against their interests... I am neglecting my duties as a mother, etc. What would they do? He says, first, they don't deal, any of them, with that type of pettiness. Second, [Cosentino] has had his problems with the first ward Italians and it would have little impact...Jerry is only concerned only with winning.

"But whether or not this can be used against me in a custody battle has to be determined...if Maureen says I can, I am going to jump at the chance. I liked Art [the campaign manager]...He is straight up and that is the kind of person I would once again enjoy working with. If I do wrong, he'll let me know. No bullshit as with the many silly dilly housewife volunteers I have worked with. Plus I love being with people. It will be just the right diversion for me."

Throughout 1981, Dianne had been cutting back on outside activities, and she planned to do more of this in 1982. She knew it was necessary if she was to be seriously considered for a paying job. "For as soon as this damn Pres. search is over and the new Pres. is in place, I plan on less of my time going to MVCC activities. I resigned from Recording for the Blind this week. I have dropped out of my Parliamentary Class, but still intend to take that test in August. No more crisis center. No more AAUW [American Association of University Women]. So time is light. Now I do have concerns about a caretaker for G...my housekeeper just announced she is pregnanet [sic]. Probably will drop out of my tennis leagues. Will plan on exercising more, in a variety of ways, during the summer."

Dianne worried how the job would affect Jim. "What do you think? Would you be uncomfortable with my dealing with the big guys. The exposure to different people? For I have to let you know, I still will always enjoy coming home to a peaceful, fulfilling environment. This [the political campaign work] is nice, and may later fulfill some financial necessities, but my home will always come first. For that is what it is all about. No doubt in my mind. (Even though Alan told his Dr. that MVCC comes first, then my political ambitions, then my daughter. He ought to be burned at the stake for that.)"

After laying out the pros and cons, Dianne ended with the question, "By fall, my life surely will be my own?" By fall, her life would be over.

Dianne was by turns frightened and determined, depending in large part on how Alan was behaving. She never knew what his attitude toward her would be, and her stomach pains were a barometer of her uncertainty. Once he went so far as to brandish a gun in front of Dianne and Georgie. On another occasion he grabbed Georgie, determined to take her to the East Coast to meet her half-brothers, but got only as far as Pittsburgh before he was turned back by snow. Instead, he told Dianne he sent the news by wire and phoned his ex-wife to tell her about the existence of a second wife and third child. He claimed, inaccurately, that the reaction of his first family was acceptance and regret that he and Dianne were having problems. He seemed surprised that Dianne refused to be swayed by this action which she had wanted for so long. He could not grasp that it was a case of too little, too late.

Alan told his brother that the only reason she was divorcing him was because she had found someone else. "Still can't accept his errors," Dianne snorted when she heard this. With his pals, Alan frequently played the role of the injured spouse. One close friend overheard her husband discussing the situation with Alan. "I'd 'off' her," was the man's helpful advice.

Dianne's attorney was badgered with phone calls from judges and lawyers anxious to attest to the level of Alan's love and adoration. Alan's counsel weighed in with a plea that Maureen McGann-Ryan persuade Dianne to reconcile. All of this pressure had the opposite effect; it served to strengthen Dianne's resolve.

Worst of all were the threats. Alan would file for custody of Georgie, and with his influence, he would win. She was used to his temper outburst by now, and while she was frightened, she was steadfast,too. "I fear his wrath," she wrote to Jim. She believed her phones were tapped, that she was being followed, and she warned Jim to be careful, too. Their attachment was growing, although they were able to be together only once or twice a week. His patience and understanding seemed boundless; the contrast between Jim and Alan was becoming ever sharper.

Dianne and Jim exchanged declarations of love, and there were discussions about living together after the divorce, together with a few tentative mentions of marriage. It was too soon to think of that, but in the meantime Dianne saw Jim as a continuing part of her life. So much so that she began introducing him to friends she had made through Alan.

They began meeting on Fridays because Jim had no classes that day and Dianne usually finished up early at the campaign office. On one such occasion, after an interlude at a nearby motel, they joined Helene Maignon at the bar of the Chestnut Street Grill in Water Tower Place on Chicago's near north side.

Introductions were made and the evening was proceeding amiably when Dianne decided to call home to check with Georgie's babysitter. Helene went with her. When they returned ten minutes later, Dianne was sobbing and trembling. Alan had answered the phone and told Dianne he would destroy her. He was furious she had gone to a divorce lawyer. Jim and Helen did their best to comfort Dianne, and finally she calmed down enough to drive home.

CHAPTER 10

$\mathcal{T}$he holiday season was a disaster. The Masters family went to Florida, but Alan returned early, leaving his wife and daughter behind. Dianne used the opportunity for some serious thinking. She flew back to Chicago on January 4, 1982, convinced that she wanted a divorce as quickly as possible, and she phoned her lawyer to set things in motion.

During the last weeks of her life, Dianne was fond of quoting from Anne Morrow Lindbergh's book, *War Within and War Without*. The title was an apt description of what Dianne's life had become. The war within was complicated by a fire in her belly: a new stomach ulcer. Tagemet was prescribed for that. She began to suffer from diarrhea as well. She could no longer tell where one anxiety attack ended and another began. These were symptoms of the stress she was under, and she believed they would taper off when the divorce suit was filed.

The war without was another question. For a couple of weeks in January, the Masters' separated. Alan stayed with his brother while Dianne remained at home with their daughter. For Dianne, it was almost bliss to be alone in the house she loved with the daughter she adored. But Alan's behavior was increasingly wild and erratic and threatening.

They had agreed he would pack while Dianne and Georgie were out so as not to distress the little girl any more than necessary. But as Dianne wrote to Jim, "Instead, because he was so 'emotional,' he made his move in front of her. Traumatic. Many tears. She scolded me that 'I made Daddy leave.' I was compelled to tell her that it was his decision because Mom had tummy troubles and we weren't happy together. Only for two weeks."

Alan also was making an issue of a herniated testicle which would require surgery and a period of recuperation. Dianne was in a quandary as to what she should do: press the divorce or postpone until Alan was well. Alan helped resolved this when he arrived home one night, complaining he had to delay a case because he felt so faint he was forced to spend the day on the couch in a judge's chambers. When Dianne suggested that this might be caused by the fact that he was "out until all hours and up at the crack of dawn," a quarrel ensued, ending only when Alan announced he was going to see his doctor.

"He called a county cop friend to take him to the doctor...Never asked me...I suggested he have [the surgery] now and I would care for him. It was a sincere offer. He refused," Dianne wrote.

Robert Rosignal, a CCSPD patrolman and friend of the couple, responded to Alan's request for a ride, only to get his Corvette stuck on the ice in the Masters' driveway. After pushing the car while Alan rocked it, the two men drove off. Alan was semi-coherent, muttering all the way to the doctor's office and back that he and Dianne had a fight.

After this argument, Dianne recognized that Alan's proposed surgery was a delaying tactic meant to get sympathy for him and paint her in a bad light. A session with her spiritual advisor, Monsignor German, at Saint Michael's Church in Orland Park, was of little help to her, but she was grateful to find she still had the courage of her own convictions. Dianne wrote Jim, "During my meeting, I decided that I have a choice, I won't nurse him [Alan]. My guilt regarding the Scarlet Letter I've placed on my chest has been removed. My relationship with you reaffirmed a number of things I had come to doubt about myself. 1) That I was experiencing life as an observer...rather than actually living my life; 2) Yes, someone does care for me in spite of my sordid past; 3) Nothing is wrong with me sexually."

In a postscript, she added, "Georgie just had another nightmare. Have to bring this to an end for all of us...Alan keeps saying he has been thinking about Mom...he also knows that this is a difficult time of year for me. Dad died April 3 and Mom on April 19. He [Alan] should have worked for Hitler."

From her work at the crisis center, Dianne knew that the most dangerous times for a woman trying to escape an abusive situation were three days after she informed her husband of her intent and three days before the final break was made. She reached out for support through religious counseling and psychiatry. When Alan discovered she was talking to Dr. Schwemer, he again tried to win the doctor over to his side by writing another long-winded missive. After asserting how much he loved and cherished Dianne, Masters complained that his wife "wishes to dissolve our marriage rather than allow me to rehabilitate myself." Once again, he wrote about Dianne as if she were a wholly owned subsidiary. Once again, he lied, especially when he indicated his approval of Dianne's attempts to find a work situation, either by studying journalism in graduate school or using her expertise as a parliamentarian. Once again, he saw to it that Dianne received a copy.

Alan Masters was not keeping his own counsel about the impending divorce. In addition to his brother, Masters phoned or appeared at the homes of friends and colleagues.

Diane Economou had worked as a lawyer in Master's office since 1978. In the fall of 1980, Alan told her that Dianne was going to take Georgie and leave him. Nothing came of it, but in October 1981, Economou attended a reunion for law school graduates of DePaul University. A few days after the reunion, Alan asked Economou to be sure not to mention that Alan and Sheila Mikel, the receptionist Dianne insisted Alan fire, had shown up. Economou agreed and did not ask any questions; she did not need to do so. Alan made no attempt to hide the intimate relationship between himself and his former employee. Economou bumped into Alan at a Halloween party at Mikel's home. Afterward, back at the office, Alan again asked Economou not to reveal his where-abouts to Dianne.

In January 1982, Alan told Economou that she would have to go it alone on a case they had been handling jointly because he was too distraught over his marital situation to function. He also told Economou that he was seeing a doctor and was on medication.

On the first weekend in February 1982, while Dianne was out of the house on MVCC business, Alan dismissed the babysitter and left home with his daughter, leaving behind a note that he was taking Georgie away for a long weekend. He knew that using the child as a pawn would not only pain his wife but frighten her as well.

Diane Economou was at her home in west suburban Oak Brook when she received a frantic phone call from Alan. He was at the office with Georgie, and he was taking the little girl to a motel because Dianne was going to leave him. "Don't take her to a motel," Economou urged Masters. "You can come to Oak Brook. I have a lot of bedrooms here." Alan replied that he would see and rung off. Later that evening, Economou answered her doorbell to find Alan and an exhausted Georgie on the doorstep.

Economou went out to get some food for her guests, and when she returned, she found Alan sitting at the kitchen table, crying over Dianne's jewelry which he had liberated from her bedroom. When he saw Economou, he looked up and said, "Look what I have done for her. Look at what I have done for Dianne. Look at all I've given her, and she's gonna leave me, and she's gonna take Georgianna from me..." Then he added, "She's not taking Georgie from me."

Masters wanted to make a phone call, so Economou went into her living room to give him some privacy. He soon joined her, saying he had talked to Dianne, placing the call through the operator so that she would think he was out of state and had taken Georgie with him. Throughout the night, Masters babbled on about Dianne's faults, how they no longer slept together, returning to the same refrain: "I've made her. She came from nothing, and I made her into everything that she is."

Economou was surprised to learn that Masters had been married to Dianne for less than two years. "But you told me that she was trying to get divorced from you before." Masters replied, "We weren't even married then."

Eventually Alan quieted down, and he and Georgie spent the night in Economou's townhouse. The following morning, a Saturday, Economou went into the office, and when she returned home, Alan and Georgianna were gone.

Economou had subsequent encounters with Alan on the matter of his marital situation. He would come into her office, sit down, fold his arms, and begin to cry. "She's just pressuring me. What else does she want from me?" Waving his bottle of Valium, he would interrupt himself, saying. "I'm going to the doctor."

Also in early February 1982, Herman Pastori went to Chicago's Midway Airport to see his wife off to Florida. As he was leaving, Pastori was surprised to bump into Alan Masters. After exchanging greetings, Pastori asked, "What are you doing here?" "I'm going to visit my kids in New York," Masters replied. "How are things going?" Pastori queried. Masters put his head down. "No good. No good at all." Pastori figured the problem had to be domestic. "Is Dianne still giving you problems?" "Yes, serious problems," muttered Alan.

Pastori thought Masters looked terrible, run down and depressed. Concerned that his friend might have suicidal tendencies, Pastori said, "Alan, you won't do anything drastic, will you?"

Masters shot back, "I won't, but I'll have someone else do it."
With that, Alan turned and walked toward his plane.

In the context of Pastori's question, the answer did not make
any sense, and he did not think anything of it at the time. After
Dianne disappeared about six weeks later, Pastori did not report
the conversation, although he did discuss it with Michael Corbitt
on two occasions after Corbitt had been dismissed as chief at
Willow Springs in June 1982.

Masters also talked to Ted Nykaza, a private investigator
working out of the law office. After listening to Alan's stream of
consciousness about how he had created Dianne and could not
understand her ingratitude, Nykaza interjected, "Alan, don't you
think it might be a part of your screwing around with other
women, too?" Masters yelled back, "That has nothing to do with
it."

As soon as Alan realized there was a very good chance that
Dianne was going to go through with the divorce, he approached
Nykaza, asking if the p.i. had the equipment to bug Alan's home
telephones. Nykaza said he did not, and Masters told him to purchase whatever he needed and install it. Alan wanted to learn
whether Dianne had a boyfriend, and if so, who the man was.
Nykaza had the equipment expressed in from a New York firm;
according to the invoices, it arrived on January 25, 1982. Five or six
days later, Nykaza installed the bugs on two of the three lines that
went into the Masters' home. The third line, restricted to Alan's
exclusive use, was left clean.

It was not a sophisticated bugging job; Nykaza placed two
fairly large tape recorders on top of a furnace air vent in the basement utility room. They ran on batteries and were voice activated.
Not long after they were installed, Masters paged Nykaza on his
beeper. Nykaza answered the summons to Masters' home to find
that Alan had tried to remove the tape recorders so that he could
listen to the tapes and had made a hash of it. Nykaza replaced the

bugs, and Masters asked him to obtain two more recorders so that it would be possible to play the tapes whenever he wanted.

The new equipment arrived on February 14, 1982, and within a few days Nykaza had a call from Masters at the Summit office the two men shared, asking him to bring the recorders to the house so Alan could listen to whatever had been recorded thus far. Nykaza agreed, taking with him CCSPD Sgt. Joe Hein, who was present in Nykaza's office when Masters telephoned.

Hein joined the sheriff's police in 1967, but at the urging of his close friend Mike Corbitt, took a leave of absence from June 1973 through May 1974 to work for the Willow Springs Police Department. Hein returned to the sheriff's office and eventually was assigned to guard then State's Attorney Richard M. Daley. Hein and Corbitt remained friends, to the extent that Hein was a witness at Corbitt's wedding.

In late 1974, Hein needed legal advice on a workmen's compensation claim, and as did so many policemen in the area, he went to Alan Masters. Masters was successful in obtaining a settlement and received a contingency fee. Hein had been divorced in 1971, and when he needed legal assistance pertaining to child support and custody matters, he again retained Alan Masters. Most of the time Alan did not charge a fee for this work which was a substantial savings for Hein.

Alan and Joe became friends; Hein's name was added to the annual summer barbecue invitation list, and he socialized with Alan and Dianne on several occasions. The two men had a further business relationship; Hein obtained a private investigator's license, using Alan's office as his business address, and Joe also worked part time as a process server for Ted Nykaza.

Through their connection with Alan Masters, Nykaza and Hein became friends. Neither remembers exactly why Hein was in Nykaza's office when Alan called, exactly why Hein decided to go to Masters' house, or whether they drove there together. It is possible that Nykaza told Hein about Alan's marital woes, and the two men thought Hein might having a calming effect on his good friend. They were wrong.

They arrived at the house on Wolf Road to find Masters waiting in the kitchen. He immediately sent Nykaza down to the basement to retrieve the tapes so they could be played on the new recorders which lay ready on top of the kitchen counter.

There were a number of conversations on the tapes, but there was one that Nykaza remembered in detail. Dianne Masters was talking to an unnamed man in an intimate fashion. As the three men listened, they heard the man on the tape ask Dianne, "Are you okay?" She replied, "There's just a little bit of spotting." "Well, maybe we won't use the bottle next time," the man said.

The conversation obviously referred to some unusual sort of sexual activity which had not been entirely successful. Much later, investigators would learn it was something the two lovers had attempted after reading a column entitled "Love and Sex: Truths the Bible Teaches Us." Written by a local media priest with some literary pretensions, it examined the *Song of Solomon*, deploring the fact that all English translations had "cleaned up the word of God," turning the song from a work of "secular erotic poetry" into "an allegory of divine and human love..." In particular, the article discussed the pouring of spiced wine between a woman's thighs as a prelude to oral sex.

An enraged Masters asked Nykaza to play the tape over and over again. It was clear his suspicious were justified: Dianne did have a lover. What's more, their relationship had advanced to the point where they were experimenting sexually, doing things that Dianne and Alan had never attempted. The more Masters listened, the angrier he became, until he erupted. "I'll kill that mother-fucker. [There will be a home invasion where] the dogs will go, the cats will go, everything will go, including Dianne. Dianne will be there, but Georgianna will not be there." Nykaza stood by the kitchen sink, watching as Alan became so furious that he literally was bouncing off the kitchen fixtures, eventually boosting himself atop the kitchen counter, cursing and swearing.

A few days later, in his Summit office, Nykaza told Diane Economou about the contents of the bugged conversation. Economou suggested that should Nykaza find out the name of Dianne's lover, Alan should not be told. Economou was worried that Masters might do something violent to the other man. At that point, Masters walked in unexpectedly.

Crying and almost incoherent, he sat down in a side chair and began to babble to nobody in particular. Both Economou and Nykaza heard Masters say that he was going to go to Nikos' Restaurant in Bridgeview to meet Jim Keating, and they were going to talk about having Dianne murdered and making it look like an accident. "Don't even think such things," Economou claims she told Masters. A couple of days went by, and Economou and Masters were riding in a car together when Masters brought up the tape recording again.

Alan was obsessed with the taped revelations and his plans to rid himself of his troublesome wife. Economou, Hein, and Nykaza were not the only ones to learn about what became known to Alan's circle of insiders as "the bottle in the vagina" tape. Michael Corbitt visited Masters at the office, and Alan played the tape for him. CCSPD Investigator Jack Bachman heard about the tape from Lt. Jim Keating.

Bachman and Masters were friends of long standing, and they had been involved in several corrupt deals, including partnership with CCSPD Sgt. Clarke Buckendahl in the Astrology Club, a suburban whorehouse. When she worked for a real estate firm in Naperville, Dianne Masters acted as the broker in Bachman's purchase of a new home there.

Bachman had seen Alan go round the bend over Dianne before; on one occasion in the mid-seventies, Masters even called Bachman saying he had beaten Dianne severely and how good it felt to do so. In 1978, Bachman received another hysterical phone call from Alan. Dianne had left him and taken the baby, and Alan wanted her found. "Where are you, and where do you think she went?" Bachman asked. "That's all right," Masters replied, suddenly hanging up the phone.

When Bachman called him at the law office the next day, Masters acted as if the conversation had never taken place. As a result of his personal experience and similar stories he had heard from others, Bachman tended to shrug off storm warnings over Alan and Dianne. The couple followed a pattern: they would fight, separate, and get back together. Some people like that kind of thing.

On the afternoon of February 18, 1982, Bachman was in his office at the sheriff's station in west suburban Maywood when he received a phone call from Lt. Howard Vanick. Vanick said he and another policeman had been on their way to lunch at the Charley Horse, a restaurant in the Orland Park shopping mall, when he spotted Dianne Masters and her "boyfriend" in a car parked in the lot outside the restaurant. Vanick entered the restaurant but came out in a short time to take another look. Vanick had jotted down the man's license number, and he wanted Bachman to pass it on to Alan Masters, making sure that Masters knew it came from Vanick. By having Bachman do it for him, Vanick would reap any benefits while avoiding any fallout when Alan received the news.

Vanick already had asked Alan to represent him in a divorce suit, and this information should guarantee no bill would ever be sent. Immediately upon hanging up the phone, Bachman walked into the office of Lt. James Keating, commander of the sheriff's vice squad and Alan's close friend (though not in that order), and told him about Vanick's call. Keating asked if Bachman wanted to tell Masters, but Bachman declined. Within a relatively short period, either that day or the next, somebody—Bachman does not remember who—ran a "10-28" (code for an automobile license plate) on the LEADS (Law Enforcement Automated Data System) computer.

A few days later, Bachman entered Keating's office as the worried-looking lieutenant was hanging up the phone. "Who was that? What's wrong?" Bachman asked.

"That was Alan. He's having troubles with Dianne," Keating replied. "Well, what kind of trouble?" Bachman persisted. Keating told Bachman that Alan had overheard a conversation between Dianne and her boyfriend during which they talked about doing "things" with a bottle. When Keating repeated the event Alan had described, Bachman dismissed it, saying, "I just don't believe that would happen like that."

Soon it became common knowledge at South Dicks and the sheriff's Maywood office that Al the Pal was a cuckold and that the man in question was Jim Church, who taught at Moraine Valley. Somebody told Bachman that Dianne and Church were having a delayed celebration of Church's birthday when Vanick spotted the couple. Not all of this information would have been included on the license plate registration, so it was obvious to Bachman that Church's driver's license had been checked and that his name had been run through the police computer, in violation of department regulations. Masters soon knew everything about Church, including how much he earned in a year, and Alan chortled to associates that Jim "would never be able to afford her."

Toward the end of February, Bachman again walked into Keating's office as Keating was ending a phone conversation. "What's going on?" Bachman asked. "Dianne is having an affair, and Alan wants to have her killed," Keating replied. Bachman shook his head. "That's crazy. He's been mad at her before. Go buy him coffee and talk to him."

But Keating was adamant that this time the marital strife at Chez Masters had reached crisis proportions. "No. He wants to have the dogs whacked, the maid whacked, and make it look like a home invasion." "Whacking" is a euphemism for murder used by organized crime.

According to Keating, Alan was offering twenty-five thousand dollars to whomever would kill Dianne, and Keating wanted to know if Bachman would be interested. Bachman responded in a joking way, "I've got twenty-five thousand dollars." Keating told Bachman that Michael Corbitt had agreed to get rid of the body if someone could be found to do the murder.

Nykaza, Economou, Buckendahl, Bachman, Hein, Keating—all of these people knew Dianne Masters, had been in her home, and could have easily contacted her—but none of them warned her that Alan was behaving in a threatening and erratic fashion.

CHAPTER 11

*M*arch 1982 came in like a conspiracy to murder. Bachman went to Keating's office on another matter, and Alan Masters' name came up. Bachman asked if Alan had calmed down. Keating said he was still ranting and raving. As Bachman prepared to leave the office, Keating admonished him, "Make sure you go home to your bride tonight." In Summit, Ted Nykaza was told by Alan Masters to make sure he had an alibi as well. The night came and went and Dianne Masters was still alive. This gave some credence to the notion that Alan's desire to have Dianne killed was merely talk.

Soon after, Jack Bachman again asked Keating how Alan was doing, and Keating told him that the person waiting to kill Dianne chickened out, and it was cold that night. A couple of weeks passed, and the same alibi warnings were issued. Once again, Dianne Masters' luck held.

Dianne was aware she was in danger those last few weeks of her life. She talked about her fears to anyone who would listen. She was sure her phone was tapped; she even wrote to Jim about her "tippy, tappy telephone." Despite this, Dianne continued to use it for intimate conversations and discussions about the divorce. She told Jim she no longer cared; she wanted Alan to be sure it was over between them.

She was positive she was being followed and compiled a list of suspicious license plates. She told friends that there was one

151

sheriff's policeman she could trust, and she was going to give the list to Lt. Howard Vanick to find out who was on her tail. She could not know that Vanick was one of the men Alan hired to stalk her or that it was through Vanick that Alan learned about Jim.

She had noticed two men watching her in the restaurant parking lot, but the glimpse was fleeting, she'd had a few celebratory drinks for Jim's birthday, and there were more pleasant things on her mind. All things considered, it is understandable that she mistook Vanick for an Orland Park policeman. Except for a few inches difference in height, the men could easily pass for each other even among people not floating in a rosy glow. Further complicating the matter was the fact that the local cop's partner also resembled Vanick's sidekick. For years these men were to live with the stigma of having been responsible for providing Alan with information to use against Dianne, information which helped tip the scales against Dianne's living to a ripe old age.

She met Jim's parents and went out with him and his small daughter. "I like being with Emily. What did she think? Didn't feel cheated, resentful, etc. that I shared those few hours with her? Keep thinking about how much the four of us can do."

Two weeks before Dianne disappeared, Brigitte had a dream that her friend was dead. She sat bolt upright in bed, shaken and perspiring, but did not tell Dianne. Instead, after Brigitte warned her to be careful, they talked about everyday things. They laughed together as they always did and looked forward to spending more time together once Dianne's lawyer returned from vacation and filed the divorce papers. Brigitte promised to help Dianne relocate and the two women made plans to travel together again. Dianne warned Brigitte, as she did other friends, that if anything happened to her, the police were not to be trusted because they would be involved.

Dianne also said she had plenty "on" Alan and his illegal dealings to prevent him from bringing all his political and judicial clout to bear against her in the divorce suit. She referred to Alan's boasts about always taking money in cash, seldom if ever giving receipts, and cheating the IRS. She assured Brigitte she had the material in a safe place as a form of protection.

Because she was sure that the local police were loyal to Alan, Dianne went to the FBI about her fears and his threats. She spoke to George Dunne, then president of the Cook County Board, and Andrew Raucci, MVCC's attorney. She also discussed the problem in detail with her hairdresser. It was almost as if by talking to so many people about it, she could keep it from happening—or perhaps she wanted to make sure that if it did happen, the people responsible would be caught.

About a week before she was reported missing, a very agitated Dianne arrived at Jerry Cosentino's Chicago campaign office. She was clutching a piece of paper, which she showed to Cosentino's campaign manager. "That bastard Alan put a threatening note on the windshield of my Cadillac," she said. She had been open about her marital situation before joining the staff and confided in the manager that Alan was "the mob's attorney for gambling interests in the Chicago area." She also was forthcoming about her affair with Jim, revealing that she and Alan had not had a sexual relationship in a couple of years.

On Tuesday, March 16, 1982, the regularly scheduled MVCC board meeting was canceled because of the statewide primary election. Dianne lunched with Bob Casey. She talked to him about the divorce, and then she went back to his home to see Pat. The two women discussed Dianne's marriage, about how she had really loved Alan, but how he had killed that love, although she still had strong feelings for him. Pat asked if Dianne realized what she was up against, how possessive Alan was of her and Georgie. "I know it's a calculated risk," Dianne replied, "but I've got to try."

From Pat's apartment in Clarendon Hills, Dianne drove to suburban La Grange to meet Jim. He was waiting for her in a furniture store parking lot when he saw her pass by and drive through another parking lot twice before finally pulling alongside. Trembling and frightened, she climbed into his car, telling him she believed she had been followed. When they got to the LaGrange

Motel, Dianne told Jim she was afraid of Alan and asked if Jim had ever seen him. He had not, so she took a picture out of her wallet and asked Jim to look at it so he would know who he was up against.

The next day, Wednesday, March 17, 1982, Dianne called Jim at the college. She asked him not to come to the rescheduled board meeting the next day, reminding him that her lawyer said they should be careful. As it happened, Jim did not plan to go because he had to teach a class at another college that evening.

On Thursday, March 18, 1982, around 6:30 p.m. Dianne Masters left her home for the rescheduled board meeting. Still trying to do the right thing, she had prepared dinner for Alan, consisting of a steak and Waldorf salad. Then she kissed her daughter good night. Georgianna would later remember that this was the only occasion on which her mother had not talked about returning.

If Dianne had any special premonitions, she did not mention them. She did tell another trustee that she had one of the worst days of her life but did not elaborate. Mary Nelson passed along a note Jim Church had left for Dianne and watched as Dianne tucked it into a large beige canvas tote bag containing a huge, heavy stack of meeting paperwork. She also gave Dianne a set of proofs of the portrait photo the college had arranged to have taken.

The meeting was uneventful, as was the expedition to the Village Courtyard, except for Dianne's initial fear that a patron there was following her. After that was dispelled, Dianne relaxed. It was a quiet, pleasant gathering. Dianne ordered a couple of glasses of white wine but did not finish either. On the way out, she walked with Mary Nelson, asking her if she could leave some material in Nelson's office the next day. Nelson explained she would be out of town, and the two women made other arrangements. When they reached her Cadillac in the parking lot, Dianne turned, smiled, and said "good night." Mary Nelson was the last person who admits to speaking to Dianne Masters.

PART II
Nemesis

Commit a crime, and the earth is made of glass.
Commit a crime, and it seems as if a coat of snow
fell on the ground, such as reveals in the woods the track
of every partridge and fox and squirrel and mole....
Some damning circumstance always transpires.

—Ralph Waldo Emerson

CHAPTER 1

*S*ergeant John Reed of the Cook County Sheriff's Police has presence. There is something about him that commands instant respect, which is very useful in his line of work. He is a big man; a solidly built six feet, two inches, he seems even larger than he is. His size helps, but there are taller, broader cops around who do not generate the same impression. Reed is pleasant looking, has a ready smile, and an amiable manner, but there are other cops who fit that description, too. He could be a menacing authority figure, but he comes across as upright and honorable, almost avuncular, making others want to gain his approval. People in trouble do not know Reed is devoted to his family, a pillar of his community, or a bulwark of his church, but they do recognize him as a man who can be trusted. If John Reed sold used cars, they would be good used cars. He is almost, but not quite, too good to be true.

Equally important to his coworkers in the Cook County Sheriff's Police Department, Reed maintains the skills he needs on the job. Even the brass, who are notorious for their ability to ignore talent, recognize this, and Reed is a frequent instructor at the police academy. All in all, John Reed is a cop's cop, the kind of guy you would want to have with you in a tight spot, watching your back.

157

Reed has a reputation as a straight arrow, a cop who works extra shifts or moonlights in security jobs to make ends meet or to buy something special for his family.

Not that there is any pietistic fallout with Reed, even after spending his high school years at Saint Jude's seminary run by the Claretian fathers. He tries to see the world as it is, rather than as he would like it to be, and to do good where he can. His friends know that after being graduated from the seminary, Reed went into the marines. Few are aware that during his hitch in the Far East, he was assigned as assistant to the chaplain and volunteered to make regular visits to a Korean leper colony and orphanage. His wife, Arlene, is proud of his concern for the most luckless of humans, but Reed never brings it up.

Reed's lack of concern about cultivating political connections also sets him apart from many of his colleagues. He is not a fixture on the golf outing/fundraiser scene which can be so important to upward mobility on the sheriff's police force. He was promoted to sergeant in 1972 because he was a good, even an inspired, policeman. Further promotion is long overdue but has nothing to do with Reed's ability. On the sheriff's PD the ranks go as high as major, but it is an open secret that rarely if ever does anyone make lieutenant without money and/or political connections. Several years ago, one man crossed the appropriate palms with fifteen thousand greenbacks in order to be promoted. The price undoubtedly has risen since then.

John Reed does not waste time worrying about these things; he was born and reared in Cook County, and he knows the score, even if he would like to change the odds a little. He just concentrates on doing his job. His wife likes to joke that a lot is expected of a Reed in law enforcement. After all, the Lone Ranger's real name was John Reid, and the Green Hornet had the same surname.

There is an air of serenity about Reed that must be infuriating to the hacks in the department. He firmly believes that all cases are solvable if enough time is allotted to them. His patient, deter-

mined, dogged style has paid many a law enforcement dividend.
Reed makes it easy for bad guys to confess to him. His avuncular
manner puts them at their ease, making them feel he understands
human frailty and that they would feel better after getting it off
their chests. "I understand," Reed would say, "these things
happen." Meaning murder, robbery, child or wife abuse, the whole
roll call of human misdeeds. And he is sincere. However, Reed's
understanding does not bring with it his approval.

John Reed was born in Chicago on July 30, 1940, to James and
Nora O'Shea Reed, the middle child between brother Jim and
sister Eileen. James Reed, Sr., came from a family of civic leaders
in Cupar, Saskatchewan, and together with his wife raised the
three Reed children with the idea that there was no higher honor
than to serve the public good. It was important to be steady and
reliable, and Jim Reed exemplified this, serving in the United
States Navy in World War II and working for Commonwealth
Edison for forty-two years as a stationary engineer.

Raised in such an atmosphere, it was natural that John Reed
initially thought of becoming a priest. When he left the seminary,
he wanted an alternative to religious life that still would permit
him to serve people. After a hitch in the marines, Reed decided
that he wanted "to serve and protect" by becoming a policeman.
His parents left Chicago for the then underdeveloped southwest
suburbs when Reed was a teenager, so he took the Cook County
Sheriff's Police exam, and on June 20, 1966, joined the force.

While he was waiting to enter the academy, Reed worked as a
volunteer fireman and taught driver's education. One of his students was pretty, vivacious Arlene Pond, who was studying education at Loyola University in Chicago. Driving lessons were certainly
more enjoyable than Arlene expected, and when Reed's tutoring
ended, she realized she would miss seeing him. A couple days later,
Reed called to ask for a date. They were married on June 24, 1967.

The Reeds knew that police marriages are notoriously unstable.
The divorce rate is high, and so are alcoholism and emotional dis-

orders. They were determined to avoid these pitfalls and they were willing to put in the work this required. The hours are daunting enough. In theory, Reed works an eight-hour shift, but criminals do not watch the clock. Sheriff's police work what is known as a "key"—six days on and two days off. Very seldom do they have weekends free, and they are home for holidays only if they fall on their regular days off. Further, every month the detectives rotate between the day and night shift, working from 8 a.m. to 4 p.m., or 4 p.m. till midnight.

The conditions of work contribute to the "us against them" attitude many cops have, and the Reeds recognized that while esprit de corps was valuable, they wanted to live a mainstream existence to the extent possible. Many police wives do not want to hear about their husbands' work, but Arlene Reed was determined to make it a family affair even before their children, Nicole and John, were born. She read textbooks, she waited up to talk over the day's events, she helped with the inevitable paperwork, she even learned to shoot a gun.

All this paid off. Despite all the stresses and strains of modern family life and the pressure of police work, there is pleasant, tranquil feeling in the Reed household. But the atmosphere is far from cloying or dull; all four Reeds share a lively wit and obvious joie de vivre. They were going to need all of the above when John began to investigate the murder of Dianne Masters in August 1986.

Dianne Masters and her daughter, for whom she was willing to risk her life. Picture was taken the summer before Dianne was murdered.

The former Dianne Turner looks like any happy young bride, but appearances can be deceiving. She later told friends that she was apprehensive that her first marriage would not last—and she was right.

Happier days: Alan Masters, Dianne, and Pat Casey during a tropical holiday in 1976.

Dianne Masters (right) receiving an award for her work with battered women through the Crisis Center of South Suburbia which she helped found. Few people knew that Dianne herself was physically abused. *Photo credit: Daily Southtown*

Dianne's house on Wolf Road in Palos Park, which is still home to her daughter.

Alan Masters' storefront law office in the little suburb of Summit. He liked to joke that the sign should read "Master Fixer." *Photo credit: Daily Southtown*

Moraine Valley Community College administration buildings. Mary Nelson's office, where Dianne and Jim used to leave notes, was on the first floor of the building on the right. *Photo credit:* Mary Nelson

Mary Nelson and Gen Capstaff (standing), the last two people to see Dianne Masters, except for her murderers.

The former site of the Village Courtyard Restaurant, where Dianne Masters was last seen alive by Mary Nelson and Gen Capstaff. *Photo credit:* Mary Nelson.

UNIFORM DONOR CARD

DIANNE G. MASTERS

Print or type name of donor

In the hope that I may help others, I hereby make this anatomical gift, if medically acceptable, to take effect upon my
death. The words and marks below indicate my desires.

I give: (a)＿＿ Any needed organs or parts
(b) **X** only the following organs or parts

eyes & kidneys

Specify the organ(s) or part(s)

or for the purposes of transplantation, therapy, medical research or education:

(c)＿＿my body for anatomical study if needed.

Limitations, or special wishes, if any: ＿＿＿＿＿＿＿＿＿

ILLINOIS SOCIETY PREVENTION OF BLINDNESS
53 West Jackson Blvd., Chicago, Illinois 60604
(312) 922-8710

The organ donor card Dianne always carried in her wallet mysteriously surfaced in the garbage behind Alan Masters' law office in the fall of 1987. No one has ever explained where it had been for more than five years. When her body was found, her eyes were gone and her kidneys were of little use to anyone.

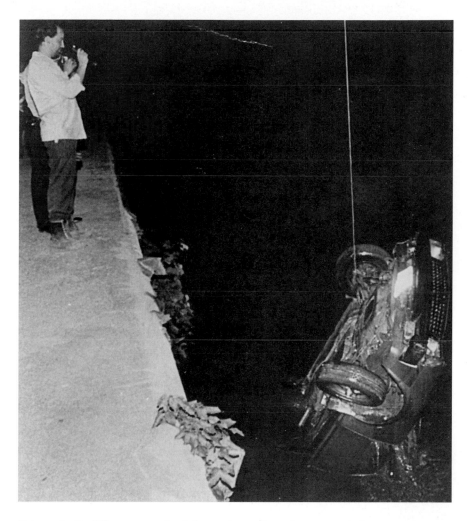

Dianne's Cadillac is winched from the polluted waters of the Sanitary and Ship Canal nine months after her disappearance. *Photo credit: Daily Southtown*

The last photo taken of Dianne before she was murdered. *Photo credit: Daily Southtown*

Dianne's grave in St. Adalbert's cemetery.

CHAPTER 2

 $\mathcal{W}$ hy did the Dianne Masters case, out of the hundreds of unsolved murders on the books of law enforcement agencies in Cook County, come alive after almost four years of inactivity? To anyone who knows Cook County, the answer is a simple one. Politics. Specifically, the hotly contested 1986 sheriff's race.

The sheriff of Cook County serves a four-year term at the will of the people. Locals have always had a provincial attitude towards higher office; the further away from home, the less desirable. Washington D.C. is the Cook County pols' equivalent of Siberia. So the sheriff's election attracted considerable attention, more than it might in other urban communities.

In 1986, Richard J. Elrod had been nominated for an unprecedented fifth term as sheriff. In fact, Elrod was the first sheriff to serve more than one consecutive term. Until the Illinois Constitutional Convention rewrote the law in 1970, county sheriffs could not succeed themselves. The uncodified but freely acknowledged reason behind the old statute was that if a man could not steal enough in four years to live comfortably, or even lavishly, for the rest of his natural span, he did not deserve a second chance at the loot. But all that was part of the bad old days, or so everyone hoped.

Elrod had been severely injured in 1969 in a confrontation staged by the Weathermen, the radical faction of the Students for a Democratic Society (SDS). Mayor Daley, an old friend and mentor, was appalled at Elrod's paralysis and the damage to his city's reputation. As Elrod neared the end of his rehabilitation therapy, the mayor had an idea.

There were two countywide offices which could be troublesome to Daley when they were held by Republicans. The state's attorney had the power to conduct investigations, convene grand juries, obtain indictments, and try public officials. The sheriff ran the jail and provided custodial and security services for county buildings, both inside and outside city limits. But more important to Daley, the sheriff's police force also patrolled unincorporated areas of suburban Cook County and provided special services to suburban police departments. A number of sheriff's police were permanently detached to work with the state's attorney. When they chose to work together, these two county officers could use their powers to harry officeholders of the opposite party. And both jobs were in Republican hands.

When it came time to draw up the 1970 county ticket, Daley decreed that Richard Elrod would be the candidate for sheriff. Everyone agreed it was a master stroke. Public support and sympathy for Elrod and the desire to stick it to outside troublemakers and critics who had given Chicago a bad name made his election a sure thing. Having a friend behind the sheriff's badge was not too shabby, either.

Daley was right, as usual. Richard Elrod swept the county and his December 1970 swearing in was a happy affair, even though his crutches were a constant reminder of the injuries that would never heal. He was easily returned to office in 1974, 1978, and 1982.

In 1986, the omens were not as promising. Daley had succumbed to a heart attack in 1976, and while the Democratic party was still powerful, it was not the juggernaut it had been. Besides, Elrod had been in office for sixteen years, and it would be easy for an opponent to plant and fertilize the idea that it was time for a change. Furthermore, recent scandals plagued the sheriff's office;

several policemen had been convicted of corruption in federal court. For the first time Elrod would face a strong Republican challenger, a man who raised the hackles of all good Democrats and more than a few Republicans. James O'Grady was one of a handful of Democrats who had recently converted to the Grand Old Party. These conversions were viewed by many pols in both parties as being based more on expediency than any blinding philosophical revelation.

But if Elrod had problems, so did O'Grady. In addition to being a turncoat, O'Grady's loyalty was in question, and loyalty is a very important quality to Cook County politicians and voters. He had worked for Elrod for almost three years as the sheriff's top deputy. Now he was going to run against his former benefactor.

O'Grady's career in law enforcement began with the Chicago Police Department, where he spent tours in the notorious First Ward and the Gold Coast, districts where vice reared its alluring head around the clock. O'Grady was superintendent of the CPD until 1979, when he was fired by Jane Byrne shortly after her surprise mayoral victory. The most visible scandal during O'Grady's tenure had been the discovery that strip searches were being conducted on women stopped for routine traffic charges. Women's groups were particularly upset with O'Grady because he was aware of this practice but had not forced its halt.

After Byrne sacked him, O'Grady enlisted the support of several fellow Irish American Democrats who held public office in finding a new job. O'Grady had a wife and kids and no job, he said, failing to mention his healthy pension, some feelers from the private sector, and his interest in Special Operations Associates (SOA), a security firm. Could the friends help him out? They could. They did. Sheriff Elrod was responsible for overseeing a police force which, while compact when compared with the Chicago PD, would be a respectable solution to O'Grady's problems and should have been to Elrod's as well.

Like every Cook County sheriff, Elrod's responsibilities were broad, and any incumbent who did not delegate authority would soon burn out under the sheer weight of the workload. The problem was to fill these jobs with honest, capable, and reliable people. Like several of his predecessors, Elrod was to discover that such people were hard to find.

About 60 percent of the sheriff's budget goes to operate the Department of Corrections, including the Cook County jail and the various lockups. Since crime is one of the growth industries of our time, the jails are always crowded, the guards are underpaid, and the potential for trouble unlimited.

In addition to running the country jail system, the sheriff has a full-time police force that hovers around five hundred in strength. Just over one hundred are assigned to the state's attorney's office to aid the county prosecutor in various ways. The remainder patrol unincorporated Cook County, widely scattered patches of real estate outside the corporate limits of the City of Chicago or the suburban villages, towns, and cities; they investigate serious and organized crime in these areas; they provide technical assistance to local jurisdictions lacking funds to support the more sophisticated aspects of police work; and they handle both outgoing and incoming fugitive warrants.

In 1979, based on references from mutual friends, Elrod hired O'Grady as undersheriff with the express purpose of raising the professional level of the sheriff's police. O'Grady stayed in the job through 1981. Among Elrod's staffers, he is remembered principally for improving his golf game and making new connections while taking care of old friends like Jim Keating. In 1986, Elrod was ahead in the polls, but it was clear that his road to re-election was to be paved with potholes, the deepest of which was corruption. The public was prepared to overlook minor police speculations and sins in any jurisdiction, believing there would always be a few bad apples. However, scandal had hit Elrod's office with particular force.

Some Democrats felt this was no accident, since or because the cases had been brought by a federal prosecutor who owed his job to a Republican governor. The office of United States Attorney frequently had been used as a political weapon or a stepping-stone to elective office. The job was appointive by representatives of whichever party held the White House, and since 1969 it had been controlled almost exclusively by Republicans. It was more or less expected that Democrat-held offices would be the targets of investigations into wrongdoing in the public sector, particularly around election time.

In 1985, a federal grand jury handed down racketeering, extortion, conspiracy, and income-tax fraud indictments against CCSPD Lt. James Keating, former commander of intelligence, and Sgt. Bruce Frasch, former head of vice control. Their trial and conviction in May 1986 would be particularly embarrassing to Elrod.

Jim O'Grady blasted away, charging that his warnings about corruption in Keating's and Frasch's departments had been ignored by Elrod. Insiders were amused; O'Grady and Keating had been so close that they were known as "The Two Jimmies" during O'Grady's employment by the sheriff.

Elrod denied that O'Grady had ever alerted him and challenged O'Grady to take a lie detector test, to which O'Grady agreed if Elrod would do so. Political watchers in Cook County shook their heads. Lie detector tests for candidates! What next?

By summer, Sheriff Elrod felt it necessary to reopen the investigation of the murder of Dianne Masters. The renewed interest was a by-product of a piece of evidence introduced against Jim Keating.

A lot of tales are told about Jim Keating. One night he was on his way into the Manor A Go Go, a tacky bar on Southwest Highway much frequented by policemen. At the time, he was involved with the wife of a local archery champion. As he was ankling up to the entrance, he felt a rush of air beside his face, and the next thing he knew, an arrow was vibrating in the door just in front of him. "Hmmm," he observed, "looks like Robin Hood is pissed that the sheriff is dating Maid Marian."

Tall, heavyset, balding, Jim Keating was a bibulous and bonhomous man, the stereotypical glad-hander. Frequently during his police career he was called upon to meet the press because he was so good at schmoozing them. He developed a reputation as a solid source, one that reporters, especially the lazy ones, liked dealing with because he made their jobs easier. From time to time, he shared tips with them that earned praise from their editors.

Keating was a dab hand at tactics; he knew it would be harder for a friendly reporter to expose his illegal activities. He worked at being a man's man, always there with a slap on the back, a "hi, slugger" greeting, and he always had great insider cop stories to tell. He drank a lot. He liked a lot of women a lot, juggling several ladies at once. No one openly questioned where he got the money to finance his lifestyle; he certainly could not do it on a lieutenant's pay, even with occasional work as a private investigator.

James L. Keating was born to a police family in Chicago in 1937. He attended a Catholic grammar school and was graduated from Harper High School on the city's southwest side in 1955. Keating's father left the force after being accidentally shot by a fellow officer, and his mother found a job as a bookkeeper to help out. Keating worked throughout high school to help support his family. Upon graduation, he enlisted in the marines, and when he was discharged, it was a given that he would he join the Chicago PD After a very short tenure, he abruptly left the force, giving various excuses over the years. Whatever the case, it is clear his departure was under some sort of cloud. Despite this, he soon joined the sheriff's police. He continued his education, receiving a B.S. in social justice from Lewis University in Lockport, Illinois, and an M.P.A. from Roosevelt University in Chicago.

Although married with two children, Keating saw himself as quite the ladies' man. He maintained an apartment in suburban

Chicago Ridge as a "party house," so he could pursue his extramarital interests. Keating told friends his wife was in frail emotional health, and many who knew the couple blamed this in large part on Keating's behavior and his treatment of her, which they describe as straight out of the movie *Gaslight*.

Mrs. Keating might have been nervous because she had heard her husband discussing what he called the "test of a true friend." According to Big Jim, you could find out who was really loyal by calling a person in the middle of the night to say, "I've just killed my wife. You've got to come over and help me get rid of her body and the evidence." A true friend would hasten to help, no questions asked. The Keatings were divorced in 1981, and Mrs. Keating moved to Michigan with the pair's young son and daughter.

It was frequently said of Keating that he was "not a tough guy." Also, he reportedly had an aversion to the sight of blood and dead bodies, a distinct disadvantage in police work. In direct contradiction to this, however, was Keating's regular appearance at crime scenes where bodies had been found in automobiles. Such remains are seldom fresh, and even the most experienced homicide investigators admit to nausea and upsets when they draw such assignments.

Dianne Masters was not the first Keating friend or acquaintance who turned up dead in a car. On June 9, 1976, Michael Curtin's body was found in the back seat of his Cadillac on a residential street in Maywood, a western suburb. The thirty-one-year-old officer of a local chemical company had been shot twice in the head, and papers from his briefcase were scattered all over the car as if his murderers had been looking for something. The Maywood policemen responding to the abandoned auto call thought they hit paydirt when they found a little black book in the corpse's shirt pocket. The book contained listings of lawyers and judges, with dollar amounts and details of traffic, drug, and other criminal cases opposite their names. Curtin was clearly not what he seemed; he was a fixer, and a fixer on a grand scale.

When the Maywood officers returned to police headquarters late that morning, they were prepared to begin interviewing everyone named in Curtin's book. Much to their surprise, they found two members of the sheriff's brass, Lt. Jim Keating and Deputy Chief Richard Quagliano, making off with the evidence. The sheriff's criminal investigations unit often is asked to assist small suburban police departments, but when it came to Curtin, Quagliano and Keating took the initiative, persuading Maywood's chief to let them take it over.

Instead of an investigation, Keating's team presided over a cover-up. Every time an honest cop like John Reed or Paul Sabin was assigned to the case and seemed to be getting somewhere, Keating would see to it that he was bounced off onto something else. The last man known to have seen Curtin alive, attorney Joseph Stillo, never was interviewed by Keating's men. Stillo, together with his uncle, former judge Adam Stillo, had close ties to Alan Masters. The case has never been solved and some of the most important evidence is missing, including the little black book and the bullets removed from Curtin's brain.

On May 24, 1979, in south suburban Blue Island, a couple of patrolmen responded to a call about an abandoned car parked in the Western Avenue business district. The weather had been warm, and the smell coming from the trunk left little doubt as to what was inside. The officers radioed back to the station and reinforcements were dispatched. When the lid was lifted, the police found the body of Timothy O'Brien, a resident of Oak Lawn who owned Irish Keystone, a chop shop just outside the predominantly black and poor nearby suburb of Robbins.

Suddenly, inexplicably, Jim Keating was at the scene. Although it was definitely out of his jurisdiction, Keating repeatedly tried to take over the investigation. Some Blue Island cops were less than happy about Keating's horning in, but once again, Keating's will prevailed.

O'Brien, one of Keating's best friends, had been shot twice in the head, like Curtin and Dianne Masters. He was last seen by his wife on May 22, 1979, when he left home for the evening with a friend. When Mrs. O'Brien became increasingly alarmed over her husband's absence, she phoned family friend and famous crime stopper, Jim Keating.

It seemed that in addition to collecting protection money from whorehouses and gambling dens, with O'Brien's help and knowledge of the industry, Keating had branched out into extorting money from suburban chop shops. During the phone call, Keating advised Mrs. O'Brien to remove her husband's business records from their residence. Further, when turning in the missing person's report, she was to say Tim had disappeared from his workplace rather than from their home. The chop shop was located in the sheriff's jurisdiction, while the O'Brien home was served by the Oak Lawn police where it might be more difficult for Keating to influence the investigation.

When O'Brien's body was found in Blue Island, it appeared that Keating's efforts to maintain control were defeated. However, once again he managed to insinuate himself. The investigation turned into a farce, and the case was never solved. Several years later, an FBI agent assigned to look into some open cases arrived at the Blue Island police station asking to see the O'Brien file, only to find that it had vanished.

Sources report that O'Brien's death was decreed by suburban mob members. Both Keating and O'Brien boosted their income by thousands of dollars per month by shaking down the chop shops. This had not pleased the organized crime figures who either owned these operations or who wanted to collect "street tax." Street tax, sometimes called protection money, is an assessment organized crime levies on businesses engaging in illegal activity which the mob does not actually own.

Killing O'Brien was the outfit's way of sending Keating a message. Around the time of O'Brien's murder, Keating reportedly received a direct threat from the mob to stay away from their chop shops. Keating sobbed over the death of his friend, but more than one snitch claimed that O'Brien felt Keating was too greedy and was killed before sealing a deal to have Keating eliminated.

For decades, Keating operated like a mobster with a badge. Then he got caught in an FBI investigation called Operation Safebet. After the death of J. Edgar Hoover in 1977, the Federal Bureau of Investigation added a new weapon to its arsenal: the sting, based on the old adage that you must set a thief to catch a thief. Under Hoover, this had not been a favored technique at the Bureau. Stings were expensive and time-consuming to mount, and Hoover feared a double danger to the undercover agents. First, they might be found out and eliminated by their partners; second, they might find the corrupt life attractive and sell out. With Hoover gone, sting operations became trendy, and several were operating in the Chicago area in the early 1980s.

Operation Safebet began in 1980. Its stated purpose was to expose vice protection rackets in suburban Cook County. FBI Agent Lary Damron, operating undercover as Larry Wright, was assigned to join National Credit Service (NCS). Given the wrong clothes and manner, Damron could carry off the slightly shady, lounge-lizard look he needed to convince suburban miscreants that he was a rascal of a businessman up from Florida, hoping to expand operations to the Middle West and not minding if he creased a few laws here and there.

Damron's double life began as the result of a gripe from Thomas Gervais, president of NCS. Gervais was an enterprising businessman who saw a need and found a way to fill it. Whorehouses could make more money if customers could use their credit cards to charge visits. However, the banks issuing the cards were highly suspicious of joints with names like Michael's Magic Touch and were too stuffy to handle their business.

Another problem with charging the occasional bit of afternoon delight was that Mrs. Blue Collar might get a tad worked up when she saw that Mr. Blue Collar had been dropping big money at the Club Taray, Plato's South, or one of the many suburban joints offering a wide array of sexual services from the missionary position to Ondinism.

So, using good old American ingenuity, Gervais had a better idea. For a fee, National Credit Service would launder these charges so that they would look like they had come from legitimate-sounding businesses, such as O'Hare Unique Gifts.

Everybody was happy with this arrangement except Vito Caliendo, a gentleman said to have mob connections. Caliendo owned the Petite Lounge in southwest suburban Lyons as well as several other boites throughout the county, and he thought Gervais should be paying the street tax. As a middleman, Gervais did not want to cut into his already narrow profit margin by complying. Besides, he was already sharing with another mobster, Victor Spilotro. Gervais complained to Spilotro, who warned Caliendo off Gervais. However, Gervais knew that Caliendo & Company had persuasive methods, and he could not be sure that he could keep Spilotro happy enough to help out. So he went to the FBI.

Damron/Wright arrived at NCS with a bold marketing plan, which immediately began to pay off. He signed up more businesses for the credit card laundering scheme and then began to diversify. He put out the word that he wanted to set up some betting and prostitution parlors of his own and that he was willing to pay for assistance. It was not long in coming.

In January 1982, Damron and other FBI undercover agents opened the Palatine Sporting Fans Club, an offtrack messenger betting service in an unincorporated area outside the far northwest suburb of Palatine. The club was never the messenger service it pretended to be; it was nothing more than an FBI-owned bookie joint.

In order to operate on a regular basis, it was necessary to make a deal with the local constables regarding the possibility of tiresome raids which disrupt business. In this regard, Damron first met CCSPD Sgt. Bruce Frasch, commander of the vice control unit. To keep up appearances, a short time after the bookmakers opened, Frasch would arrange to raid them. But he would give them advance notice so they could prepare for the bust. This had a price and Damron paid it: two hundred dollars per month.

But Frasch proved to be unreliable and hard to reach at times. He seemed to enjoy generating vice as much as controlling it. Before throwing in his lot with the FBI, Gervais owned Sunkissed, a tanning studio that was a front for a brothel. Like Damron's bookie joint, it was located in unincorporated Palatine. Frasch and another member of the sheriff's police provided protection from the vice squad for four hundred dollars per month. Frasch also enjoyed taking out part of his fee in trade.

In the fall of 1980, CCSPD Lt. Errol Levy was on patrol with another officer when he saw the lights go on inside Sunkissed at about 2 a.m., long after operating hours. The two officers checked the front door, and found it open, so they went inside. Nobody was in the foyer, so they proceeded to the rear. There they found several naked people in a hot tub. One of them was very familiar to Lieutenant Levy; it happened to be Sgt. Bruce Frasch, who was bouncing a naked woman on his knee. Levy gave Frasch five minutes to dress and meet him out front. When Frasch appeared, Levy reminded him that as a member of the vice unit, Frasch was supposed to prevent vice, not participate in it. Frasch apologized, admitting he had made a mistake—by not locking the door.

Frasch's welcome was wearing thin with the management elsewhere. Herbert Panice, owner of the Show Club in Chicago Heights at the far southern end of Cook County, processed his credit card charges through NCS. During a conversation with Damron, Panice bellyached that he paid Frasch a deuce (two hundred dollars) per week but only received a couple hours' notice of raids. Others had worse experiences. Something would have to be done.

Damron thought he had a solution. After setting up NCS' basic laundering service, the agent became friendly with Joseph Marren, who managed "My Uncle's Place," a "show" club (a euphemism for house of prostitution) in Lyons. Eventually, the topic of finding really reliable crooked cops came up. Marren, a resident of Willow Springs, said he had connections with policemen and public officials who could be helpful in setting up legal business fronts for illegal ventures.

At the end of January 1982, as agreed upon, Frasch arranged a raid at the Palatine Sporting Fans Club. One FBI agent, calling herself Sharon Wright, was arrested. Almost immediately afterward, Damron called Marren about his "wife's" arrest. Marren had been talking about having a highly placed contact with the sheriff's police, and Damron decided it was time to find out who this person was. He asked Marren to consult his contact about direct dealings, bypassing the flaky Frasch.

Within ten days, Marren was back to Damron with the news that the contact could take care of everything. The cost would be one thousand dollars to have the case against Sharon Wright thrown out of court. In addition, Damron would have to pay six hundred dollars per month in protection money for the betting parlor. The money, in cash, was to be passed through Marren at the beginning of each month.

Damron agreed to this arrangement, which continued until spring 1982. Because Marren was about to go to prison, a new conduit for the payoffs would have to be found. Also, Marren agreed to help Damron develop more business before he went away.

In May 1982, Marren personally introduced Damron to Michael Corbitt, chief of the Willow Springs Police Department. The meeting was particularly memorable to Damron because it took place outside the Willow Springs police station. What's more, Corbitt appeared in full uniform, name tag, badge and all, and drove up in a marked squad car. Even in Damron's wide experience with known ne'er do wells, this was bizarre, arrogant behavior.

On first encounters with lawmen, it was Damron's practice not to wear a wire or carry any recording devices, because such men were apprehensive about the motives of new acquaintances and a quick frisk might precede any negotiations. As soon as possible after these meetings, Damron would prepare a report about each session.

The discussion took place in Corbitt's squad car. Damron gave Corbitt his resume as Larry Wright and told him he wanted to open another "messenger" service in Corbitt's area. He described how the operation worked in Palatine and that he needed to know how much it would cost to duplicate it in Willow Springs. Corbitt told Damron that they could work together, so long as Damron was cleared by the "county" (meaning the sheriff's police) and by alleged mobsters Carmen and Sal Bastone. Because Damron's outfit connection was with another man, representatives of the two factions would have to work out the details, Corbitt said. Once this was accomplished, Corbitt would give Damron an idea of the cost. Corbitt suggested some possible locations, then went into the station. Marren and Damron went off to scout the suggested sites.

Willow Springs never got its new bookie joint, because in June 1982, Michael Corbitt was forced out of his job as chief of police. Marren told Damron not to worry; Corbitt was to be appointed to the same job soon in Summit. As a result, Marren and Damron began looking for locations there.

In July 1982, Marren and Damron tried for a repeat meeting with Corbitt, this time at the Summit police station, but Corbitt was not there. Instead, the two went to the Holiday Inn at Ford City, a shopping mall on the grounds of an old Ford plant at Seventy-sixth Street and Cicero Avenue in Chicago.

Marren was concerned about maintaining a smooth flow of bribes while he was in jail. The high-ranking county police officer Marren dealt with had a couple of women friends, quickly dubbed "the bag ladies," who worked in the bar at the Holiday Inn. Marren thought it would be a good idea for Damron to meet these women so that they would know he was Marren's friend. By doing this, Damron could establish a line of communication with Marren's county cop pal. After several telephone calls, a face-to-face meeting was arranged.

Lt. James Keating, head of the sheriff's police intelligence unit, introduced himself to Damron on September 3, 1982, in the lounge of the Ford City Holiday Inn. Keating used Herb Panice and Joe Marren as references. Relaxing over drinks, the two men discussed opening a combined strip club and bordello in Summit. Keating said he could arrange for Damron to meet a lawyer with the right connections to put the deal together. Damron told Keating he wanted to be certain that Keating had been receiving his cut every month. Keating replied that he had and, ever the thoughtful friend, was putting some away as a nest egg for Marren when he got out. Damron then passed Keating the regular monthly payment of six hundred dollars.

The next meeting took place on October 25, 1982, at Nikos', a restaurant on Harlem Avenue in suburban Bridgeview. This time, Damron was wearing a wire. After engaging in a little male bonding, Damron got down to business.

"I talked to him [Corbitt] a little bit about Summit, you know, and I said...I want to do something out there. And he said well ...it shouldn't be any problem and he talked to somebody, and he got back to me and he says, 'Look,' you know, 'go ahead and find your-self a location... Get back to me when ...you know where it is. I'll tell ya what it's gonna be and, you know, you can go ahead. 'Cause what I really like to do is, if I could...is lock that thing up before Joe gets out...'"

"What are you talking about?" Keating interjected.

When Damron said he wanted a show club, Keating asked, "Have you got somebody official?"

"Well, it's according to whether that guy ever gets in as chief or not," Damron answered, referring to Corbitt. "See, I know him."

"Don't bet on that," Keating cautioned Damron. "You know, it may happen...But he's a bullshitter and he's, 'Don't worry, Larry, it's gonna be a week from tomorrow at 10:30,'" Keating explained. "...you fucking signin' the lease... You spend a lot of fucking money remodeling it, and he says, 'Well, it might be another year.'"

Damron picked up on the opportunity to find another fixer. "I can't make a move as long as the guy's not in a place to do it...you said you might know somebody out here so we could go that way."

Keating wanted more specific information. "Okay, what are you gonna do? Just straight out hooking or just a promise?"

"It's according to what they'll let us do," Damron responded, "...we'd like to be wide open...like they do in Lyons. If not, you know, maybe we can build up to it. Maybe we can open up and say well look, we're just gonna dance, and, you know, we'll see how the heat's coming and then we'll do the other things. But, you know, once you get those customers coming in there, and they know what they're gonna get, and they're not getting cheated and screwed over, you know, they're gonna come back and back and back."

"How much we talking about?" Keating asked. "You go and open a joint up...you can't give me a number until you see what the place looks like... I'm gonna talk to a guy tomorrow...or right next to Summit is a town called McCook."

The two men discussed the market for whorehouses in the McCook area, and Keating went on to talk about the "guy" he had in mind. "The guy's a lawyer," Keating said. "All right? And he runs that area...He's very close to the mayor in Summit, and he's very close to the chief of police.

"He's very close to the mayor of McCook," Keating continued. "It's just how much balls they got...If push comes to shove and there's a fucking beef in the joint, take your fucking license...stay open on an appeal and then run for another six to eight months on appeal."

"Yeah, see that's it," Damron agreed. "That's all you gotta have. If you can get a year out of it...Geez, you're makin' money."

Before the men parted, Damron gave Keating eight hundred dollars in marked bills, two hundred more than the usual payoff as a tip for his good advice.

Damron continued his efforts to find a southwest suburban base. On November 27, 1982, he and Keating met again at the Holiday Inn. No recording was made, but Damron wrote up a "memorial" of the conversation immediately afterward.

Keating said that Joe Marren would be furloughed from prison over the holidays and that they would get together then. Proving that honor among thieves is a myth, Keating promised that while Marren was a close friend, Keating would not reveal any conversations or deals Keating and Damron might make.

Keating was anxious that Damron had been cleared by the mob to open up in the Summit area. Damron described a plan that he had to launder money in banks in the Grand Cayman Islands and asked if Keating could help obtain false identification documents. Keating assured the agent that not only could he help obtain phony driver's licenses through a friend working in the office of the Illinois secretary of state, Keating also would be willing to help carry the cash to the islands.

Keating revealed that he had recently taken the captain's exam and that he expected to be promoted soon. He believed he would then be put in charge of all the investigators detailed to the Cook County state's attorney, and that would make it impossible for the prosecutor's office to raid any establishments that were under Keating's protection without Keating's foreknowledge. Life just seemed to get better and more lucrative for Jim Keating.

Keating identified Alan Masters as the lawyer who "runs the area." Keating had already discussed the situation with Masters, and the lawyer was waiting for Damron's phone call. To further impress Damron with Masters' power, Keating described how

Masters had achieved his hegemony: he paid the cops who made the cases, he paid the judges who tried the cases, and he paid everybody in between. He wanted to assure Damron that Masters was reliable; he had a lot of experience with him in referring cases, received referral fees from Masters, and he knew other cops who had successfully done business with the lawyer.

It was during this meeting that Dianne Masters' name entered the Operation Safebet file. After revealing Alan Masters' identity, Keating added that Mrs. Masters had filed for divorce, but did not show up the day before the divorce was to be final. Then Keating chuckled; he thought it was rather humorous that she had disappeared on such a timely basis. He hastened to assure Damron that even though Alan Masters had been questioned by the police, he had been released and did not have any more worries.

Keating then picked up a cocktail napkin, wrote Alan Masters' name and phone number on it, and handed it to Damron, with instructions to phone the lawyer as soon as possible. Keating was going to Michigan for a few days, so he gave Damron another paper napkin with a "safe" telephone number there.

Damron's contact with Keating continued until 1984, when the lieutenant began to feel some heat. On June 19, 1984, Damron and another undercover FBI agent visited Joe Marren, back on the job at his whorehouse in Willow Springs. Keating had visited the joint a few days earlier, according to Marren, but was keeping a low profile. Even though Keating trusted Marren, he checked to make sure there were no bugs under his table before he sat down.

Keating still had control; Marren received advance warning that two sheriff's vice cops would be visiting the Saints and Sinners. Marren said the two policemen "had a good time" and gave the place a pass.

As the agents were leaving, they noticed that one of the female employees had passed out. Marren left the men to check her out. When he returned, Damron asked if the woman was okay. "Well, if she's not okay, she'll just be dumped in the woods," Marren replied. Women were expendable; garbage was treated better. After all, antilitter laws were enforced in Willow Springs.

The Keating-Frasch trial began in May 1986. During the trial, the prosecutor described the squad they commanded as "the cesspool of corruption that the sheriff calls a vice unit." Witnesses against Keating and Frasch included three former sheriff's deputies who had entered guilty pleas to similar charges. Robert Wiencek and Robert Napora described how the payoffs from operators of whorehouses and bookie joints were divided among other members of the sheriff's force. They also named unindicted officers, including Richard Quagliano, the sheriff's deputy chief of police; Sgt. Clarke Buckendahl, former commander of vice control; Sgt. William Barbat, Buckendahl's successor; and Ronald Nardini, Jack Newman, and Rick Urso, former officers in the vice control unit.

Quagliano denied the charges and the others refused to comment. Sheriff Richard Elrod promised to cooperate with the federal government in investigating these men when the Keating-Frasch trial ended, but in the interim, they retained their positions.

The bribery was handled without finesse. Wiencek recounted how he and Urso met Frederick Aprati, Jr., a south suburban lawyer, in the hall of the Markham branch of Cook County's Circuit Court. Aprati represented Western Hills Spa and Plato's Castle South, two houses of prostitution posing as massage parlors. Both had been raided recently. "I'm going to have this case tossed," the lawyer told the lawmen. It was dismissed, and afterward Aprati and Wiencek got into a courthouse elevator, where Aprati stuffed four envelopes totaling two thousand dollars into Wiencek's pockets. Wiencek described how he and Urso almost drove off the road in their excitement, because "Attorneys don't go around giving out this kind of money." The bribery did not come as a surprise, but the arrogant, public manner in which it was handled was shocking.

At Keating's trial, Lary Damron testified that he paid Keating $5,900 in cash—not a lot over a four-year period. However, it was clear that Keating was obtaining bribes from other sources as well. Patrick Gervais, brother to Thomas of NCS, told the court how he transferred $22,600 to sheriff's police in return for being allowed to operate the Portrait Des Femmes, a bordello disguised as a nude photography studio. What's more, Gervais paid an additional $26,000 to organized crime figure Victor Spilotro. Spilotro's brothers, Anthony and Michael, also reportedly in the family business, were found shot to death and buried in the Indiana dunes in June 1986, not long after the trial ended.

Although the defense lawyers for Keating and Frasch did their best to cast doubt on witnesses against their clients, saying they were admittedly corrupt policemen or proprietors of vice dens, the jury quickly found both guilty.

Keating startled the courtroom when he rose from his chair, walked to the prosecution table, and shook hands with the prosecutor. "You did a great job. Thanks a lot," he added, perhaps grateful the revelations about him hadn't been worse. Those who heard him did not think he was being sarcastic.

In July, Keating appeared in federal court for sentencing. To waiting reporters, he said, "I'm ready to be sentenced to my time and get on with my life." Keating faced a maximum on all counts of 133 years in prison and a fine of $140,000, but no one expected he would receive anything near it.

When Judge James Holderman ordered fifteen-year terms for both Keating and Frasch, there were gasps from spectators.

"The evidence...was absolutely overwhelming," said Judge Holderman, adding that the corruption "turned my stomach." Fifteen years was one of the longest sentences ever imposed in a case of police corruption. After processing, Keating was sent to the federal correctional institution (FCI) at Seagoville, Texas.

The media turned their attention toward one of the by-products of the trial: Keating's remarks about the disappearance of

Dianne Masters. Doubly interesting, some of the sheriff's police who were responsible for investigating Dianne's disappearance were named as bribe recipients. Jim Keating's private investigator's license was registered at the law office of Alan Masters. The two were obviously close. Some observers wondered why Alan Masters had not been indicted or at least called as a witness.

Until then, Alan Masters, Michael Corbitt, and James Keating, had every reason to believe they were home free on Dianne's slaying. The crime itself was more than four years old. There is no statute of limitations on murder, but by now the trail was cold, to say nothing of being well nigh obliterated, and Dianne's name had been relegated to the growing list of long-term unsolved murders.

True, some of the trio's decades of illegal activities seemed to be catching up with them. Keating was in prison as a result of Operation Safebet, and the feds were sniffing around Corbitt. Still, Alan Masters seemed secure; even though he had been a target during one or two investigations of legal and/or judicial chicanery, nothing came of it. Rumor had it that in one case, another lawyer had taken the fall and that Alan had paid him so well to do it that the man had been able to open a profitable business while still in prison. So even if the two cops had to do time on these other charges, there would be compensations. Al would take care of his friends; after all, he paid mouthpiece-about-town Herb Barsy to represent Keating and was taking care of Keating's finances while the ex-cop was in the joint.

The state's attorney's office repeatedly proved it had no stomach for convening a grand jury to investigate the circumstances surrounding Dianne's death. Many of the people who had direct knowledge of the murder but were not among the principal players kept silent, some because they feared discovery of their own illegal activities, others out of fear for their own safety. It was not the perfect crime, but the chance of anyone being punished for it seemed nonexistent.

But political realities necessitated some action on Sheriff Elrod's part. In August 1986, Chief Samuel Nolan of the sheriff's police announced that the investigation into Dianne's murder would be reactivated. There was some question about jurisdiction, especially since the sheriff's police had been invited out of the murder case by Willow Springs Police Chief Jim Ross back in December 1982. In the intervening years, the political power in Willow Springs had shifted; there was a new mayor and a new chief of police. As a result, Elrod's staff anticipated no dispute. With Elrod's approval, Nolan assigned the case to sheriff's investigator Paul Sabin.

John Reed remembers this period well. "If anyone asks me who reopened this case, I tell them it was Jim Keating with his comment about 'isn't it humorous that Dianne disappeared a day before she was going to file for divorce'—it was inaccurate, should have been three days, but that's how it was quoted and how it was played in the paper. Masters, Corbitt, and Keating were living a criminal's fantasy: commit a crime and then investigate it. That's some heady wine. Like having Ted Bundy investigate his own cases. Kind of scary.

"The Masters case was a domestic homicide. Any investigator should have exhausted the mere possibility that Alan might be involved first. And some of the men who were legitimately investigating it tried to, but they couldn't go anywhere. Alan had his people in place. Masters, Corbitt, Keating—they thought they could get away with it, and why not? They had gotten away with so much for so long," Reed mused.

"But they were arrogant. Arrogance leads to the assumption that everyone else is stupid. In turn, that leads to carelessness. Keating's wisecrack about Dianne got Elrod off his duff, and he got hold of Paul Sabin. That was a brilliant choice."

CHAPTER 3

On Friday, August 8, 1986, the
same day the news of the renewed activity on the Masters case was
released, Paul Sabin began reviewing the file. Sabin's name was not
included in the release, but among his peers he was known as one
of the best investigators in the department. Bright, determined,
and scrupulously honest, Sabin's appointment was a signal to those
who were paying attention that this would be a serious investigation rather than a cosmetic campaign effort.

Born in Detroit in 1949, Sabin grew up in Niles, a suburb just
across Chicago's north boundary. He joined the sheriff's police in
1977. Even as a rookie, he stood out because he already had a bachelor's degree in psychology. His goal had been a job in federal law
enforcement, but due to budget cuts, there were none available. By
1986, Sabin had acquired a master's degree in public administration from Roosevelt University, a law degree from John Marshall
Law School, and had passed the Illinois bar examination.

Although he had experience in all aspects of the sheriff's PD,
he was not familiar with the geographical area in which he would
be conducting his investigation. For help and advice, Sabin turned
to one of his best friends on the force, Sgt. John Reed, who lived in
Orland Park and knew the southwest suburbs. If Elrod's choice of
Sabin was brilliant, so was Sabin's decision to call upon John Reed.

By the time it landed in Sabin's lap, the Masters' case was four
years old, and investigations by the sheriff's police, the Willow

183

Springs police, the state police, and the FBI had come to nothing. Sabin was aware of the basic details; it had been a high-profile murder in the media and in the department's rumor mills, but he had not been personally involved in any aspect of the original investigation, nor had John Reed.

For Sabin, there was only one way to handle it: ignore everything he had heard and start from scratch. The first step was to pull all the available records. He had just begun to do this when the public responded to the news that the case was off the back burner.

On Saturday, August 9, 1986, the day after the announcement appeared in the newspapers, the sheriff's police communications center logged a call at 3 p.m. A woman who refused to give her name said she had read the papers, and she had a theory about Dianne Masters' death.

The woman claimed that a neighbor's daughter had been represented by Alan Masters in a divorce suit in 1982. In the course of the case, according to the tipster, Masters had suggested to the attractive young woman that she participate in what Masters called a high-class call girl operation. The client was shocked and upset by the suggestion.

The caller believed that Dianne Masters might have found out that her husband was offering love for sale and might have threatened to expose him. Because the news stories linked the cases to the recent convictions of sheriff's policemen, the caller felt that the murder of Dianne Masters was the result of a conspiracy by her husband and the police to prevent her from going to the media or other authorities.

The south suburban beauty salons were packed that Saturday morning, and Arlene Reed reported back to her husband that topic A was once again the Masters case.

Many factors would distinguish this case from the others Reed and Sabin worked on, but this first tip brought a taste of what was to come: more than the usual number of sources who were too frightened to go on the record. In most cases, the two officers knew the identity of the informants but for various reasons agreed to protect them.

Apparently it had become trendy among husbands and boyfriends to threaten the women in their lives with ending up like Dianne Masters. Promised anonymity, the women were anxious to share the threats. Then there were the barroom braggarts who liked to boast of their inside knowledge of how Dianne met her death. Plenty of listeners were happy to phone in about them. For a while, it seemed as if half the south suburbs was tattling on the other half. Even the most unlikely sounding leads had to be checked out.

Because it was widely believed that the police were involved, Sabin and Reed would have to be especially meticulous. Investigating fellow officers is not a popular thing to do; it violates the code among police. Reed and Sabin believed in the code as much as the next cop, but they also believed that somewhere a line had to be drawn. Murder was certainly one place to draw it.

For several months, Sabin and Reed worked the case together unofficially. Reed began spending substantial amounts of his own time advising Sabin and conducting interviews. The sheriff's race was heating up, and allegations of a cover-up in the murder of Dianne Masters continued to surface as one of the issues, but Reed and Sabin were so engrossed in the case that they barely noticed when election day came and went, with James O'Grady squeaking into the sheriff's office.

Shortly before his December swearing in, O'Grady assured reporters from a south suburban newspaper chain that he would make the Masters case a "high priority item."

On December 16, 1986, Chief James Walsh, Sam Nolan's replacement, phoned Reed to inform him that he was assigned to the Masters case full time. Now he was official.

Reed and Sabin continued to review the existing files, going back again and again. They found the rumors about the slipshod quality of the sheriff's initial investigation were true, which meant they had to try to reconstruct events that were more than four years old. Inconsistencies in witness accounts provided leads as well. Far from being high tech or flashy, this was general dogsbody work, tiring for everyone concerned. For all intents and purposes, the detectives lived with one foot in the present, and the other in 1982-83.

CHAPTER 4

*A*t 6:30 a.m. on Friday, March, 19, 1982, Alan Masters was awake and playing the role of the distressed husband. He telephoned several MVCC trustees, expressing his anxiety about Dianne's failure to make it home, told Georgie's sitter how worried he was, then went to his office. Jim Keating's act began at about 10:30 a.m., when Masters called to discuss what official steps he should take about Dianne's disappearance. By arrangement, Keating told Masters that a missing person's report could not be filed until Dianne had been gone twenty-four hours. After calling his house several times to find Dianne still had not arrived, Masters went home.

The official paper trail began in the early afternoon when Masters again called Keating, this time insisting that the sheriff's police take some immediate action. Masters' home was part of an unincorporated area of Cook County known as Beat 44 to the sheriff's police. Beat Officer Nick Johnstone was patrolling in his squad car when the dispatcher radioed him at 2:34 p.m. to proceed to the Masters' home on Wolf Road.

As Masters was telling Johnstone that he had last seen Dianne about 6:30 p.m. the previous evening when she left to attend a meeting of the board of Moraine Valley Community College, three other sheriff's cops arrived.

Sgt. Clarke Buckendahl and Investigator Mark Baldwin were on their way to a late lunch together when they heard the radio trans-

187

mission. A few minutes later, Lt. Howard Vanick called to confirm that Baldwin and Buckendahl had heard the report, telling them to meet him at Masters' home. All three men were assigned to South Dicks, in Markham. This was pretty heavy artillery for a missing person's report, but Alan Masters had connections. Among them were Vanick and Buckendahl, who were tied to Masters in business ventures.

Buckendahl and Baldwin arrived about 2:30 p.m. to find Patrolman Johnstone in the kitchen with Alan Masters. Vanick showed up about forty-five minutes later. Masters was explaining that the other MVCC board members with whom he had spoken said that after the board meeting the group had gone to the Village Courtyard for drinks. Dianne was last seen leaving the parking lot, driving toward home at about 1 a.m. Friday morning.

Although Alan claimed he had gone to sleep at about 10 p.m. and slept through the night, Mark Baldwin found this hard to believe, given Alan's appearance. "He was shaking. Very drawn and haggard looking, bags under his eyes like a person that didn't sleep," Baldwin noted.

After obtaining a description of Dianne's car and the clothes she was wearing when Alan last saw her, Baldwin asked Masters whether anyone else had been home with him during the night. "My daughter, who is four and one-half," Masters replied. During the six hours Baldwin spent at the house on Wolf Road, he never saw Georgie.

When Baldwin asked Alan about his relationship with Dianne, Masters said that "things were not well" between them, that he suspected she was seeing another man, and that he anticipated divorce proceedings. "It is not completely irreconcilable," Masters added.

"Has there been any previous occasion on which your wife has been out all night?" Baldwin queried.

"Yes, on more than one occasion, she hasn't come home till the following day," Masters replied.

An alarm went off in Baldwin's head. Masters' appearance belied his words. Masters seemed too agitated, too nervous, if this was really run-of-the-mill behavior for Dianne. After more questions from Baldwin, Masters revealed that he more than suspected there was another man; he actually had the man's name. He identified Jim Church by both name and employment.

About forty-five minutes after he arrived at the scene, Buckendahl asked Masters for permission to search the house. It was granted, and Baldwin walked through each room to see if there was anything out of place, checked the floors for marks, looked for broken furniture, peeked into closets to see if any clothing appeared to be missing. It was preliminary in nature, not the type of search conducted on a suspected crime scene. No scientific methods were used nor were any dogs brought in. A more thorough search was conducted the following week, but there had been plenty of time to dispose of any evidence of what had transpired in the house on Wolf Road.

Baldwin also checked the driveway and the grounds in the same fashion but found nothing that immediately indicated foul play to the naked eye. Neighbors told him nothing of interest.

On returning from his sortie, Baldwin asked Masters, "Where do you think your wife might be?"

"With her friend Jim Church," Masters answered.

"Would she have picked up a stranger on the highway?" Baldwin continued.

"No," Masters stated, "she's not the type to stop or pick up a hitchhiker."

About this time, Lt. James Keating drove up to the house. As far as Baldwin knew, no one had summoned him; Keating was commander of the sheriff's Criminal Intelligence Unit (CIU), and he did not usually get involved in a missing person's investigation. Baldwin was aware of Keating's presence, but the two did not speak as Baldwin went about his job.

However, shortly after Keating's arrival, Baldwin was standing inside the Masters' front door when he saw the two lieutenants, Vanick and Keating, engaged in what Baldwin described as an "animated" conversation, although he could not hear what they were saying.

Clarke Buckendahl also observed his two colleagues, and to him it looked as if they were arguing. No description of this encounter was included in the official report by Vanick or the officers who witnessed the disagreement. According to Vanick, he told Keating that Dianne Masters had not disappeared voluntarily and that Alan was responsible. This angered Keating, who accused Vanick of not being objective and admonished him that Alan was to receive the benefit of any doubt.

Vanick ordered a foot search of the route Dianne Masters would have taken from the Village Courtyard to her home. It was completed by members of the CCSPD with the assistance of the Cook County Forest Preserve Police. Although it was March, the top level of soil had softened. If a heavy car like Dianne's Cadillac had been forced to the shoulder of the two-lane road, it would have left tire marks. After walking the area on both sides of the roadway, the joint force found no signs of such a stop nor any clothing or other personal property.

At 5:30 p.m., Vanick assigned two investigators to go to the United Savings Bank in Orland Park where Dianne had an account. The detectives showed their identification and a written authorization from Alan Masters to the night teller and were told that during the previous week there had been two withdrawals and one mail deposit. The teller would not provide the men with the amounts on that occasion, but they were later found to be inconsequential, not what might be expected if the woman had been preparing to run away with a lover.

At sunset, Mark Baldwin was ready to leave the Masters' house. There was little else he could do there. As the assigned case officer, he asked Masters to let him know immediately should there be any word from Dianne.

At about this point, Mary Nelson was letting herself into her home after returning from a meeting in downstate Normal. When she checked her answering machine, she found messages asking that she call a sheriff's detective about a missing person. She was familiar with an individual on the MVCC campus who suffered from a recurring memory loss and would occasionally disappear for short periods. She assumed that the calls were about this person.

She returned the call from Lt. Howard Vanick. He began by asking if she "really" had been out of town that day. It seemed to her a curious way to begin an interview and not the best method of obtaining cooperation.

"Yes, I was away, and I can prove it," she shot back.

"Do you know where Dianne Masters is?" countered Vanick.

Surprised at the question, Mary replied, "No, I don't."

"She never reached home after the board meeting," Vanick explained. "Did she tell you where she was going when she left you in the restaurant parking lot?"

Mary was perplexed. "She said she was going home. She had to get up early in the morning to drive downtown. We walked out together. She wanted to drop some material off at my office on her way to the Loop, but I suddenly remembered I would be away. I told her she could leave the packet with my secretary. By that time, we were standing outside her car. I saw her open her car door, and I turned away to get into my car."

Vanick thought for a minute. "Was there anything unusual that you remember?"

"No, we just said good night. By the time I pulled my car around, Dianne was in her car at the parking lot exit. The left turn blinker was on. A car driven by another member of our group was between us, but I had a clear view of her Cadillac. She pulled out going west, and that's the last I saw of her, because I was going east."

When questioned, other members of the college party group who left the Village Courtyard with Dianne agreed with Mary Nelson's account. There was nothing suspicious or alarming in the parking lot, and they had not heard from Dianne since. Several members of the group who left the restaurant about thirty minutes before Dianne and Mary were not interviewed.

Helene Maignon was in her native France in March 1982. Immediately after Dianne disappeared, Maignon received a phone call from Alan Masters asking if Dianne was with her. When she answered "no," he hung up. During a May 1982 interview, she told the sheriff's police that she had last seen Dianne at dinner in mid-February before Maignon left on vacation, and that Dianne was concerned but not "distraught" about her marital troubles.

Maignon's knowledge of any problems in the Masters household was not probed nor were the circumstances of the friends' last meal together with Jim Church, during which Dianne related Alan's telephone threat, adding, "My husband is a very violent man, and I think he's going to hurt me."

Also omitted from Helene's first interview was the fact that beginning on January 14, 1982, Maignon's birthday, she received phone calls from Alan Masters on almost a daily basis. During the first call, he told her that Dianne had asked for a divorce, that he was desperate and contemplating suicide as a result. Helene was so upset that she canceled plans for her birthday celebration. During subsequent phone calls, Masters would tell Helene that as one of Dianne's close friends, she should work on changing Dianne's mind, "or else." If Dianne could not or would not change her mind, "she [is] going to pay for it. Remember, as much as I love her, I will hate her, and you know what I do to people I hate." He said he would hurt Dianne and that he would never let his daughter go.

On Saturday, March 20, 1982, Masters called his employee Dianne Economou and asked that Economou contact Sheila Mikel, requesting that Mikel phone Alan. Masters explained that he did not want to make the call himself because he was afraid the police were tapping his phone. This did not make sense, because as a defense attorney would know, if a line is tapped, it picks up incoming as well as outgoing calls. Alan Masters was aware that the only person tapping Alan Masters' phone was Alan Masters himself. What did make sense is that Masters was worried that the police might request from Illinois Bell a record of calls made from the Masters' house. The MUDS (Message Unit Details) would list all the numbers dialed except for a small area in the immediate vicinity. Masters did not want the police to discover he was calling Mikel because too many people knew that Masters had been seeing her on the side. It would be best not to call attention to the liaison; the thing with Sheila was not serious, but some might see another woman as a motive for getting rid of Dianne. Economou complied with Masters' demand.

On Sunday, March 21, 1982, the investigators talked with Dianne's lawyer, Maureen McGann-Ryan, at her home. She had just returned from the Florida trip which had prevented earlier filing of Dianne's divorce complaint. She told the detectives that the minimum discussed was joint custody of Georgianna and half the proceeds from the sale of the couple's home, but that Dianne expected the alimony she would receive would be somewhat limited because of short term of the marriage. No specific financial demands had yet been made, according to the attorney.

McGann-Ryan also said that friends of Alan Masters had called in his behalf, requesting that she try to talk Dianne out of the divorce. When Dianne was told of this, she reiterated her determination, saying that "through therapy and a lot of soul searching (she had) reached a decision and that the marriage was over." She refused to go through any further counseling, adding that it was just another delaying tactic on Alan's part.

Dianne also had placed her jewelry in a safe deposit box, McGann-Ryan informed the police. Earlier in the year Alan had taken it with him when they were separated. He did return it eventually, but Dianne believed that he would continue to use this as another way of pressuring her, so she wanted these items in a safe place, out of Alan's reach.

Jim Church was not interviewed until Monday, March 22, because he had gone on a long-planned skiing trip over the weekend. There was a part of him that would cling for months to the hope that Dianne had found the situation too difficult and had gone away to distance herself from home. But deep down, he worried that Dianne's worst fears had come true. If she was right about the first part, that Alan would hurt her, she probably was right about the second part—that the police would be involved. As a result, Church was not in a good mood when he arrived at South Dicks in response to a request from sheriff's investigators. His attitude did not improve when it became clear that he was being treated as a suspect. "I don't believe you can perform a serious investigation, not with your connection to Alan Masters," Church told Clarke Buckendahl.

The session was not a pleasant one for Church. Asked by Sergeant Buckendahl to take a polygraph test, Church replied, "I will, if Alan Masters takes one, too." Church was dismayed by what he saw as the beginning of a cover-up and hoped to shame the sheriff's cops into doing their job. As yet he was unaware that corrupt dealings and money combine to wash out feelings of shame. "I knew I hadn't done anything to Dianne and could pass the test, but I was sure Alan was involved. I was also sure that the sheriff's cops, especially Buckendahl and Vanick, wouldn't do anything that would expose their pal." Church was correct.

CHAPTER 5

*B*y midweek after her disap-
pearance, photos of Dianne Masters had been sent to the Chicago
Police Department and the Illinois State Police, and descriptions
of her car went out on the stolen auto computer listing.
Investigators obtained her credit card numbers and were watching
for any charges that appeared after March 18th. Her bank account
was monitored for withdrawals. There were none of the above, confirming the theory that she had not disappeared voluntarily.

On March 26, Alan Masters phoned the sheriff's police to
notify them that one of Dianne's friends in Maryland had received
flowers from Dianne on March 23. It seemed like a promising lead.
Upon checking with Fehser Florist, where Dianne had a weekly
account and her voice was well known, it was discovered that she
had placed the order by phone on March 17, and asked that the gift
be delivered on March 20, the friend's birthday, but because of a
glitch at the florist, the order was delayed.

The following Monday, Mark Baldwin paid a visit to Alan
Masters' family jeweler to obtain descriptions and photos of
Dianne's jewelry. The value at that time was less than $20,000, a
good deal less than the reported $200,000. Later that week when
Dianne's safe deposit box was opened, the jewelry was found
intact.

Those women who were close to Dianne believed she had met
with foul play immediately upon learning that Georgie was still at

195

home. The men who were working on the investigation were equally convinced when they found Dianne had left her jewelry behind. These men could have learned something from that most famous of all sleuths, Sherlock Holmes, who said that when a woman is threatened, "her instinct is at once to rush to the thing which she values most. A married woman grabs at her baby—an unmarried one reaches for her jewel box." Dianne did neither.

As Sabin and Reed went through the old files, Alan Masters' efforts to manipulate the investigation were increasingly obvious. Although news of Dianne's disappearance had gone through several word-of-mouth cycles, the first media accounts did not surface until March 25, 1982. Vanished women were a dime a dozen, and it was always possible that Dianne had taken some cooling-off time after a spat and would be returning. After almost a week with no word from her or about her, it began to look serious.

"Woman missing; reward offered" read the teaser under Dianne's photo on the front page of the *Chicago Tribune*. The story ran on page 3, and immediately it was clear Alan was trying to put his own spin on it. Alan Masters well knew that he would be the prime suspect. Offering a ten thousand dollar reward was one way Masters could assure himself of being portrayed as a loving and bereft husband. It was an easy, empty gesture; Masters knew the men involved in getting rid of Dianne were not going to be filing any claims.

But Masters did not stop there. Through Buckendahl, he admitted that he and Dianne had been having difficulty with their marriage and that "once" she had told Alan she wanted to file for a divorce. Contrary to all the information uncovered in the investigation and his own personal knowledge of the Masters' situation, Buckendahl went along with this, adding that Dianne had "never initiated divorce proceedings, however, and the couple were reconciling." Dianne "was believed to be carrying $200 to $300" when she disappeared, according to Buckendahl, and had removed "approximately $200,000" in jewelry from her home at the time of the marital difficulty. All strung together, these details made Dianne sound like a pampered, spoiled brat who had abandoned her wifely and motherly responsibilities, probably for a little fun in the sun.

The *Chicago Sun-Times* ran a somewhat different story under the headline "Wife gone; reward is $10,000." This article referred to "fear" on the part of relatives and the sheriff's police that Dianne had been the victim of foul play. It painted a more accurate picture of the Masters' marital situation. Dianne's lawyer was quoted on her plans to file for divorce. Dianne was described as "a wonderful mother...[who] wouldn't have left without talking" to her daughter.

The games had only begun.

The same day the news story broke, Alan Masters reported a demand for twenty-five thousand dollars in ransom to be delivered to Waukegan, a city near the Wisconsin state line. Because the caller was wrong about several details, including the color of Dianne's car, Lieutenant Vanick concluded that it was a "parasite call," made by a crank, and he refused to pursue it. Jim Keating took over, sending sheriff's police to cooperate with Waukegan officers, but nothing came of it or subsequent ransom calls.

Reed and Sabin encountered further evidence of attempts by sheriff's police to hamper the initial investigation. As the leads dried up and nothing was heard from Dianne, Howard Vanick called the CIU to talk to Robert Neapolitan, an investigator who was an expert on chop shop operations. Vanick wanted a list of such establishments near the Masters' house.

"I'll get back to you," Neapolitan promised.

Vanick did get a return call that same day, but it was from Jim Keating. "If you want to know anything about the disposal of cars, you ask me and nobody else," Keating ordered Vanick bluntly and then slammed down the phone.

In mid-April 1982, two investigators interviewed Brigitte at her home. Brigitte told them that during a trip to Germany in July

1981, Dianne expressed fear about disappearing and never being found.

Brigitte also said she had been present when Alan and Dianne were arguing and had heard him say, "I will take Georgianna, and you will never find her." Exactly a month had passed since Dianne's disappearance, and Brigitte was even more firm in her belief that Dianne was dead. She was haunted by the dream she had two weeks before Dianne went missing, visualizing Dianne in dark water.

The regular monthly meeting of the Moraine Valley Community College board rolled around again. The disappearance of their pretty, outspoken vice chairman hung over the session like a dark cloud. The women especially were nervous. After adjournment, it was decided that the group would return to Artie G's for some post-meeting refreshment. As usual, they drove separately. Mary Nelson's car was a little balky and she was tired, so at the last minute, she decided to go home instead. She had barely taken her coat off when the phone rang. It was one of the male board members.

"Where did you go?" the caller asked, obviously relieved that Mary answered the phone. "You said you were coming, and when you didn't show up, we were worried." Until that moment, no one had been willing to articulate the apprehension each person felt. After assuring the caller that all was well, Mary sat down with a severe case of the chills.

On the night Dianne disappeared, Genevieve Capstaff, a professor at MVCC, was part of the group that left the Village Courtyard about a half hour before Dianne and the remainder of the party. When she realized the sheriff's investigators were not going to interview her, she came forward on her own, saying she had hung around the parking lot until the others emerged from the restaurant.

In response to her disclosures, two sheriff's cops interviewed Capstaff on April 30, 1982. She told them that she had to turn west out of the parking lot in order to go to her home and that the car ahead of her was Dianne Masters' easily recognizable Cadillac. She was behind Dianne until Dianne turned south on Wolf Road, and she had seen nothing unusual about Dianne's car or driving.

Despite the Capstaff revelation placing Dianne a few seconds from home, the investigation slowed to a crawl as far as the public was concerned. Dianne's friends and family worried that Alan had been successful in putting a lid on the case, and they decided to stir the pot a little. They mistrusted local police departments, and those who knew Dianne had gone to the FBI about her fears were worried about approaching the Bureau as well. But something had to be done, and the federal level seemed the only one left.

There are several instances, including suspicion of kidnapping, where the FBI will step into a missing person's case, preferably at the request of the police having jurisdiction. However, the Bureau does not require an invitation especially if police corruption or collusion may be involved. It would be impossible for the FBI to check out every such allegation because many of them are crank calls, but in the case of Dianne Masters, most of the callers who identified themselves proved to be solid citizens who phoned back repeatedly. The FBI would have to move. And it did. Sort of.

The FBI runs a little school for local policemen, and Vanick had attended a course there. The stated purpose of this school is to train the police in the latest methods, but there is an unstated purpose as well. By making selected local cops feel a special tie to the Bureau, the FBI creates what many other policemen regard as lapdogs or "pooches." It does not help the FBI's general unpopularity with local police that candidates are chosen primarily on the basis of political clout rather than on merit.

On April 26, 1982, Howard Vanick wrote a "Dear Richard" letter to his friend FBI Special Agent Richard Stilling. Vanick enclosed the missing person's bulletin the sheriff was distributing on Dianne, adding "Hopefully [sic] this effort will be productive although I am not very optimistic at this time that we will find her.

"Everything that we could possibly do to locate her has been done, and the evidence pointing to the missing person theory is non-existant [sic]. We don't believe at this time that Diane [sic] G. Masters is a voluntary missing person, nor do we believe that she was the victim of a random criminal act. Rather the evidence seems to point to a contrived and planned act eliminating Diane Masters."

Not "everything" had been done, especially with regard to Alan's involvement and that of his friends among the police. Doing "everything" would expose Vanick's role in the events leading up to Dianne's disappearance: providing Alan with details about Dianne's lover; following Dianne; not revealing that Dianne had given him a list of license plates she had accumulated from cars she believed were tailing her.

Vanick continued to contradict himself. "We have, indeed, received information, which at best is questionable as to accuracy, that Diane G. Masters has been killed and her body and her automobile destroyed. Although our sources are questionable, this theory certainly seems viable. As you know this is not a difficult task to accomplish if you have the necessary contacts.

"At this point in time the elements necessary for formal FBI involvement are not present, however, I would like to ask your assistance by requesting that any information you possibly receive, from whatever source be relayed to us. Again Dick, thanks for your help. " It was signed "Howie."

Vanick's letter helped get the FBI off the hook. The local office could tell those pesky complainers that everything that could be done had been done. No one was going to mention the fact that Dianne had told the FBI about her fears.

It was all very cozy, but Dianne Masters' was an unquiet corpse. On May 19, 1982, Vanick received another phone call from the FBI. Agents John O'Rourke and Robert Pecoraro arranged to meet Vanick the next day to discuss the case.

During this session in the sheriff's Markham office, the agents told Vanick that telephone calls to the FBI and the U.S. attorney's office were continuing. There was a common theme: that Alan's close association with the police and inside the judicial system precluded an honest investigation.

According to Vanick's memo summarizing the meeting, the U.S. attorney had directed O'Rourke to "determine the need for an investigation into the allegations of official misconduct as it related to the allegation of judicial bribery, with the underlying thought of providing information to the [sheriff] relative to the missing person's investigation." In the face of evidence to the contrary, such as Keating's admonition in the Masters' driveway and subsequent involvement, Vanick assured O'Rourke that reports of police "non-objectivity are totally unfounded."

With regard to Dianne's statements that Alan was a lawyer for the south suburban mob, FBI Agent Stilling wrote Howard Vanick that these allegations had been checked out with Joseph Cullotta, a former mobster in federal protective custody. According to Cullotta, Alan Masters "was not that well connected" to the outfit. This seemed to preclude the involvement of organized crime in Dianne's death.

The days turned into weeks and months, and those who loved Dianne struggled with their emotions. It seemed like everyone had forgotten their friend. Even the FBI refused to help. The media turned their attention to other breaking stories, although there were periodic "still missing" articles.

One of these appeared in a suburban paper on July 29, 1982, slugged "Board to Replace Masters as Family Tries to Cope." "I've had a dream about her [Dianne] every night for the last four months," Howard Vanick told the reporter, who unfortunately did not ask about the content of the dream.

"The case will never be closed until it's brought to a successful conclusion...The FBI also has an open case...What we're interested in is the disappearance." Vanick added a tantalizing tidbit:

"There's something else that the FBI is interested in...We were given some information that at the very best is extremely questionable as to its authenticity and validity." Vanick's statement to the press did not correspond to his written communications with the Bureau.

Asked if there was any truth to the rumors that the sheriff's office was investigating a mob connection, Vanick said "That is just one of a million areas that we could possibly investigate."

Toward the end of July 1982, Alan Masters phoned Clarke Buckendahl, asking that the sergeant come to Masters' house to discuss something of interest. After informing Howard Vanick, Buckendahl left South Dicks for Palos.

"My daughter's birthday is July 20," Alan told Buckendahl. "On July 23, there was a card in the mail addressed to her. It might be from Dianne."

Buckendahl studied the greeting card. The address had been typed on the envelope, but there was no zip code; the postmark read "South Suburban, Il. July 20, 1982." The card itself bore a picture of Snoopy, the "Peanuts" dog. Inside, it read "Thinking of you" and was unsigned. The sergeant inventoried both card and envelope and sent them to the laboratory to be checked for fingerprints. The tests were negative.

During this visit, Masters showed Buckendahl an eavesdropping device he had found in the bedroom. He claimed to have no knowledge as to how the battery-operated bug got there or who was receiving transmissions. He permitted Buckendahl to examine it on the premises but insisted on keeping it.

"You should report this to the state's attorney or the U. S. attorney general," Buckendahl advised Masters before leaving. Masters did not follow through.

However, a report of the bugging surfaced in the press in September, along with an account of an August telephone call received by one of Masters' law office employees. A man, identifying himself as "Jack Springer," allegedly phoned to say that while paddling down the Des Plaines River in Lake County, Illinois, he had heard the voice of a woman who identified herself as Dianne Masters calling through the padlocked door of a ramshackle cabin on the riverbank. The woman said she had been kidnapped and asked "Springer" to notify her husband, giving him two phone numbers.

As with the ransom demands, Vanick did not take the story seriously, but he did report it to Lake County police. A search of both sides of the riverbank failed to turn up any trace of such a cabin, let alone of Dianne. It was another hoax.

Despite an occasional burp in the media on a slow news day, the investigation by the sheriff's police of Dianne Masters' disappearance ran out of steam by the fall of 1982. However, the ransom demands and rumors again brought the case to the attention of the FBI, and two agents were assigned to interview sources. This was not public knowledge, and as the holiday season approached, it seemed as if the mystery surrounding Dianne's disappearance would never be solved.

In early December 1982, Alan presented Pat Casey with a package wrapped in festive paper. "Here's a little Christmas present for you from Dianne," he said. Appalled by the cruelty of Alan's gesture, Pat was also touched by Dianne's thoughtfulness. Pat knew that Dianne liked to get a jump on her Christmas shopping; she began preparing for the next holiday immediately after New Year's, ordering from catalogs and buying special items. Dianne believed there was something magical about finding exactly the right gift, and it was never too early to start. She would wrap the presents immediately and put them away until December. It was all part of Dianne's attempt to create an atmosphere of affection and thoughtfulness, to build a sort of substitute for the warm family life she had always lacked.

The two women had a running joke about armadillos, and when Pat opened the gift, she found a small armadillo figurine. For the past nine months, Pat had tried to come to grips with Dianne's disappearance, and in one moment, all her defense mechanisms were destroyed. Alan could not have hurt her more if he cut her to the bone. Pat had tried so hard not to believe the gossip about Alan's involvement in the mystery surrounding Dianne's departure, but he was making it difficult for her. Like Brigitte and Jim and Mary and Dianne's other friends, she clung to the hope that Dianne was alive someplace and that someday Pat would hear from her.

On December 2, 1982, Lary Damron finally reached Keating's guy who ran everything. Far from the distressed husband, Alan Masters' main concern seemed to be the work that had piled up while he was in Florida on vacation. "What part of the world do you live in, Larry?" Upon being told that Damron lived in Palatine, Masters replied, "Okay, the other part of the world from me."

"But I can be in there probably about forty-five minutes to an hour, or so, you know," Damron hastened to add, not wanting to let geography stand in the way.

"Okay, well...I'm gonna start a trial tomorrow morning that'll take me away from the office all day...I'm only gonna be here for a few short hours Saturday, but I will be available Saturday afternoon or Saturday evening to sit and talk to you. But it would have to be out southwest at my house, if that's okay," At this point, Masters felt sufficiently comfortable that Damron was just what he claimed to be to invite the agent to his house.

Damron was anxious to make the connection. "That would be fine, yeah, that'd be great."

Before the conversation ended, Masters provided Damron with his unlisted home telephone number, and the two men agreed to talk on Saturday afternoon.

On Saturday, December 4, 1982, Damron and Masters spoke on the telephone about land values and the availability of liquor licenses in Summit, and then Damron said, "...You know we want...to make sure that we can get the necessary help," meaning protection for the proposed house of prostitution.

"Yeah, there's no problem," Masters replied. "I would imagine for the first month or so... you would not have that and then after a month or so you would have it."

"Right...we want to start off just as a nice business... and gradually move into it as long as we're assured of...what we need," Damron responded. He understood Masters' comment to mean that for the first month, Damron would not have to pay protection. By "nice business," Damron was indicating that during the start-up phase when people might be paying attention, the club would operate legally and only gradually would move into prostitution with the proper protection.

On Friday, December 10, Damron had a lengthy telephone conversation with Alan Masters. It was their second chat in two days, and Alan was in a bubbly mood. They continued to discuss various sites around Summit for Damron's bordello. Masters joked about leaving the practice of law to become a television evangelist.

Getting in the spirit of the thing, Damron said, "Oh, do these people make money, or do they make money? ...What do they say, 'Give your money to God, but send it to my address.'"

Masters asked Damron if he had heard of the Reverend Ernest Ainsley..."if you touched a television set where his hand is at, hemorrhoids, leukemia, or ingrown toenails and headaches all go away. He did the counting himself; he opened up the envelopes last year and his count was thirty-eight million, Larry."

"Well, listen, I'll be glad to be your road manager or whatever the hell you need," Damron laughed.

"I mean, can you fuckin' believe that?" Masters asked. "I mean, it's unbelievable. That's the greatest thing since Wonder Bread, you know...And he doesn't get arrested for that shit, can you imagine?"

"There's something wrong, you know, I'm in the wrong profession obviously," Damron observed.

"I have a client whose wife is a born-again Christian, and God bless her, she sent one of those people $33,000 last year," Masters confided. "I sat her down, and I said, 'Honey, I don't tell you to be a Protestant, a Jew, a Catholic, a Moslem, but there are orphanages, there's this Mother Theresa who's doing all this work.' I mean what she could have done with $33,000 was unbelievable...she could have given it to me."

After playing along with the evangelism joke, Damron got down to business, wanting reassurance about not having any "problem" in the future.

"I'll talk to you in person, okay?" Masters said.

"Okay...but I won't see you for two weeks, right?" Damron had heard that Masters was leaving for Florida the next day.

"Well, you can see me next week," Masters explained. "I'm not leaving this Saturday..."

Indeed, Masters would have to put off his trip for more than a week. The next day, Saturday, December 11, 1982, Dianne Masters' body was discovered.

CHAPTER 6

*I*mmediately after Dianne's remains were located in the jurisdiction of the Willow Springs PD, Chief Jim Ross announced his intention of replacing the sheriff's team with the Illinois State Police. As a longtime courtroom bailiff in the Fifth District, Ross knew Alan Masters and his reputation, and he also was aware of the gossip swirling around Dianne's disappearance. It did not help matters when Howard Vanick asked Ross for a piece of evidence, one of the license plates off Dianne's car, as a souvenir. Vanick claimed that Sgt. Clarke Buckendahl wanted the plate for his collection, but Buckendahl denied ever soliciting Vanick's aid in this matter, saying, "It would be lousy police work, and besides, Howie Vanick's not the type to do anyone any favors."

A few days after Ross' request, Illinois State Police Special Agent Charles Kitchen was assigned as the case agent. While reviewing information made available by the sheriff's office, Kitchen and his partner, Edward Miller, began interviewing Dianne's colleagues, friends, and family members, some of whom were firmly convinced that the case would never be solved.

Kitchen was particularly interested in the detailed results of the postmortem performed on Dianne's remains. On arriving at the morgue on December 11, 1982, the medical examiner, Robert Stein ordered that the body bag containing Dianne's remains be X-rayed, and this revealed two bullets lodged in what was left of her brain. The cause of death had been listed as "bullet wound

207

(head)." The condition of Dianne's body was compatible with her having been in the canal since her disappearance, so the "date of death" on the certificate was changed to "date found," December 11, 1982. Because the two small caliber bullets found in Dianne's skull had not been enough to cause massive fractures of her cranium, Dr. Stein called upon the department's consulting forensic anthropologist, Dr. Clyde Snow, to reconstruct Dianne's skull.

The two experts agreed that in addition to being shot twice in the left cheek, Dianne Masters had been struck by forceful blows from a blunt weapon, which could have been anything from a blackjack to a baseball bat. It was Dr. Snow's opinion that Dianne's skull had been shattered before she was shot and that the fractures were enough to cause death.

The recovery of Dianne's car and remains in Willow Springs opened a whole new area of investigation. Kitchen obtained a list of all the cars that had been dredged out of the canal to date and queried taxi companies serving the area in case they had picked up any fares nearby at the time of Dianne's disappearance.

At the same time, Kitchen reinterviewed all the MVCC people, including the early departures, who had gone to the Village Courtyard the previous March; Dianne's decorator friend who now lived in Florida; her housekeeper, who had been ill for several months prior to Dianne's disappearance, and Donna, the housekeeper's daughter, who had filled in for her mother and who arrived the morning of March 19, 1982, to find Georgie eating her breakfast. After asking his daughter to go to her room, Alan had told Donna that Dianne had not come home the previous night and that he was worried. If she did not arrive soon, he was going to call the police, but in any event, he was staying home that day and Donna need not stay. According to Donna, she left soon after. It was her last day of work for Masters, as her mother returned on March 23, 1982.

Donna told Kitchen and his partner that she occasionally used Dianne's car and that she was familiar with Dianne's large brass key ring which had five or six keys on it, including both the car and house keys. The description fit the ring attached to the key found in the Cadillac's ignition, but when recovered there were only two keys, both of which belonged to the car.

Shortly before Dianne vanished, she mentioned her concern that she was being followed and asked Donna to watch for cars parked near the house when Donna used the Cadillac to drive Georgie to preschool. Donna said she had never seen any.

Dianne's medical records might hold some important information, especially her psychiatrist's notes. Although the law protecting patient/doctor confidentiality ends with the patient's death, Dr. Schwemer's concern about ethical considerations made it necessary for Kitchen to obtain a subpoena. Then the state trooper met with the doctor, who told them about Dianne's long road to self-discovery, her genuine alarm over her husband's threats, and Schwemer's conversations with Alan.

Jim Church was more receptive to the state special agents than he had been to the sheriff's investigators, and finally he agreed to take a lie detector test at the state bureau of scientific services in Joliet.

Although the results of such tests are not admissible in court, properly administered, with the right questions asked, the police have considerable confidence in the results. The test measures changes in blood pressure, pulse, and respiration, the galvanic skin response, and muscular activity, especially in the forearms and legs.

Church was first interviewed briefly by the licensed examiner. After having the procedure described to him and answering some questions about the case, he was asked what medications he was taking, if any. Then he was seated in a chair and a corrugated rubber tube was placed around his chest; a blood pressure cuff, attached to one of his arms; and a set of electrodes, to the fingers of the other arm. Any changes were transmitted to a recording pen.

Church was told he would be asked several control questions, and he would be asked to give several incorrect answers in order to establish a pattern for his responses. After this was done, he was asked four specific questions: Were you with Dianne Masters on March 18 or 19, 1982? Did you shoot Dianne Masters? Did you help or plan with anyone to cause Dianne Masters' death? Do you know for sure who shot Dianne?

To all of these queries, Church answered "no." The examiner concluded, based on the polygraph procedure, that Church was telling the truth.

On February 18, 1983, Kitchen met Jim Ross at the Willow Springs police station. Ross gave the agent an envelope post-marked South Suburban, Illinois, on February 10, 1983. Inside was a handwritten letter filled with errors in syntax and spelling that read in part:

"I will not say where I was when I overheard the conversation. Now don't get me wrong. I really feel sorry for that beautiful lady 'Masters.' And I would bet anyone Mr. Masters is 100% behind the whole matter.

"I know... that Corbitt and Masters have to be guilty... I just hope you can nail both of these bastards—especially Corbitt—he was never nothing but a crooked prick."

It was signed "a friend."

The next day, Kitchen and Miller visited Alan Masters in his home. As they were about to begin, Alan produced a portable tape recorder and demanded that he be permitted to record the interview because he had been "misquoted in the past." The agents informed Masters that they did not wish to have a recording made, but they did agree to permit Alan to record their refusal.

Masters repeated his story about arriving home as Dianne was preparing to leave for her board meeting. He did add one homely detail; as she was leaving Dianne promised, "If I get a chance, I'll call before Georgie goes to bed so I can say goodnight."

According to Masters, Dianne did call at about 8:30 p.m. during a break in the board meeting. By that time, Georgie was asleep, so Dianne was not able to speak to her little girl.

"I'm not sure when the meeting will be over," Dianne told Alan, adding that she probably would be stopping off for drinks when it did end. Masters claimed that this was the last time he spoke to his wife.

Masters went to bed about 9 or 9:30 p.m. and slept until about 5:45 the next morning. When he awoke, he went to his wife's bedroom. Finding her bed had not been slept in, he began to call the other board members.

Kitchen asked if this had ever happened before. Masters answered, yes, once in January or February when she did not get home until about 6 a.m. When he questioned her, she said she had fallen asleep in the parking lot outside Artie G's. It was a transparent excuse, if indeed Dianne used it.

Masters contradicted the temporary housekeeper about what happened after her arrival around 7:30 a.m. He claimed he went to his office, leaving Donna in charge. At about 10:30 a.m., he called home to find out if Dianne had arrived. Told she had not, he called his friend Jim Keating, then went home and dismissed the hired help. Several hours later, he called Keating again, and this time a report was filed.

Kitchen already knew about Dianne's affair with Jim, but he had to find out if Alan knew, too. "I believe she did have a boyfriend, but I don't believe she was having an affair," Masters asserted.

"How did you learn about her involvement with another man?" queried Kitchen.

"I overheard her talking on the telephone to him," Masters said, protecting Lieutenant Vanick.

Masters pooh-poohed the seriousness of his marital troubles, saying, "...we've had our difficulties in the past, but right before she disappeared, we were getting along very well." To add to this lie, Masters claimed no knowledge that Dianne's lawyer was about to file for divorce or that his attorney had been so informed. When Kitchen asked Alan if he had ever physically assaulted Dianne,

Masters replied that in 1970 or 1975 he had assaulted her when he learned she was having an affair during one of their separations, but he could not remember if she had required medical attention. In fact, she had been physically abused repeatedly, and he had paid her medical bills.

Then Kitchen shifted gears to ask Masters if he had ever placed eavesdropping devices on the telephone or hired anyone to follow Dianne. Masters became very agitated and began to perspire. This was the same reaction Mark Baldwin noticed nine months earlier.

"I'm being treated as a suspect, and I don't appreciate that. I won't answer any more of these types of questions," Masters complained.

Dropping that line, Kitchen inquired about Dianne's key ring. Alan described it as made of brass, with a hook on the end, and said Dianne kept five keys on the ring: two automobile keys, two house keys, and one alarm key.

Next Kitchen produced the key ring with the two car keys that had been found in the ignition of the Cadillac and asked if Masters could identify it. He recognized it, but said he could not account for the missing keys.

Before the state troopers left, Masters showed them a Valentine's Day card he said he received on February 18, 1983. The envelope was hand-addressed and was postmarked Willow Springs, February 17, 1983. Inside the card was written "now is the time to tell all." It was signed with the letter "D." Masters told Kitchen that the writing was very similar to Dianne's. Masters asked, "Has Dianne been positively identified?" "Yes, through her dental records," Kitchen answered, although he knew Masters was well aware of how the body had been identified. The state forensic lab found no similarities in the handwriting.

Sometimes Kitchen followed tips that took him on a wild goose chase; on other occasions, he met with half truths or a stone wall. For example, a source told Kitchen that Masters had used Ted

Nykaza to follow Dianne and that the private investigator had photographs of her with other men, but when confronted, Nykaza denied this. He also denied tapping Alan's home telephone or placing other eavesdropping devices at the house on Wolf Road. When Kitchen tried to interview Michael Corbitt, the former WSPD chief hired a lawyer who blocked such a session.

There were a number of discrepancies in statements Kitchen obtained, especially when compared with those given the sheriff's police, but these contradictions were not explored. By April 1983, Kitchen felt he had explored all possible leads, with no positive results. The investigation by the state police had ended.

CHAPTER 7

*T*heir study of the official files left Sabin and Reed with more questions than answers. Over the years, potential witnesses and sources had been interviewed by the sheriff's police after Dianne's disappearance, by private detectives hired by her brother, by state troopers, and by the FBI. Each time they answered questions, it was like opening an old wound, each time hopes were raised that some action would be taken, and each time, these hopes were dashed.

As a result, some people who had no fear of self-incrimination were too afraid or too disgusted to talk. Others were determined to put the whole sad business behind them. They were in the minority, however; most wanted some sort of justice for Dianne. They simply did not believe they were going to get it. Some were frightened because Alan Masters seemed to have very good information as to what people told the police in earlier investigations.

Her friends remembered Dianne's premonitions and her statements that if something happened to her the police could not be trusted because they would be involved. Now, four years later, there were two more plainclothesmen on the doorstep. There was simply no reason to think anything had changed. More than one interview began in an atmosphere of hostility.

It was time-consuming, frequently tedious work, and it threatened to take over the lives of both men. Some informants were reluctant to make any contacts through the sheriff's office.

Policemen do not like to give out their home telephone numbers, but in this case, they made an exception. John and Arlene Reed had trained their children Nicole and John to carefully note messages, and the Reed offspring frequently found themselves soothing nervous sources. The investigation of Dianne Masters' death became a family affair.

John Reed had a couple of advantages over Paul Sabin in the investigation. Besides twenty years on the job compared to Sabin's nine, Reed was on familiar ground. Sabin knew Alan Masters only by reputation, but Reed had seen him around the courts, especially in the southwestern fifth district, for years.

When it came to Dianne Masters, Reed and Sabin were even. Neither had ever met her. "We did that part by remote control," Reed observes. "We never saw the body or the car, except in photographs. At the time Dianne disappeared, both of us worked out of central investigations in the sheriff's west suburban Maywood office. You couldn't help but pay attention, because everyone was talking about it. Everybody had a theory."

Although he never expected to work the case, in June 1982 Reed was sufficiently intrigued with an article in the *Southtown Economist* that he clipped it out of the paper and kept it. Columnist Ray Hanania asked Masters if he would comply with police requests and take a polygraph test. Several people connected with the case had already done so. Masters' reply was, "I don't believe in trying a case in the press."

Reed found this curious because, so far, there were no grounds on which to build a case, much less a trial. Hanania also asked if Masters believed his wife was still alive. "It's been a mind-boggling experience. I hope so," Masters responded.

Masters added that he had no faith in polygraph tests and usually advised clients not to take them. However, as Reed discovered while combing through the state police file, on at least one occasion, when Dianne's cash and jewelry disappeared from a friend's house, Masters did take a lie box and pass it. Masters used the polygraph results as a means to effect a reconciliation.

Sabin and Reed read through all the newspaper clippings they could find about the case, noting areas to be explored. The day after Dianne's body was recovered, Alan told investigators for the county medical examiner and Willow Springs Police Chief Jim Ross that he wanted to have her remains cremated immediately.

Dianne's family protested that they wanted her buried; her friends said that she was afraid of fire and as a Catholic would have never opted for cremation, even though there was such a provision in her will. It was theorized that since Alan had prepared the will, he might have slipped it past Dianne.

Dr. Stein, the medical examiner, refused permission because, "it's a homicide case...Possibly we might even have to exhume the body sometime for further examination." Stein went so far as to have a court order issued preventing cremation, which was duly served upon Alan Masters.

After the postmortem, what remained of Dianne Masters was placed in a body bag and released to Tower Funeral Home in Lyons, owned by Alan Schiefelbein. A retired policeman and chum of Alan Masters, Schiefelbein also handled Annie Turner's funeral. A memorial service was held for Dianne at Saint Michael's Church in Orland Park on December 16, 1982. The service was attended by Alan and Georgie, as well as Dianne's close friends and associates. The mourners were not told about the final disposition of Dianne's body, leading several friends to believe she had been cremated after all.

What Reed called Dianne's second secret burial took place on December 17, 1982. Because of the condition of the body, there was no question of any preparation. The remains of Dianne Masters were left in the medical examiner's body bag and placed inside a coffin, which was then driven to Saint Adalbert's, a Roman Catholic cemetery on Milwaukee Avenue just outside the Chicago city limits. Schiefelbein, his wife Elaine, and Alan Masters rode with the casket. The small party was met at the cemetery by a priest who read the short graveside service as Dianne Masters was laid to rest a few rows away from the graves of her parents. Afterwards, Alan went to dinner with the Schiefelbeins.

CHAPTER 8

*T*he first big lead in the Sabin-
Reed investigation came at the end of August 1986, when Paul
Sabin interviewed a deputy sheriff named Joseph Danzl. Danzl's
former stepfather was Ted Nykaza, the private detective who operated out of Masters' office. After reading newspaper accounts of
possible participation in Dianne's murder by sheriff's police, Danzl
went to the internal affairs office.

Danzl recalled that around the time of Dianne Masters' disappearance, Nykaza talked about installing voice-activated bugging
devices on Masters' home phone. Nykaza also said that when the
tapes were played back, he had heard Dianne mention a boyfriend.

Danzl told Sabin that Nykaza had a serious drinking problem,
which increased after Dianne's disappearance, and that Nykaza
had asked the then teenaged Danzl and his younger brother to
destroy a number of audio cassettes. Danzl believed that these
were the tapes that had been used in the bugging equipment at
Masters' house.

Sabin also began to turn up information that confirmed the
gossip about Masters' extremely close ties to several members of
the sheriff's force, particularly those intimately involved with the
investigation of Dianne's disappearance and death.

Sgt. Clarke Buckendahl admitted that he knew Masters well in
a "professional" capacity and that he had retained as a lawyer one
of Masters' former partners, Diane Economou.

219

Sabin knew that Buckendahl was licensed as a private investigator as well as a private security and an alarm contractor, and that the address listed on one of these licenses belonged to Alan Masters' law office in Summit. Buckendahl said that while he had not done any private work in some years, he kept his license current and shared in an insurance liability pool with Nykaza, as did several other sheriff's policemen, including James Keating. Buckendahl's name also was registered with those of Keating and Jack Bachman in two separate p. i. agencies.

Sabin next talked to Lt. Howard Vanick, who headed the 1982 missing person's investigation. Vanick acknowledged that he had a long acquaintance with Masters and that Masters had represented Vanick in a divorce suit in 1981. The Vanicks were reconciled and the suit was dropped, only to be reinstated in 1983. At that time, Vanick was represented by another lawyer, unconnected with the Masters firm. Frederick Aprati, Jr., withdrew from the case when he was implicated in Operation Safebet. Several lawyers later, the Vanicks were divorced.

Vanick told Sabin that during the course of his interview with Masters on March 19, 1982, Vanick learned that the couple had been having problems, that Dianne had a boyfriend on the Moraine Valley faculty about whom Alan had detailed information, and that Dianne had stayed out all night with this man. Vanick again did not reveal his role in discovering the identity of the "boyfriend" or in other events leading up to Dianne's murder.

Sabin inquired about Vanick's encounter with Keating on Masters' driveway on March 19, which had been observed by both Clarke Buckendahl and Mark Baldwin. According to Vanick, when he asserted that circumstances indicated the investigation should focus on Alan, Keating became visibly upset, saying, "Why don't you give the benefit of the doubt to the client?" Sabin's ears immediately pricked up. Referring to Alan Masters as the "client" was odd. The police do not have clients. But private investigators do, and Sabin wondered if Vanick might have done some moon-lighting for Alan.

Vanick thought it "ironic" that among the officers Keating pro-vided to conduct the search of Dianne's route home were Robert Neapolitan (nicknamed "Ice" after the ice cream of the same name), Robert Cadieux, and Ronald Sapit. All three would later be convicted in federal court on corruption charges relating to chop shops.

Three days after the missing person's investigation began, Vanick recalled being summoned to the office of Deputy Chief Richard Quagliano. Masters had complained to Quagliano about Vanick's investigative methods. Because Masters had been uncoop-erative, Vanick claimed to have told the chief it was necessary to increase the pressure on Alan by giving statements to the media. Quagliano warned Vanick not to try the case in the newspapers.

The evidence of unseemly interest and/or interference in the Masters' case on the part of officers who had been involved in cor-rupt activities was mounting.

According to Vanick, the 1982 investigation had been marked by complaints from people that anything they told the sheriff's investigators found its way to Masters. Vanick said he believed Keating was reading the team's reports and passing their contents on to Alan. He knew that Keating and Buckendahl had private investigator's licenses and that both were somehow connected with Masters' office, although Vanick did not put this information in the file. Also, he neglected to mention that he had himself used Alan's office as an accommodation address.

Vanick said that on September 15, 1982, he and Buckendahl and several other investigators met with Dennis Dernbach, head of the state's attorney's special prosecutions unit. The sheriff's police wanted the state's attorney's office to convene a grand jury in order to obtain the testimony of several uncooperative witnesses. Dernbach said he would think about it, but his immediate reaction was that a grand jury investigation would be "unproductive." No county grand jury was ever summoned.

Finally, Vanick told Sabin that the case reports were forwarded to the FBI, and the matter stood there until Dianne's body was found in December 1982. There was no record of communication with the FBI in the file Sabin pulled, and he suspected that it was incomplete in other areas as well.

In response to Sabin's request for these documents, Vanick omitted his letter to Agent Stillings but did provide Sabin with the file memo on a May 1982 meeting with FBI Agents John O'Rourke and Robert Pecoraro. "Why you could not locate this [in the file] is a mystery to me," Vanick wrote Sabin, adding "The Agents...provided some additional information and they requested that the information as well as the source, including what is included here be kept confidential. Hence the 'black out of their names.'" Using a marker, Vanick had carefully gone through the memo, obliterating the agents' names.

Vanick's slaughter of English grammar aside, the memo did not make sense. Whatever sensitive information he provided to the agents was not detailed in the file, but even if it had been, Sabin was supposed to be furnished with a complete record. There should have been no reason to protect the FBI men from Sabin's inquiry.

On September 11, 1986, Sabin sent Vanick a "to/from" (sheriff's jargon for interoffice memo), requesting the files on Vanick's interviews with Michael Corbitt and Alan Masters' secretary. Vanick's response was definitely testy. The interview with Corbitt, which Vanick characterized as "a real accomplishment," was pitifully short. Corbitt admitted to knowing Dianne and Alan but said he had no information of interest as to Dianne's disappearance. With regard to Masters' secretary, Vanick could not find any paperwork indicating she had been interviewed.

"By the way I wish to see a copy of your investigation when its [sic] done," Vanick added. Reed and Sabin thought this was an interesting way to put it. Not when it is solved; just "when its done."

So far the ladies in the beauty parlors were ahead on points. Every suspicion that had been voiced was turning out to be true. John Reed paused to contemplate this from time to time. Seldom had he found gossip, rumor, and innuendo to be so on target. The most disturbing aspect was the behavior of his own department and the obvious failure to conduct the original investigation in a proper manner. The question was just how much of this was due to incompetence and laziness and how much to a cover up. Like all cops, Reed felt a loyalty to fellow members of the force, whether or not he liked them personally.

He knew that what he and Paul were doing was not going to be popular, but they had sworn to protect the public, including Dianne Masters. If police were involved in her murder, they would have to be exposed. Then it would be up to a jury to punish them.

The fact that Dianne Masters was young, vibrant, and attractive made no difference to Reed. The status or qualities of the victim had no bearing on his determination to solve a case. Both his religious and professional training told him that murder of even the most unattractive victim, the kind of person the general public might regard as no loss to society, was wrong. An innocent child or the most depraved biker gang member, it was all the same to Reed. He derived just as much satisfaction from solving what cops call pork-and-bean homicides, the kind that don't even rate a column inch on the back pages of the local newspapers, as he did the high-profile cases.

So it was not necessary for John Reed to identify with the victim; indeed, it could work against the professional edge the detective wanted to maintain. It could also lead to early burn-out; Reed saw it happen all the time. But studying the victim frequently enabled him to identify the murderer, and so he would subject all the information he could gather about Dianne to merciless scrutiny.

There was Dianne's correspondence, which Reed thought of as "letters from the grave."

She wrote to an out-of-town friend in February 1982, "You were right in assuming that since I haven't written in so long there is something wrong. I have asked Alan for a divorce. He doesn't want to separate...I made a commitment in 1979 that I would give him one last chance to change and he hasn't." Dianne wrote that Alan finally took Georgie to meet his family, something Dianne wanted for years. ""I am happy for Georgie for the extended family is important in the development of children and their conception of what family life is all about. But it is too late for me." She hoped that Alan would find comfort in being able to share his daughter's existence with his folks. "Perhaps he won't feel quite so alone. As alone as I have felt all of these years, being the one looking through the looking glass."

She talked about visiting the marriage counselor on returning from Florida. "Until that moment I had no idea how angry he was at me for making this decision...My inherent values are very different from Alan's. I'm not judging him, just saying that through the years I have grown into a full, cognizant individual. We are worlds apart. I am leaving this relationship knowing fully that I have given all any human being could give." She felt regret, not guilt, for leaving what she termed "this sinking ship."

She still did not recognize the full dimension of Alan's anger. "I returned home Fri. night to find a note from Alan saying he had taken Georgianna and I wouldn't see her till Monday. On Monday he intended to file papers for custody of her. He said it was all fixed with the Chief Judge. He also took all of my jewelry and the guns that were in the house. He called me in the middel [sic] of the night. First to say he was going to destroy me and that I may never see Georgianna again; second, that he really loved me and wanted to reconcile. I never know what kind of mood he will be in and I find that mentally exhausting."

With the benefit of hindsight, Reed found parts of the 1982 letter particularly pathetic. "I know I will survive this only to go on to be a better, probably more productive person, I believe that I have God's imprint in my heart and that is why I have worked hard and long for the good of others. Right now the focus has turned to me and I am confident that God is with me in my decision." Dianne was sure her parents and other family members who were dead were in heaven, "making a beer toast to my courage."

The letter ended, "Forgive me if I have saddened you...I can only write the truth such as it is. Take good care of yourself. And, if I may ask, say a prayer or two for me. I know it isn't going to be easy...I treasure our friendship..I promise I will be in touch."

In some instances, her writings confirmed information gleaned from other sources or Reed's suspicions. Other promising leads went nowhere. In a note to Jim Church, there was a tantalizing reference to having the phones checked for bugs, but she did not say who was going to do this or how it came out, only that "Am certain now that ALL phones are tapped...Must be more cautious. Also you."

She was trying to keep a positive outlook, but her frequent reference to the rather mawkish poem "Little Boy Blue" seemed ominous. It was written by Eugene Field before the turn of the century, about a son who died suddenly when small, but whose faithful toys gathered dust and rust as they waited his return. "'Time was when the little toy dog was new/And the soldier was passing fair/And that was the time that our Little Boy Blue/Kissed them and put them there.' The time is here with all my tugs in different directions, that I feel not new nor even passing fair."

After talking to the college attorney, she wrote, "Andy indicated that the best tact [sic] in a situation is to swallow hard, stop procrastinating in the hope that reason will strike, and bite the bullet. He thinks, w/o knowing all of the details that I will do OK. He cautioned me several times not to get paranoid and let this part of my life overwhelm me...he did say that there is always an end. It may not be in direct view, but it does exist." Reed shook his head. The advice had been half right; there was an end, and it was in direct view.

Despite her anxiety and fear, Dianne continued to function. She tended her child, she met her commitments to the college and the crisis center, she visited friends. She compiled a breakdown of her projected expenses and tried to put together a postdivorce budget. She looked for a new home for herself and Georgianna. Still she wanted to keep the old one. "As I sit here with a jungle of house plants strangling my typewriter, I know how much I love this house...I am going to fight for it. There is too much of me here." Again, what seemed liked prophecy, written the week before she was slain: "I really thought, after all of the places I lived that this was the last."

Reed also had a bundle of correspondence from Alan, which Dianne had passed along to her lawyer. Except for letters of apology, promising never to beat her again, Masters seemed unable to approach Dianne directly, going through another male authority figure instead. To Dr. Schwemer, Alan wrote that he would do any-thing for Dianne, including diet down to 180 or 190 pounds, by cutting his calorie intake to 900 per day and becoming more active. He would join a nearby TOPS weight loss group, or better still, perhaps Dianne would be his "conscience." This way, it would be Dianne's fault if once again he failed to lose the weight or keep it off.

Alan would take an interest in Dianne's views and activities, and he would cut back on his workweek, freeing up two full week-ends per month for Dianne and Georgie. He promised to visit his parents, who had not yet been told about his new wife and daughter, during the week rather than on weekends. And he would accompany Dianne to art galleries, museums, and so on. This would be no great sacrifice, as he had grown tired of his legal work, adding "Dianne believes this is not true." He guaranteed that he would alter his "focus from the office to the family."

"I have the same sexual desires as Dianne (she doubts this). Her words, body language etc. have told me that I am not physically desirable to her..." Alan put this down to his overweight condition, but it was more a result of combined neglect, fear, and a longing for a fresh start. Even if poundage was the problem, Masters had another excuse. "I have without intentionally doing so, created a mental block about overly aggressive [women]. I have been wrong. Dianne's complaints tell me that my shell is too soft..." Everything was Dianne's fault, including the rages and beatings. It was "my upbringing that when you love someone you show it by kindness, generosity, warmth and jealousy." Masters seemed to sense this argument did not exactly follow, because he added that now he knew what problems this had caused, and "I can say that I have not exhibited it [violent behavior] to her to any extent for some time, and will in the future continue not to do so because it was unwarranted and not right."

In all, Masters wanted to convince Dr. Schwemer that he was an average reasonable, overweight, overworked, undersexed, middle-aged professional, game as hell to save his marriage. The impression he tried to create was completely dispelled at the end of the letter. "I must say that I wish so much to love my wife and child and know that I am the person she wants that I cannot agree to a divorce."

The old need to dominate and control Dianne was still there. He was not going to let her go. Dianne no longer believed his declarations of undying love, but perhaps he could persuade others, thus isolating his wife.

After Alan taunted Dianne about Jim, Dianne wrote her lover, "A word of caution: ...Be careful. Also watch driving while under the influence and any parking lot purchases. We're alert to the obvious, but not giving heed to the less obtrusive."

Everywhere Reed's experienced eye looked, he saw over-whelming indicators that a domestic tragedy was in the making. Alan was talking freely about having her dispatched. Any one of a number of people—Jack Bachman, Howard Vanick, Joe Hein, Ted Nykaza, Dianne Economou, Clarke Buckendahl—could have con-firmed her gut instinct that she was in danger, but none of them did. Perhaps in the beginning they believed it was all conversation; people do say things they do not mean when they are caught in the whipsaw effect of strong emotion. But as the days went by and it was clear that Alan was determined to construct a plan, it would have been a simple matter to phone Dianne and tell her to watch out. Nobody did.

The cops who handled the case had been close to Alan person-ally and were tied to him professionally. He had represented them in court and allowed them to work out of his office. He had been bugging his home phone and telling his cop friends about Dianne's extramarital activities. Several of the policemen who played some part in the investigation had already been convicted or were about to be indicted for some sort of corrupt activity.

It seemed clear to Sabin and Reed that for those who cared about the reputation of the Cook County Sheriff's Police, things were going to get worse before they got better.

CHAPTER 9

*O*n September 25, 1986, Sabin and Reed had a crack at the elusive Michael Corbitt, who had been questioned so fleetingly by Howard Vanick in 1982. Corbitt refused an interview with ISP Sergeant Kitchen in 1983 on the grounds that he was the target of both federal and county investigations. The detectives met the former Willow Springs police chief in his lawyer's office.

"I became a suspect as soon as Dianne's body was found," Corbitt griped before denying any knowledge of how she met her death. He acknowledged that he and Alan Masters had been friends for at least twenty years and that Masters had acted as attorney for Corbitt and a number of other Willow Springs policemen in civil cases. Corbitt said he had met Dianne once, at a party in her home. He had heard that the couple were having difficulties and that Dianne wanted a divorce. He believed that because of Masters' connections and skill as a lawyer, he would have no trouble obtaining custody of his daughter. He also did not believe that Alan would have participated in killing Dianne in any way because of the damage it would do to Georgianna, to whom Masters was devoted, according to Corbitt.

With the air of someone imparting a precious bit of naughty news, Corbitt suggested to Reed and Sabin that they talk to Willow Springs Sergeant and resident troll Charles "Sonny" Fisher. According to Corbitt, the night before Dianne disappeared, Fisher called Alan Masters, saying that several weeks earlier, he had spotted Dianne in a compromising position with a black man in a car parked under the bridge.

Sabin and Reed had quickly determined that when questioning sources in the Masters' case, it was useful to ask for the individual's "scenario" as to what might have happened to Dianne. Corbitt had several based on allegations about Dianne's sexual promiscuity. One of Dianne's boyfriends might have gone too far in the course of sexual activity. Possibly, she might have met someone new at the Village Courtyard who went with her to the lover's lane on the canal bank, and that person might have become enraged by something and killed her. Or a disgruntled former client of Alan's might have decided to get revenge by murdering Masters' wife.

As to method, Corbitt suggested there was just one person involved in Dianne's death. That person had placed a bicycle in the trunk of Dianne's Cadillac; after disposing of the car, that person rode the bike back to his own car or home. The sheriff's detectives found this last bit amazing. The idea of placing a bicycle on top of a corpse in order to make a getaway was a novel approach in their broad experience of the bizarre.

Before they departed, Corbitt reiterated that he did not believe Alan Masters would be involved in his wife's murder. If Corbitt were reappointed to his old job in Willow Springs, he promised, he would make the Masters case top priority. Even the remote prospect of such an event boggled the detectives' minds. A lot of strange things happened in Willow Springs, but they hoped the only way Corbitt would be welcome in any police station was as an arrestee.

"Do I look like I just fell off a turnip truck?" Reed asked as he and Sabin returned to their unmarked squad after talking with Corbitt.

"Well, you might," Sabin replied, "but I sure don't."

On October 3, 1986, Sabin and Reed interviewed Jim Ross, Mike Corbitt's successor. Ross said he was "fed up with the criminal justice system in Cook County," and he had left police work to operate a discount store in Summit, just across the alley from Alan Masters' law office.

Ross firmly believed that Alan Masters was responsible for Dianne's death and that he had the assistance of Jim Keating, Mike Corbitt, and a Chicago cop named Anthony Barone, Corbitt's former brother-in-law. As the interview wound down, Ross declared that he was not telling everything he knew because he did not trust the sheriff's police. He did confirm what Reed noticed in the evidence technicians' reports: that several potentially important observations were not noted, including the position of the seat, the gearshift, ignition, the steering wheel, the windows, and so on.

Throughout the fall of 1986, Reed and Sabin continued to interview sheriff's police who were known to have close business and/or personal ties to Alan Masters. Reed and Sabin expected some resentment over the questioning of fellow officers, but the reaction was so out of proportion that Reed and Sabin were convinced the subjects had something to hide.

A list was obtained of the names of principals in the private investigation firm called Ted Anthony & Associates Ltd., one of Ted Nykaza's business names. As expected, that list contained the names of several sheriff's policemen, in particular Jack Bachman and Clarke Buckendahl. The state of Illinois requires that every corporation have a registered agent; Alan Masters served that function for Anthony & Associates.

In many states, it is against the law for a policeman, sheriff's deputy, or state trooper to moonlight as a private investigator because of the many opportunities for conflict of interest. Illinois is not one of those states, although such a law has been suggested, partly because of revelations from this case.

Like several other veteran officers, Jack Bachman explained that having his p.i. license issued through Ted Anthony & Associates was an attempt at insurance cost-cutting. Paying part of a group premium on the insurance required of p.i.'s was a lot cheaper than paying as an individual. Similarly, Bachman's name appeared on a number of Ted Anthony checks as a convenience because he did not have a separate account of his own.

By this point, Sabin and Reed were aware of gossip that Bachman and Masters and possibly other policemen were partners in the Western Health Club, a bordello on Western Avenue in south suburban Dixmoor. It was a shabby working-class joint which had gone through several incarnations, beginning as the Isle of Capri, which catered to men who like to wear women's clothing and hang around in bars.

Bachman denied ever having any sort of financial interest in the club. He claimed he did not know any members of the sheriff's police who did. He advised Sabin that the whorehouse, which had recently been converted into an adult bookstore, might be operated by Philip Caliendo, a Chicago mobster. Technically, Bachman was telling the truth. When Bachman, Masters, and Buckendahl owned the property, it was called the Astrology Club. Bachman also neglected to mention that he and Buckendahl had owned two other whorehouses, one in Blue Island and the other in an incorporated area near the Indiana state line.

Also interviewed, although not on the Nykaza list, was Robert Rosignal, another sheriff's policeman. Rosignal, who had been both Alan and Dianne Masters' friend for several years, admitted to house-sitting for Dianne when the couple was out of town. He rejected the idea that he held any interest in the Western Health Club or that he knew of any coworkers who did. On March 18, 1982, he called in for a medical day so that he could study for exams at St. Xavier's College. He did not know that Dianne was missing until several days later.

When Masters took his daughter to Florida a few months after Dianne disappeared, Rosignal was asked to watch the house and look after the pets in their absence, something which had happened regularly in the past. Rosignal recalled that one of the dogs had an eye condition and had to receive daily medication.

On the day of Masters' scheduled return, Rosignal received a phone call that Alan and Georgie had been in a serious auto accident and would not be home as planned. That evening, Rosignal returned to the Wolf Road house unexpectedly to feed and medicate the pets. As he glanced out the kitchen window, he observed a man inching his way across the front lawn, moving from tree to tree, then from shrub to shrub, rather like a cartoon detective. As the man crept closer to the entrance, Rosignal decided it had gone far enough. He opened the door, stopping Inspector Clouseau in his tracks. "Who are you?" the startled man asked.

"I'm a county police officer, and I'm supposed to be here. Who are you?" Rosignal responded. The man said he was a federal investigator who was there to help Rosignal, but produced no identification. Rosignal told him that unless he had a search warrant, it was time to scoot. Finally, the man flashed an FBI badge identifying him as Agent Robert Pecoraro. When Pecoraro admitted he had neither a search nor an arrest warrant, Rosignal refused to let him inside the house.

Exasperated, the agent played what he clearly thought was his ace. "I'll tell Lieutenant Vanick on you," he said. Actually, he probably could not have come up with a worse ploy. Like most of the sheriff's rank and file, Rosignal had little or no respect for Vanick as a cop or an individual.

"I don't care if you tell my mother. If you haven't got a warrant, get off the property," Rosignal yelled. To emphasize the point, he released Dianne's three large and enthusiastic dogs. Pecoraro could not know that the dogs just wanted to lick him all over, and he fled, shaking his fist at Rosignal, the dogs in hot pursuit. Fifteen minutes after Rosignal arrived home that night, he had a call from his superior officer, who was not Howard Vanick. "Why did you set the dogs on that poor little FBI man?" he inquired. When Rosignal explained the circumstances and the absence of a warrant, the matter was dropped.

On October 20, 1986, Reed and Sabin caught up with Ted Nykaza in his home in unincorporated Orland Township, near the Will County line. They already had spoken to Nykaza's estranged wife, the former Sheila Mikel, who had kind things to say about Alan Masters, but not about her soon-to-be ex-husband. To explain her affair with Masters, Sheila observed that "some men and women require a variety of relationships." She described Masters as a "bubbly, outgoing person" and said she had never seen him angry. She did not have much to say about Ted. Yet.

Nykaza was just a few days shy of his thirty-ninth birthday, but years of alcoholism had aged him. He grew up on Chicago's south-west side, attending Saint Rita High School and Bogan (now Daley) Junior College. In 1965, he joined the Chicago Police Department, resigning in 1977 when the city began enforcing its residency requirement. During twelve years as a Chicago cop, Nykaza received more than fifty commendations for his work. There were also some disciplinary matters related to Nykaza's growing alcoholism, which began when he was a teenager. Such problems were not unusual among members of the Chicago PD Although no official records are available, there are quite a few alcoholics who function as police officers on a daily basis.

In 1978, Nykaza established himself as a private investigator. Although he had space at Alan Masters' law office, he operated out of his home for the most part. He did p.i. work for Alan and in return, did not pay rent. It seemed like a good arrangement. The two men had known each other since the sixteen-year-old Ted was cited for drunk driving and damaging a parked car three doors away from his home. Alan Masters was the guy who could get Ted off the hook, advised Ted's maternal uncle, and uncle knew best.

When Reed arrived, Ted was obviously hung over, and while he expressed reluctance at becoming involved, he was willing to be asked specific questions. Asked for his scenario or theory, Ted asserted he did not have one. Nykaza's second wife had told him she had been interviewed by Reed and Sabin, adding that she hoped that "slime ball Masters" got what he deserved. Nykaza also knew that the investigators had talked to his incumbent wife, claiming he did not care what she said. But if Ted was aware of his former stepson's revelations about the Masters' tapes, he did not indicate it, claiming he knew of no specific incident that might have triggered Dianne's murder. He observed that Alan would have gone "nuts" if he had learned Dianne was having an affair.

He added that Alan never discussed the case, and if it was brought up in conversation, he would ignore it. Nykaza did say that the walls were thin at the Summit office, and during the period immediately preceding Dianne's disappearance, he heard Masters on the phone, presumably with Dianne, begging, crying, yelling, and pleading with her not to divorce him. After one of these sessions. Masters asked Nykaza, "Why would she do this to me?" He expressed bewilderment after all he had done for her, including dieting, submitting to hypnotism in an effort to cure his snoring, obtaining a hairpiece, and buying her fur coats. Nykaza commented on how Masters always tried to buy his women.

It was Nykaza's opinion that if Alan did plan Dianne's disappearance, he would "screw it up" because Masters did not think well under pressure, especially in situations where physical activity or manual dexterity was required. Nykaza never heard Dianne publicly criticize Masters, but sometimes she would mock him about his ineptitude around the house.

After sharing some opinions about other people involved in the case, the interview ended. It was to be the first of many with Ted. Compared with those that followed, it was relatively tame.

Reed and Sabin were more than ready to tackle Alan Masters, and on Monday, October 27, 1986, they did so. Alan seemed comfortably ensconced in his law office and proceeded to repeat his basic story about Dianne's 1982 disappearance.

Masters did admit that right after New Year's in 1982, Dianne had asked him for a divorce. As a result, he prepared a praecipe for summons. This is an infrequently used legal device which would assure that any divorce case would be heard in Cook as opposed to any other Illinois county. Friends and Dianne's lawyer suggested he did this because he was concerned that she would file in one of the collar counties where Masters' judicial connections were not as far-reaching.

In March 1982, Masters said he "heard" Dianne planned to file for dissolution of the marriage and had hired Maureen J. McGann-Ryan as her attorney. As a result, Alan called McGann-Ryan's father-in-law, Judge Daniel Ryan, and persuaded the judge to ask his daughter-in-law to stop the filing of the divorce petition.

In an attempt to control the interview, Masters began to question the questioners. He wanted to know what Sabin and Reed had found out about his wife's murderers, while asserting he knew of no reason for anyone to kill her. He tried to direct their attention toward serial and mass murderers who were allegedly operating in the Chicago metropolitan area, such as Henry Lee Lucas who was in the process of confessing to hundreds of murders in several states. In addition, Masters brought up the disappearance of the wife of Chicago Cubs' star Milt Pappas. If these leads failed, Masters suggested that members of Jerry Cosentino's campaign staff might have been involved. Another campaign worker, a man, had been found dead in a downtown hotel room.

Masters also observed that he felt the case would have been solved if the sheriff's police had been more objective, which was laughable in light of the facts the detectives had already determined.

Masters explained that he did not believe his wife ever reached their driveway. The pair had separate bedrooms due to his snoring, and his room was right next to the garage. Although Dianne always left the car in the driveway, Alan felt he would have heard her pull up. On the subject of Dianne's $100,000 life insurance policy through the college, Alan claimed that he had not known about it until after her death.

When asked about business relationships with members of the sheriff's police, Masters declared that none were in his employ. With reference to Ted Nykaza, Masters said that he had a small office on the premises but that Nykaza was there only to collect mail or to meet clients after hours. He expressed his "disgust" with Nykaza and observed that Ted's experiences in the Chicago Police Department had ruined the p.i.

Masters made an effort to divert Reed and Sabin into other areas. He said that before Dianne's disappearance, a client in a divorce proceeding assaulted him in the Daley Center in downtown Chicago, but that person had recently died. He also turned in the name of a former client who had been calling the law offices, blaming Masters for Dianne's death.

Masters denied ownership of Western Health Club and said he was not aware of any sheriff's officers who were involved in its operations. When Reed and Sabin confronted Masters with the fact that the real estate tax bills for the property were sent to Master's secretary, he explained that Barbara Klimek was the beneficiary of a land trust for the property, and he suggested Reed and Sabin ask her since that is what "she testified to." This struck them as an odd response, because insofar as they knew, no testimony had been taken on the question. If she had testified anywhere, it would have to be before a federal grand jury, possibly because of Operation Safebet or Operation Greylord, another federal investigation into judicial corruption. Although Masters had practiced law for twenty-eight years in the area, and his father had owned a currency exchange across the street for years before that, he claimed that until Dianne's body was found in the Ship and Sanitary Canal, he thought the only nearby body of water was the Des Plaines River. Masters also said he was "confused" as to how a car could be launched into the canal. Increasingly the interview had turned into creative fiction, but even Masters' lies were important because they were an indicator of what areas he wanted to avoid.

Before the detectives left, Masters voiced his unhappiness with the media coverage of the murder and said he was consulting with a law firm specializing in defamation of character suits.

"I hope I read that I was uncooperative," Masters concluded. Reed and Sabin took this parting shot as Alan's boast about his easy access to the sheriff's files.

CHAPTER 10

$\mathcal{I}$n November 1986, the focus of
the investigation shifted slightly. Reed and Sabin spent more time
with sources who were not suspects, with people who wished to
have their anonymity protected, with peripheral figures, and with
Dianne's friends.

It was during this period that the investigators heard most of
the scurrilous stories about Dianne Masters: that she had once
been some kind of a nightclub or go go dancer, that she had a wild
background, that Alan occasionally offered her to judges and
policemen for their sexual enjoyment, citing one particular
instance which allegedly happened in the Bahamas or Bermuda
and involved oral sex. Reed and Sabin were unable to confirm any
of these stories.

Barbara Klimek ran Alan Masters' law office and her devotion
to her boss was legendary. Klimek was a local girl who grew up in
Summit. She had been at school with and learned to dislike Mike
Corbitt. Although she characterized her relationship with Dianne
as friendly, she said they were not "bosom buddies," and Dianne
did not confide in her. To those who knew Dianne, this was not
surprising. It had been Klimek who came to Dianne's home with
the plane tickets to New York and the money to pay for Dianne's
abortion.

According to Klimek, when Dianne disappeared, the responsibility for keeping Alan's business afloat fell on her shoulders, and

239

she did not have time to think about what had happened. The same was true after Dianne's body was found.

Klimek admitted owning the Astrology Club, the predecessor to the Western Health Club, as an investment, but claimed that no sheriff's policemen were involved. She was vague as to the name of her club's manager, declaring she communicated with him only by telephone, and said that the RVS Corporation was also involved in the club. On checking, the investigators found that RVS was dissolved in July 1986. Philip Caliendo was president of the corporation, and his brother Vito, secretary. Jack Bachman had told a partial truth.

Bachman was feeling the pressure, and he became a confidential source known in the file as EOL, for "end of the line." He revealed that Ted Nykaza talked about the tap he placed on Masters' home phone and that Ted was remorseful because this might have been a causal factor in Dianne's death. Nykaza told Bachman that on one tape Dianne could be heard telling her boyfriend how good it felt when he inserted "a coke bottle up her pussy." When Alan listened to the tape, he went berserk. Bachman believed Nykaza had something on Alan; before Dianne was murdered, the lawyer treated Ted like a gofer, and after, he seemed to have a whole new respect for the p.i.

Bachman did not believe Nykaza would be a good participant in a murder plan because of his drinking, but Mike Corbitt was another matter. Corbitt had an itchy trigger finger and liked to boast that he kept track of his kills by notching one of his guns. However, Bachman observed that if Dianne's corpse still had jewelry on it, Corbitt either was not involved or was afraid it could be traced back to him because he was notoriously greedy.

With regard to Jim Keating, Bachman thought Keating might line up the players, but would stop short of the actual deed. Keating could fill in a lot of blanks, but he was safely tucked away in federal prison, off limits to Reed and Sabin.

As Bachman saw it, Nykaza set up the phone tap, Masters was responsible for Dianne's death, and Corbitt handled the disposal. As for Lieutenant Vanick, head of the original investigation, he was characterized as a slow man with a buck who was looking for a free divorce and was worried that the press would find out he used to swim in Dianne's pool.

Things were beginning to fall into place. What Reed and Sabin needed were a few confirmations of important incidents leading up to Dianne's murder. They were about to get one.

On November 23, 1986, Paul Sabin and John Reed met with Jim Church at the Purple Steer Restaurant in Calumet City. The meeting had not been easy to arrange. Church was suspicious of the cops and felt he had been hassled and treated like a suspect by Alan's police cronies. Over the next four years, the failure of law enforcement authorities to charge anyone with the crime did nothing to change Church's attitude and his cynicism increased.

John Reed needed someone to break the ice with Church. He found that person in Jim Kaszuba, another sheriff's policeman. Church had grown up with Kaszuba and trusted him. With Kaszuba to vouch for Reed, Church was ready at least to give it one more try.

By prearrangement, Sabin left his partner and Church alone at the restaurant. Reed began slowly, going over background details. Soon Church began to tell Reed about his intimate encounters with Dianne. He had even spent one night at the Masters' home when Dianne and Alan were living apart and Alan had taken Georgie for the night. They had cuddled and talked in front of the living room fire until dawn. On March 2, 1982, the pair had arranged to meet after the postboard gathering at Artie G's and go to a motel. They left Dianne's Cadillac in the restaurant parking lot. A soft white snow was falling, giving the wooded area a picture postcard look, so instead they decided to park on a quiet, isolated street near the adjoining forest preserves. They never made it to the motel that night; when their lovemaking and snow gazing were over, Jim drove Dianne back to her car.

This verified something Jack Bachman said. Earlier that same day, March 2nd, Jim Keating advised Jack Bachman to "make sure you go home to your bride tonight." On March 3, 1982, Bachman stopped in at Keating's Maybrook office and asked Keating how Alan was doing. Keating replied that whoever was waiting for Dianne "chickened out," Dianne didn't show up, and it was cold that night.

On the morning after Dianne disappeared, Church received an odd phone call at home. He recognized the voice as that of Alan Masters, though the caller pretended to have reached a wrong number. At first, it seemed to Church that Masters was surprised when Church answered.

Church denied that he and Dianne had ever visited the area where Dianne's body was found. He did confirm that on February 18, 1982, he met Dianne for lunch at the Charley Horse Restaurant in Orland Square to celebrate his February 17 birthday. When they were saying goodbye in the parking lot, Dianne thought she recognized two Orland Park policeman watching them. Jim believed that these men copied the license number off his car and gave it to Masters, who in turn had Howard Vanick run the plate number through the police computer to determine Church's identity and to check for any criminal history Jim might have had. Church had just a few details wrong; Dianne had mistaken Howard Vanick and his partner for two look-alike suburban cops, and Howie used a middle man to get the information to Alan.

Since Dianne's 1982 disappearance, Church felt that Masters was having him followed. Jim told Reed that as recently as the summer of 1986, Alan had been seen driving around the Moraine Valley College Campus.

Church seemed to feel comfortable with Reed as the meeting progressed. Finally, Reed raised the delicate subject of the bottle-in-the-vagina incident. Although he had never discussed it with anyone before and had not heard the rumors about salacious tapes, Church confirmed that Reed had the basic details right. However, it had been a partly filled bottle of Gallo chablis, left over from a faculty party, not a Coke. And Jim had not placed it inside Dianne but merely poured the wine on her.

When he called Dianne the next day, Church thought it odd that Dianne would speak so freely about their unusual sex play over the phone she was sure was bugged. Church felt she was talking as if she was aware that someone was listening, but no longer cared.

Eureka.

Bingo.

Jackpot.

Now the detectives had something, a litmus test for inside knowledge. However unreliable Ted Nykaza might be because of his drinking, he was telling the truth about hearing tape recordings of Dianne's telephone conversations right before she disappeared and about the content of one of them. Without the tapes, there were only two people who knew about the wine bottle incident, and one of them had been murdered shortly afterward. The other had told nobody about it until tonight.

Concrete evidence of the depth of police involvement in the murder was piling up. Details confirming the widespread gossip were beginning to come in so fast that the two detectives could scarcely keep up with them. According to Arlene Reed, the family would be having dinner or watching TV together, when suddenly John would get up, go to the phone, and call a source. He was never off the job. She had learned over the years that when an investigation reached a critical stage, the best thing was to try to help out. She typed reports, but more importantly, she listened to theories and contributed her ideas.

CHAPTER 11

*I*n early December, Reed and Sabin interviewed Dianne's divorce lawyer in her suburban Evergreen Park office. Maureen McGann-Ryan spoke to Dianne on almost a daily basis beginning in January 1982.

Dianne rejected McGann-Ryan's suggestions about marital counseling, because she had already tried it, and was convinced her marriage was over. McGann-Ryan confirmed that she was prepared to file for dissolution of the marriage when she returned from vacation on Monday, March 22, 1982. She claimed she did not inform Ken Denberg, Alan Masters' attorney, of her intention, but somehow Alan found out.

McGann-Ryan characterized Dianne as "deathly afraid" of her husband and said they had not lived together as man and wife for some time. Dianne was in a good position to obtain sole custody of Georgianna, although she was amenable to joint custody. Dianne also still clung to the hope that she might ultimately take title to the family home on Wolf Road, but she knew that would be a long struggle. For her own peace of mind and that of her daughter, she was reconciled to moving as soon as the papers were filed.

McGann-Ryan based her belief in the strength of Dianne's case for custody on several factors, including the fact that Alan had kept their daughter a secret from the rest of his family even after his divorce and marriage to Dianne.

Once Alan got wind of this, he mounted frantic efforts to introduce the almost five-year-old Georgianna to her grown half brothers, who were attending colleges on the East Coast.

McGann-Ryan knew that Alan abused Dianne physically; he admitted as much in letters to Dianne and her psychiatrist which Dianne turned over to the lawyer. In a cover letter addressed to "Mo" Ryan, Dianne wrote, "Enclosed is correspondence dating from 1970. It required many years of study with the FBI before I was able to master them. I do not expect you to attempt such a struggle. If and when necessary [I will] type them for you." Dianne had the FBI on her mind; she thought they would protect her.

Dianne outlined the contents of the package: statements acknowledging abuse, both physical and mental; acknowledgment of little effort to maintain the marriage on Alan's part; a statement about his first wife having signed income statements and his fear of IRS prosecution; promises, "almost all broken"; and so on.

While the divorce complaint was in preparation, Alan told McGann-Ryan that "she [Dianne] would be sorry if she hurt him." She had heard from others that Alan indulged in another form of abuse, forcing Dianne to have sex with judges and policemen, but Dianne had never spoken of this.

Dianne told McGann-Ryan of her certainty that she was being followed by men hired by Alan and gave specific instances of such surveillance. She also told her lawyer that she would not pull her car over on a traffic stop if the Cook County Sheriff's Police were involved.

McGann-Ryan declared that never had so many judges called her in regard to a divorce case, urging that she effect a reconciliation. Based on her father-in-law's experience, McGann-Ryan believed Alan was behind the calls.

John Reed sees Genevieve Capstaff as the Miss Marple of the case. There is some resemblance to Agatha Christie's fictional sleuth. Both of them have soft white hair and admit to being snoopy old ladies, but Miss Marple never packed a gun, admitted to a couple of face lifts, drank martinis straight up, or dated.

Now professor emeritus of humanities at Moraine Valley Community College, in 1982 Capstaff was an instructor who was active in the faculty union and regularly attended board meetings. When the March 18 session ended, she drove on to the Village Courtyard to join the rest of the group. She recalled hearing Dianne complain about a stranger whom she suspected of following her.

At about 12:30 a.m. on Friday, March 19, 1982, Capstaff left the restaurant and got into her car. Her "nosy" instinct was at work and she decided to pull into the shadows to await the departure of the rest of the college crowd. Capstaff was intrigued by the fact that Jim Church had not shown up as usual. She thought the pair might have had a falling out, and she wondered if Dianne had found someone else, possibly a board member. That information might be useful in future negotiations. After waiting thirty minutes, the rest of the group emerged. Instead of approaching her colleagues, Capstaff watched as Dianne Masters got into her Cadillac and made a left turn onto McCarthy Road. Gen had to drive in the same direction to get home anyway, and she might learn something interesting on the way, so she followed Dianne. Another auto was behind Capstaff's, but it turned off at LaGrange Road. As the two cars proceeded west toward Wolf Road, Capstaff noticed that theirs were the only vehicles visible on the road.

As Dianne made her left turn, Capstaff slowed for a deer crossing, a hazard in that area, then continued due west. Genevieve Capstaff was the last person to admit to seeing Dianne Masters until her body was discovered nine months later.

Several members of the college group expressed doubt that Capstaff could have hidden in the almost empty parking lot without being recognized in her large maroon station wagon. No matter who criticized the Capstaff account, Reed and Sabin found her absolutely unshakable, a very credible witness.

Everyone told Sabin and Reed that Brigitte Lunde, now married to Dan Stark, was Dianne's oldest, closest friend and that Dianne would never go into hiding or leave town without Brigitte knowing. Brigitte recounted that Lieutenant Vanick had called her in the wee hours of Saturday, March 20, and asked if Dianne was with her. She asked him where the baby was. "Georgie is with Alan," Vanick replied. This told Brigitte two things: Dianne was dead, because she would never leave Georgianna, and Vanick was part of Alan's ingroup, because very few people knew Georgianna's nickname.

Before ending the telephone interview, Brigitte heard someone whose voice she recognized in the background. Later on Saturday morning, she called Alan at his office. "Was that policeman calling me from your house?" she asked. When he said "yes," she hung up.

Brigitte cited endless episodes of Alan's bragging about his clout-heavy contacts, about his wealth, about his control of the criminal justice system. "We have the best judicial system money can buy," he liked to boast. He claimed that he could fix any kind of case, all the way up to murder, and gave specific instances.

Dianne confided in Brigitte that she had enough papers on Alan to put him away for life, but she did not say where she was hiding them. John Reed's scrutiny of lists of unclaimed safe deposit boxes did not reveal Dianne's name or any variant of it. About three weeks after Dianne's disappearance, Brigitte was approached by a private detective agency hired by Dianne's brother. Perhaps during a visit to Georgie, Brigitte could take a look around the house to see if anything was out of the ordinary? Brigitte agreed. She was anxious to see for herself how Dianne's daughter was coping, and she wanted to do everything possible to help find out what had happened to Dianne. She found Dianne's clothing and shoes gone from the armoire in her bedroom and her furs from the hall closets. This confirmed Brigitte's theory that Dianne was dead, and Alan knew it.

Just before Christmas 1986, Sabin and Reed interviewed Dianne's brother, Randall Turner, and his wife Kathy. Aside from an aunt and a few cousins, the Turners were virtually the only living relatives Dianne had. From the moment Alan Masters called to ask if Dianne was with them on March 19, 1982, they believed she was dead and that Alan was responsible. They hired Special Operations Associates, a firm of private investigators, shortly afterward, but the file was closed in June 1982, without developing any firm leads. Unfortunately, the savaging of Dianne's reputation continued based on SOA's report which contained unsubstantiated gossip and half truths.

As 1986 drew to a close, Reed and Sabin took stock. They had found some of the missing pieces, and had plenty of new leads to follow. They knew that some of their sources were holding back or just plain lying. Reed was now assigned full time, and the new sheriff had given the two men carte blanche to continue their efforts. Every time it seemed they had hit a dead end, something new came up. Reed put it down to divine intervention. He believed that Somebody wanted this case solved.

They tried to check out all the people whose cars had been discovered in the canal. They talked to members of the Willow Springs PD who had been employed around the time Dianne disappeared. Because there had been almost a complete turnover when Corbitt was finally ejected, the cops who were present when her remains were located also had to be interviewed. They talked to everyone who had attended the Moraine Valley board meetings around the time of Dianne's death. They pored over the files from the first sheriff's investigation and from the state police to make sure they had not missed anything. They followed the paper chase left by the life insurance claim filed by Alan with the Hartford Insurance Company, resulting in a $100,000 payout Alan deposited in a tax free mutual account at the investment firm of Stein, Roe & Farnham.

Most important of all, the detectives were willing to back off when they sensed a source was becoming annoyed or frightened. The partners agreed it was better to plan a return engagement than to wear out their welcome. If they had a "door slammer"—a question which when asked would effectively put an end to future sessions—they were willing to bide their time before asking it.

Nonetheless, despite the solid progress, it was not entirely a happy work situation for the two detectives. Policemen may hate criminals, but reserve their greatest scorn for their own internal affairs division (IAD), the unit that investigates complaints and possible wrongdoing within the force. While Reed and Sabin were not attached to IAD, they still were questioning fellow officers. Their colleagues were already sensitive about the number of sheriff's police who recently had been found guilty of misconduct. Many colleagues felt that any such knowledge should be kept among themselves and that giving witness against a fellow cop was a violation of the policeman's Eleventh Commandment against speaking ill of another officer.

In January 1987, Ice Neapolitan called John Reed's home. Ice knew that Reed had interviewed Ice's former wife and wanted to know who suggested this to Reed. Reed took advantage of the incident to ask Neapolitan for his theory on the case, especially because Ice knew all the most likely suspects.

In talking to fellow officers, Reed would say he understood the importance of loyalty, but that sometimes a line had to be drawn. Murder was certainly one place to start. After being approached in this fashion, Neapolitan responded, "Ask yourself who does Masters trust the most, and who is it that has been the closest to Masters for the longest period of time? There is only one guy, Mike Corbitt."

CHAPTER 12

$\mathcal{T}$he new year began with some new faces for Reed and Sabin. They continued to call on Dianne's friends, starting with Jude Fogerty, with whom Dianne had been staying when she left Alan for a brief period in August 1979. It was during this separation that Dianne's jewelry and George Turner's cash were stolen. Fogerty said she began receiving threatening phone calls from Alan Masters, which stopped after she told friends that she asked the telephone company for assistance in finding the source of these calls.

What Fogerty did not know was that Alan had not stopped with phone calls. She was under surveillance by Ted Nykaza and his operatives, and a couple of nasty pranks were played on her at Alan's request. A funeral wreath was placed at her door, and on another occasion, Nykaza blew up her mailbox with a combination of cherry bombs and M80 firecrackers lit by a sparkler.

The detectives also paid a call on one of Georgianna's former babysitters. The woman's husband, an orthodox priest, had been described as a strange man who boasted of his prowess with prostitutes and was capable of doing anything, especially for money. When Reed and Sabin interviewed him, he denied having visited the Astrology Club, Alan's personal house of prostitution, or taking advantage of any of Alan's other vice connections "because such things were forbidden to priests." He admitted to having borrowed money from Dianne on one occasion, but swore he had paid it

251

back. He now supplemented his clerical income by delivering pizzas. His superiors reported that the man had a problem with writing bad checks which sometimes took him into court. On the whole, it was one of what was to become many bizarre side trips Sabin and Reed would take.

Then there were the anonymous sources. Some checked in on a continuing basis, while others were one-shot deals. It appeared that Alan Masters had a habit of talking too loud for his own good, especially in front of strangers in the Fifth District courthouse. One caller said that two or three months before Dianne's disappearance, Alan was talking about the possibility that Dianne would leave him and said he would find it easier to defend himself against murder than divorce.

Another remembered seeing Alan in court the day Dianne was reported missing. Masters was hurrying to obtain a continuance in a case, but stopped long enough to be overheard telling a courthouse functionary that Dianne "was not coming back."

Another group of informants who required anonymity were women who feared for their own safety. Like Dianne, they came from homes where there was a pattern of physical, sexual and/or substance abuse. Like Dianne, from their earliest childhood their emotional growth was stunted by what they perceived to be a lack of real affection. Like Dianne, they quickly got the message that they were of little or no worth, and therefore, whatever they might accomplish in their lives had done little or nothing to increase their self-esteem. Like Dianne, they escaped an unhappy homelife by marrying or attaching themselves to a man only to perpetuate the same cycle they had witnessed as children. Like Dianne, most were attractive, although years of beatings and fear of being abandoned had taken its toll. Like Dianne, the majority have children whom they love.

Unlike Dianne, with a few exceptions, the women remained in these situations. Those who divorced their abusive husbands or left their abusive lovers have married or taken up with men who are just as harsh. Unlike Dianne, most had begun to overindulge in drugs or alcohol. Unlike Dianne, they did not seem to realize the harm their lifestyle almost certainly had on their kids, particularly their daughters. A few stood by while these children were molested or beaten, almost guaranteeing repetition of the cycle. Unlike Dianne, they are alive, if you can call it living.

Some are quite intelligent. A few are rumored to have lurid pasts, but most come under the classification of "vulnerable." They have no faith in their ability to establish themselves as independent people. They equate this with an existence devoid of male companionship. When it is pointed out that this need not be the case, one woman replied for them all. "I don't know any men who would stay with an uppity woman for five minutes." To her, an uppity woman is any female "with ideas of her own." These women play games with themselves and the men in their lives; they try to manipulate and are manipulated; they fear abandonment more than constant humiliation, threats, battering, or even death.

They range in age from their mid-twenties to fifty-something. Not all live on the wrong side of the tracks; some have comfortable-seeming suburban lives. Most work, although they have jobs rather than careers and cannot expect much in the way of advancement, especially economically. Only a few ever met Dianne. None were close friends. Others knew about her from gossip. A few never heard about her until they were threatened with her fate after she was dead. Some envied her life: the substantial home in Palos and getaways in Indiana and Florida; big cars; designer clothes and furs; a nice collection of jewelry (although the worth was vastly inflated in their minds); expensive vacations to exciting places; household help; and so on.

Even when the unhappy reality of Dianne's life and the gruesome details of her death became known to them, a few still think she "didn't have it so bad." The reasoning may sound tortured, but it goes something like this: life is a bitch, all men are shits, you might as well grab as much as you can while you can get it, everyone dies sometime, so you might as well do it young and leave a good-looking corpse.

Reminded that Dianne did not leave a good-looking corpse, they shrug.

After four months on the case, Paul Sabin and John Reed progressed further than previous investigators, but they refused to congratulate themselves. They were fairly sure they knew what had happened to Dianne Masters, but complacency could be fatal to acquiring the facts necessary to prove the case. Not that they had much opportunity to be smug; for every new lead, every successful interview, there seemed to be matching frustrations.

Both detectives were keenly aware that the subjects of their interviews to date had answered questions with varying degrees of openness, let alone truthfulness. This meant extra work trying to obtain confirmations from other sources as well as return engagements.

Wherever possible, anonymous sources who provided critical information needed to be coaxed onto the record. This was not going to be easy. People who have guilty knowledge of a crime like murder are going to be preoccupied with their own legal problems. When recruiting potential murderers, a prospective employer naturally chooses people who are likely to be receptive, and at the very least, unlikely to call a cop. To get such individuals to flip over, or become a government witness, it would be necessary to cut a deal, and Reed and Sabin could not do that without the cooperation of a prosecutor.

So far, the state's attorney office was not involved in the investigation, and anyone taking a look at the history of the case might wonder if it ever would be. Rumor had it that too many former and present assistant state's attorneys were worried that they might be called to testify about the corrupt antics of Messrs. Masters, Corbitt, and Keating over the years. Embarrassing questions might

be asked about how these men were able to fold, staple, and muti-
late the suburban justice system without the representatives of the
people noticing anything was amiss. Better just to leave well
enough alone.

Despite this, the two sheriff's detectives kept going.
Indeed, their investigation was at a critical point. "You've got to
watch out that you don't try to make the evidence fit your theory,"
John Reed recalls. "Guys bend a little here, and stretch a little
there, and come up with the right solution. It all feels pretty good
until you get to court. Then a minor detail, something subtle, a
nuance, pops up. It does not destroy the overall case but casts just
the tiniest fragment of doubt, and the whole prosecution collapses.
Paul and I didn't want that to happen here."

The two men were putting in an incredible number of hours
per week on the case. It was important for them to stay fresh and
alert at all times because they did not take notes or tape-record any
interviews. This is a common practice, contrary to movie and TV
depictions of cops whipping out their notebooks. The rationale is
that having a law officer write down or record every "hem" and
"haw" is too intimidating to the innocent bystander, let alone
those who have good reason to be skittish.

Although they were well trained and had plenty of practice in
this technique, it was essential that the results of each interview be
recorded immediately. Sabin and Reed would go straight to their
unmarked squad, where they took turns doing the actual writing.
Then they reviewed each other's work. If there were discrepancies,
they were resolved to the benefit of the subject. Finally, the report
was typed up and filed.

It was becoming increasingly clear that Dianne Masters had been
caught in the middle of a situation where male bonding had run
amok. Although Reed and Sabin did not have Charlie Bates' testimony, they knew that for at least a year before it happened, Alan
Masters had been discussing his plans to murder his wife and

trying to recruit his pals to do the deed. He left a trail that a child could follow, and without his close and illegal connections to members of various law enforcement agencies, Alan Masters would have long ago been charged with homicide domestic.

Instead, Reed and Sabin were sitting on a powder keg that could destroy a number of professional and political reputations. This was not the most comfortable prospect for two men who were just trying to do their jobs. Nor was the fact that they had to approach so many policemen, particularly members of their own department.

The top cop on the list of suspects was CCSPD Lt. James Keating, and this had created special problems for John Reed. He and Jim Keating had been friendly coworkers for more than twenty years; Keating had been Reed's supervisor early on. Everyone on the sheriff's force knew Keating, and most cops liked him.

Ultimately Reed came to the conclusion that, "There are two Jim Keatings. A good man and his evil twin. And it looks like the evil twin won out."

John Reed believes that all cases are solvable, given enough time and shoe leather. Despite the frustrations, he never wavered in this belief.

CHAPTER 13

$\mathcal{T}$he John Reed/Ted Nykaza
marathon sessions continued. To say that Nykaza has a problem
with alcohol is like saying that the Pacific Ocean is damp. Reed frequently found Nykaza the worse for drink, resulting in interviews
which had a surreal quality. On one such occasion, the sergeant
rang the doorbell and then identified himself over the intercom at
the front entrance. Ted opened the door, brandishing a fully loaded
snub-nosed Colt revolver. After being satisfied that it really was
Reed, Ted unloaded the gun and asked the policeman for a lift to
the local purveyor of fermented fluids in order to replenish his
stock.

There was no need for Nykaza to exaggerate his success as a
policeman; he had a wall full of commendations for his work on
the Chicago PD However, when sloshed, he had a tendency to
boast about his body count and to reenact some of the instances in
which he allegedly had killed others in the line of duty. After a
good night's sleep and a lot of coffee, Nykaza would admit that
these episodes were imaginary.

Even inebriated, Nykaza was a gold mine of information, some
of it trivial, all of it interesting. For example, Reed learned that
Rusty, Dianne Masters' golden retriever, had been living with Ted
since 1982. Ted explained the dog had become a behavior problem
after his mistress' disappearance and had suffered from recurring
nightmares ever since. Alan threatened to have the dog put down

257

unless a home could be found, and feeling sorry for the "sad" animal, Ted took him in.

More important to the case, Nykaza revealed that Masters had wanted to run the take from the Astrology Club through Ted's p.i. agency. Ted agreed, on the condition that Alan or one of his partners pay the IRS. When he heard that, Masters lost interest.

Nykaza occasionally revealed more than he wanted. After such an instance, he reproved Reed, saying, "I think your bumbling routine was just an act, right?" Reed's Columbo-type approach frequently stood him in good stead: bit by bit, even through an alcohol-induced haze, Nykaza was confirming other sources as well as supplying new leads.

Because Ted was a night person, rarely awake or sufficiently sober to be interviewed during regular working hours, and because Paul Sabin lived at the other end of the county, Reed volunteered to handle the nocturnal meetings. The relationship between the investigator and the p.i. became sufficiently close that Nykaza warned Reed that Alan Masters still had many good friends on the sheriff's police who rushed to tell the lawyer whenever Reed filed a report. Reed was aware of the leaks, but he took Nykaza's gesture as a kindness.

Nykaza's drinking was on the upswing. His ex-wife refused to permit their son to visit Ted. Sheila Mikel, his wife of four months, had moved out, and Ted discovered she was having affairs with a couple of men and was reporting back to Alan Masters about Ted's discussions with Reed and Sabin. Early one January morning, Reed received a call from a fellow officer regarding one of Ted's cars burning. It appeared that the car was torched and that Ted was responsible; a trail of blood led from the burning car to a gas can to Ted's home, where Ted displayed a fresh wound to his arm. Reed was concerned that Ted would do something desperate and asked to be kept informed about new developments.

Not all the encounters were as successful as Nykaza; some were called "threshold" interviews because Sabin and Reed never got further than that. In mid-January Sabin and Reed tried to talk to Anthony Barone, whose name kept popping up on everyone's short list of accomplices in the Masters' murder. A Chicago cop allegedly under investigation for official corruption, Barone had once been on the Willow Springs force and was a former brother-in-law of Michael Corbitt.

The detectives identified themselves when Barone opened his door. "Do you have a subpoena?' Barone asked. "No," Sabin replied, "but a source told us that you bragged of having knowledge about who killed Dianne Masters." An attractive young blonde standing behind Barone, said "Oh, shit," when she heard Dianne's name. "Go back to your snitch, look at your own police department—if you don't have a grand jury subpoena, I have nothing to say to you," Barone snapped as he slammed the door.

The first Mrs. Masters was cooperative but very uncomfortable when Reed and Sabin met her in her office in a small Jewish college on Chicago's South Michigan Avenue. Obviously embarrassed, the former Mrs. Masters wanted to know how the detectives had found her; she was concerned that the press would not be far behind.

She mentioned that in 1983 she had been called to the FBI's Chicago office by Agent Dave Parker. Until Reed and Sabin arrived, she said, her only contact had been with the FBI, who asked her about Alan's possible involvement in a number of illegal activities, including child pornography and prostitution. She said that during their marriage, Alan introduced her to a few selected associates only, and that while he changed during the 1960s, she never saw his violent side. When he moved to the south suburbs, he became a different person, who did not like himself, she asserted.

Mrs. Masters recalled that in 1970, Alan's name surfaced in the newspapers as part of a ticket fixing scandal in the Fifth District. The entire family found the exposure shameful, and because of the revelations, she was careful about signing joint income tax returns.

On returning to the office, John Reed pulled the clippings of the now defunct newspaper *Chicago Today* for June 1971. In December 1970, an eighteen-year-old Palos Hills man was arrested in nearby Bridgeview for drag racing and failing to notify the Illinois secretary of state of a change of address.

Later the same day, the man was contacted by a Bridgeview cop who suggested that Alan Masters would be a "good lawyer" to hire. The man made an appointment to see Masters, taking with him an investigator for the Better Government Association (BGA) and a *Chicago Today* reporter.

After looking over the two tickets, Masters said, "OK, I'll represent you for five hundred dollars. I'll get the drag racing thrown out." He was asked if he could get the second ticket dismissed because the change of address had in fact been reported but not yet recorded. Judges routinely throw such charges out upon proof of notification. But Alan Masters did not think this would be possible. "They're losing a big charge," he explained, "so we've got to give them something."

Three months later, the men returned to Masters' office to pay another installment. Before the cash changed hands, the BGA investigator asked how Masters was going to have the drag racing charge dismissed. "Just let me handle it. You didn't ask Blackstone how he did his magic tricks while he was on stage, did you?" Then the visitors left, taking with them the vivid memory of Alan's tank of piranha in the midst of a goldfish feeding frenzy.

Another man arrested on the same charge told investigators that he hired Masters on the advice of the Bridgeview cop, and that Masters guaranteed success for a fee of seven hundred dollars. Alan explained that the fee was so high because "some money would go to the judge and some to the cops to keep everybody happy."

When a reporter contacted Masters for his reaction, he denied the allegations, saying about the first case, "I did not receive his name from a police officer. That would be unethical." Those in the know around southwestern court buildings collapsed with laughter at this and at the statement that the investigators from the BGA, the courts, and the newspaper, "found no judges were involved in the racket or took any money."

Reed shook his head. All the "investigation" did was contribute to the legend of Alan Masters' invincibility.

Reed and Sabin scheduled a coffee shop meeting with John Waters, a Chicago PD officer, who worked temporarily for SOA, the private detective agency hired by Dianne's brother in 1982. Despite the fact that Sheriff O'Grady was a partner in SOA, the agency was refusing to cooperate with the sheriff's investigators. Waters agreed to pull a copy.

The possibility that Alan Masters was involved in child pornography and/or was molesting his daughter and that Dianne had discovered it was a recurring theme in the investigation. According to one source, Alan was dating a divorced woman with two preteen daughters. One day while their mother was at work, Alan persuaded the girls to admit him to their home, claiming that their mother sent him to make sure that the girls bathed and that he had to observe. When informed of the incident by her daughters, the girlfriend was angry, but given Alan's connections, she felt no one would ever listen to her.

An anonymous source who had been dribbling information out told Reed that a drunken Jim Keating revealed that one of the men involved in Dianne's murder was "bitching" that Dianne's Cadillac had a flat tire en route to the disposal site. The source was still more afraid of Masters and Company than the law; Reed's reaction was to advise some additional "soul searching."

CHAPTER 14

$\mathcal{W}$hile studying the Willow Springs police duty roster and radio log for March 19, 1982, Reed and Sabin discovered a notation at 11:03 p.m. about shots fired on the canal. The officer responding to the call was Robert Olson, a WSPD auxiliary patrolman. There were a few honest cops in Willow Springs, and Robert Olson, a part-timer who lived outside the village, was one of them.

Reed and Sabin located Olson in his office at Montgomery Ward where he was working while finishing law school. At first, Olson did not remember the exact date of his encounter with Corbitt, but he did recall the event. Even for Willow Springs, it was an unusual night. Olson punched in at 10:57 p.m. on Friday, March 19, 1982, for an eight-hour shift that would end at 7:05 a.m. Saturday. The interesting part happened at the beginning of his shift.

His memory refreshed as to the specific date, Olson said he arrived at the station at 10:45 p.m. to meet with the officers who were finishing the previous shift, a regular procedure to provide continuity. That completed, Olson encountered George Witzel, the man he was relieving, on the station steps. Witzel handed Olson the keys to squad car number 52. As Olson was still standing outside the station with a couple of fellow officers, he heard two shots fired, just seconds apart. To Olson, they seemed to be coming from the area west of the police department, more specifi-

263

cally the bank of the canal, a short distance as the crow flies. He volunteered to check the canal, and then all three officers went to their respective squads, going in different directions.

As he took off west on Archer, Olson called the station at 11:03 p.m., "52, broadcast to base. Nature of traffic was 1041 and 8." This informed the radio operator that Olson was on duty, giving his vehicle number and mileage. Logged at the same time was Olson's report that he was responding to the sound of gunfire.

Olson estimates it took him between thirty seconds to one minute to arrive at the canal, where it was very dark. As he was driving over the railroad tracks just south of the canal, the lights of another automobile flashed on. Worried, Olson slowed to unstrap his gun and flip on the squad's spotlight, aiming it in the direction of the other car, which was now moving towards him. As it came closer, Olson recognized the license plate and the vehicle as belonging to Michael Corbitt.

Soon Corbitt's personal car was close enough that the driver's windows were next to each other, forming what the police call a "signal eight." At this point, Olson saw that Corbitt was driving, and that he was not alone. In the passenger seat was a dark-haired, dark-complected, forty-something Caucasian male whom Olson judged to be of medium build, somewhat smaller than Corbitt, clothed in a leather jacket. Although Corbitt's passenger had a familiar look, Olson did not recognize him.

After pulling alongside Olson, Corbitt made a dismissive motion and said, "I've already checked, and everything is okay." "All right," Olson replied, turning the squad around and leaving the canal bank. He did not reflect upon the incident, as Corbitt was frequently observed tooling around the streets of Willow Springs late at night in his own car. Nor did Olson call in a report on what he had found since the chief had emphasized that everything was under control. Olson estimated the encounter took less than a minute and that he left the canal area by 11:06 p.m. The next log entry from car 52 was at 11:16 p.m., when Olson made a traffic stop at Archer Avenue and Colonel Street, a short distance away.

At this point, Olson was not aware that Dianne Masters had been reported missing earlier that day. Even if he had known, there was no reason to connect the two events. A couple of weeks later, while eating in a local restaurant, Olson overheard other diners discuss her disappearance. Specifically, he remembers one person saying, "I bet her husband did it," to the general agreement of the others.

He did not know Dianne Masters, but Olson had good reason to remember a couple of meetings with her husband. The first time, Olson stopped a speeding car on Archer Avenue. Approached by Olson and asked for his identification, the driver said, "Hold on, I'm robbing a bank over the telephone." If it was meant as a joke, Olson did not think it droll. Then Masters handed Olson the car telephone. Mike Corbitt, Olson's boss, was on the other end. "Alan Masters is a friend of mine," Corbitt informed Olson. No ticket was issued. Olson's second meeting with Masters was not as cute; Masters was representing a person who had been arrested by Olson.

In June 1982, when Mike Corbitt was finally kicked off the Willow Springs police force, Bob Olson was one of a number of officers who also were discharged. Olson felt this was unfair, since he had patently not been one of Corbitt's team, and Olson took it up with the new chief, Jim Ross. During this discussion with Ross, Olson mentioned the incident near the canal. Still, there was no reason to connect it to Dianne.

By fall of 1982, Olson was reinstated, still in a part-time capacity, but now he was making undercover drug buys. He was also working another job and attending college. It was a busy life.

On December 11, 1982, Olson attended a Saturday morning class and was taking care of typical Saturday chores when he received a call from the Willow Springs PD to report for special duty. It was late afternoon when he arrived at the canal to find the sodden, canal-muck covered mess that constituted what was left of Dianne Masters and her car. Evidence technicians from the sheriff's office were already there, and the medical examiner came soon after.

Once the car had been trucked to the fire station, Olson rigged up a closed circuit television surveillance system. Willow Springs simply did not have enough men on the force to provide a twenty-four-hour guard, and it was a concern that curiosity seekers or people with something to hide would tamper with a vital piece of evidence. When Olson was finished, it was possible for the radio operator to monitor any activity in the boarded-up garage.

At the end of January 1983, Olson was interviewed by FBI Agent Dave Parker about sighting Corbitt the previous March. In the intervening years, Olson heard nothing further, until Reed and Sabin showed up at his office.

In the interim, Olson had left the Willow Springs PD, this time for good. There had been a mayoral election in Willow Springs in the spring of 1986. Frank Militello was out and a friend of Mike Corbitt's was in. The incoming mayor did not renew Olson's appointment. Although he was told this was due to a campaign promise to appoint more local residents, Olson believed he was laid off because of an unfortunate habit of trying to bust people with influence. During the Corbitt days, Olson arrested the chief of police of the Cook County Forest Preserve District for driving under the influence and refusing to stop his vehicle. Just before the '86 election, Olson made a traffic stop; the violator turned out to be a close friend of the successful mayoral candidate. "I'll have your job!" the man threatened. Olson wrote the ticket anyway.

As Reed and Sabin were preparing to leave Olson's office, the former Willow Springs cop said, "I can't understand how Corbitt, who never made more than $25,000 as chief of police, can afford a house worth $150,000, a Corvette, and all his other cars." It was a question Sabin and Reed had heard before. They had a pretty good idea how Corbitt did it, and a lucrative paper route was not the answer.

The investigators were aware that Alan was kept well informed about their activities. If they needed confirmation, they got it in a telephone call from Jack Bachman in his EOL persona. Bachman told John Reed that Sgt. Clarke Buckendahl was repeating EOL's information verbatim to Bachman, without realizing that Bachman was the source. Buckendahl said his source was another cop, Bill Waldron. Reed confronted Waldron, who admitted encountering Buckendahl in a south suburban bar, but denied repeating any revelations about the Masters' case. However, another source at the bar claimed that Buckendahl and Waldron spent more than an hour in "heavy conversation."

Besides interviews, there were investigative nuts and bolts to be completed. On 1 a.m. on Saturday, February 21, 1987, the weather and road conditions were similar to those on Friday, March 19, 1982, so John Reed retraced Dianne's last known drive from the restaurant to her Palos Park home, meticulously recording starting and ending mileage and departure and arrival times. The distance was 4.1 miles, which he traveled in eight minutes. He caught the same red light that had stopped Dianne and Gen Capstaff almost five years earlier. Next, Reed drove from the Masters' driveway to eastbound 123rd Street to northbound Willow Springs Road to Archer Avenue, turning west off Archer to northbound Colonel Street, arriving at the canal launch site, a distance of 6.2 miles. Reed had the green all the way, and the trip took just nine minutes.

On March 19, 1987, the fifth anniversary of Dianne Masters' murder, the sheriff's team staked out Dianne's grave at Saint Adalbert's cemetery. The plain, flat marker read:

Wife/mom

Dianne G. Masters

1946-1982

No one showed up.

The thaw was on its way to suburban Cook County and to the Masters' case as well. Every obstacle proved to be a turning point in the evidence, but John Reed and Paul Sabin needed more to bring the murderers of Dianne Masters to trial. They needed a scrupulously clean, relentless prosecutor who could not be reached by any of Alan Masters' high-placed pals. They were about to get him.

PART III

A Federal Case

"Mother of mercy,
is this the end of Rico?"

—Edward G. Robinson
in Little Caesar

CHAPTER 1

$\mathcal{J}$t is common for one law enforcement body not to know what another is doing. This is true of police and/or prosecutors at the county, state, or federal levels. The general public tends to believe that except for the crooked ones, all these people are working on the same side and that jurisdictional disputes and personality clashes should take a backseat to the public good. As so frequently happens, the general public is misled.

Problems arise, and not simply due to disagreements over who gets the credit for a job well done. They may work together on a regular basis, but the foot soldiers in the war against crime do not necessarily trust each other. Cops from one suburb may not trust the Chicago PD, the state troopers, or the sheriff's police. The one area on which they agree is that none of the above trusts the FBI.

Many agents from the Bureau have an attitude of disdain toward local law enforcers, as if they are several notches above the police on the food chain. The entry of the FBI into a local investigation can mean the destruction of days, weeks, months, or even years on a case. The disregard for the bureau is not restricted to Cook County; as one out-of-state policeman put it, "Working with the Bureau can be like pissing into the wind and usually is."

If there is common ground among the FBI and local police deparments, it is their mistrust of lawyers. For one thing, today's prosecutor may very well be tomorrow's defense attorney. When

271

prosecutors switch from one side of the courtroom to the other, they take with them all the knowledge of how the police and the FBI operate as well as specific information on current files. As a result, there is an inclination to give the prosecutor only as much information as he or she absolutely must have to make a case.

Paul Sabin and John Reed were too professional and too determined to let such attitudes stand in their way. If anything, the detectives felt a special responsibility to the public because of the allegations against members of their own force. If the FBI or the state police or the Chicago PD had information that would help, that was fine. The two men agreed to reach out to other departments in case they could help.

As part of this effort, John Reed spoke to a Chicago FBI agent with whom he had cooperated before. In turn, this agent put Reed and Sabin in touch with FBI colleagues Roger Griggs and Ivan Harris, who were working with Assistant U. S. Attorney Thomas J. Scorza, who was investigating Mike Corbitt and Alan Masters. When Scorza learned that two honest sheriff's officers were vigorously investigating the death of Dianne Masters, he summoned them to the Dirksen Federal Building in downtown Chicago.

This was another major turning point in the case. It was almost as if the Fates, having realized that they slipped up, were making doubly sure that the murderers of Dianne Masters would be punished by setting yet a third bloodhound on their trail.

Actually, Tom Scorza resembles a pit bull rather than a bloodhound. Where John Reed tends to rely on an indirect, friendly approach, Scorza targets a vital organ. Maybe several vital organs. While Reed is willing to lay back in the weeds, returning again and again until he gets what he needs, Scorza proceeds at one speed: fast forward. The men could not be more different in appearance, either. Scorza is slight, wiry, balding, bearded, and intense.

The prosecutor is aptly named. The Italian verb *scorzare* means to peel or to decorticate. After a session with Terrifying Tommy,

"The Scores" or "The Scourge," as he is sometimes called behind his back, people have emerged feeling brain damaged.

Scorza does not suffer fools. Period. His manner ranges from brusque to charm school dropout. He does not interview sources, he interrogates them, and many—even cops who are experienced at being cross-examined by top defense attorneys—crawl away from a close encounter with Scorza as if they had just been run over by a freight train. He is not particularly popular among his colleagues, but he gets results, especially in risky cases.

A fairly recent arrival to both Cook County and the law, Scorza was born in Brooklyn in 1948. He was graduated from Notre Dame in 1969 and went on to acquire both a Master of Arts and Ph.D. in philosophy and literature from California's Claremont Graduate Schools by 1972. His doctoral thesis on Herman Melville's *Billy Budd* was later developed into a book. He lives near the university with his wife Judy and their three daughters, Gina, Anne and Caroline.

After teaching philosophy for seven years at small, prestigious colleges in Illinois and Ohio, Scorza became bored with some aspects of teaching and its limited financial rewards. It was time for a career change, and in 1979, he entered the University of Chicago Law School, emerging after three years with a law degree. His goal was a job with the U. S. attorney's office, but due to a hiring freeze, he went to work clerking for a federal court judge. In September 1983, the freeze was lifted in order to start up a narcotics task force, and Scorza was one of six people hired. In 1988, he was named assistant chief, and in 1989, chief of the Organized Crime and Drug Enforcement Task Force.

Scorza's involvement in the case that came to be known as 88 CR 500, the *U. S. vs Masters, Corbitt, and Keating*, began in 1985, just before the FBI transferred Agent Dave Parker to another city. While assigned to the Chicago office, Parker worked on the FBI's investigation of suburban corruption, which led to Mike Corbitt's activities in Willow Springs. During the course of this inquiry, the names of Alan Masters and his murdered wife began popping up on a fairly regular basis.

Initially, Scorza and Parker concentrated on Corbitt. Operation Safebet, the sting operation aimed at the exposure of suburban vice, was in the hands of a separate federal strike force, but Parker eventually learned of the May 1982 meeting between Mike Corbitt and undercover agent Lary Damron. Even on an intramural basis, the FBI finds it hard to share, and it took three or four months for Parker to obtain the records of the meeting.

Before Parker's reassignment and before the dimensions of the case against Alan Masters were known, Scorza decided to separate allegations against Masters, opening a new file. In retrospect, Scorza sees this as one of several acts, such as the assignment of Sabin and Reed, which could only be explained by divine intervention.

Parker's legacy to Scorza was a huge file of FBI interview reports known as 302s. It took Scorza two months to consume the contents of the file and to organize it. When he was finished, it was clear that Corbitt was connected to an old arson case. Because the statute of limitations was about to expire, Scorza was under extreme pressure to put obtain an indictment. It was the kind of pressure Scorza thrived upon.

Michael Corbitt was born in Oak Park, Illinois, on March 17, 1944, and was reared in Willow Springs and Summit. He came from an average lower middle class background, although occasionally he liked to boast that he was from aristocratic and/or wealthy stock. He attended Saint Procopius Catholic Seminary in Lisle, where it quickly became clear that he was not cut out for the priesthood, and he left at sixteen without obtaining a diploma. He is remembered as a restless teenager, often to be found at the scene of trouble. He idled around until he was twenty-one, when he became a policeman.

Corbitt enjoyed his reputation as a tough guy. At six feet, two inches and 240 pounds, with a shock of white hair, a face pitted by terminal acne, a macho swagger assisted by his high-heeled cowboy boots, and his record for "justifiable" homicides, Corbitt was a menacing figure.

Corbitt loved to tell stories about himself. One of them is what John Reed calls the "Case of the Terrified Tourist." Willow Springs was a wide-open town, but for some reason Corbitt hated hitch-hikers worse than poison. Whenever he saw one, he sent out his pal Shaggy to pick up the hiker in Shaggy's big Cadillac. Soon after, Corbitt would be right on the Caddie's trail, sirens and lights blazing.

When Shaggy showed no sign of pulling over, the hitchhiker understandably became nervous. "Gee, sir, I think that policeman wants you to stop. Don't you think..." "Listen, kid, I just robbed a bank [a 7-ll, whatever Shaggy favored that day], and I shot a man." With that, Shaggy would pull out a gun. "I ain't stopping." By now the hitchhiker would be a complete wreck. Finally, Corbitt would fire blanks over Shaggy's head, forcing the car onto the shoulder. He would pretend to drag Shaggy out of the car on his knees and fire a couple of blanks toward Shaggy's head. Shaggy would oblig-ingly play dead.

By now the hitchhiker was usually a quivering mass of Jello. "I'm giving you a break, kid," Corbitt would tell the poor wretch, "but I never want to see you in Willow Springs again." The hapless hiker would take off as fast as his fear would permit, frequently with more of Corbitt's blanks whistling around him. Then Shaggy and Mike would go off to some local wateringhole for a few drinks and a good laugh.

On one occasion, this little act was interrupted at its most interesting point by a semitrailer. When the trucker saw a policeman engaged in what appeared to be a shoot-out, he became so nervous that he ran right into Corbitt's squad. No report of the collision ever made it into the file.

Shaggy and Corbitt had another mutual interest: stock car racing. In an excess of cuteness, Corbitt named his car the 10-4.

Corbitt might protect the citizens of Willow Springs from the dread hitchhiking menace, but schoolteachers were not safe in their own school yards. One young woman was being harassed before and after class by an overgrown, overage eighth grader who kept trying to run her down with his bike. After trying reason, she called the police, and Chief Corbitt responded. At first, the teacher thought her troubles were over, but to her dismay, the problem only got worse. When she called again, Corbitt laughed at her, explaining that the youth was the son of a minor mobster, and the teacher would just have to bear with the situation. The principal and district superintendent claimed their hands were tied because the harassment was not taking place inside the school building. She believed they were afraid of Corbitt and the lout's father. Rather than buck the system, she left teaching and Willow Springs.

His approach earned him the title King Corbitt. When he was deposed in June 1982, Corbitt tried to become chief of police of his old home town, Summit. But that fell through, and Corbitt was hired by Circuit Court Clerk Morgan Finley as a special investigator for southwest suburban Circuit Court Districts 4 and 5. He was still in business. Corbitt's new job enabled him to carry both a badge and a gun.

In October 1968, when then Patrolman Michael Corbitt claimed he found a peeping tom outside an apartment window. According to Corbitt, even though he identified himself as a police officer, the suspect jumped him and took his weapon. But Corbitt had a backup gun, which discharged during the scuffle. It was ruled justifiable homicide, although there were rumors that Corbitt was visiting his girlfriend at the time of the incident and may have stretched a point in order to show off.

In September 1971, now-Sergeant Corbitt added another notch while trying to subdue a man terrorizing patrons in a Willow

Springs tavern. When the drunk waved his gun at Corbitt, the cop said he had no choice but to shoot.

In November 1976, news surfaced that for the past year, the Better Government Association (BGA), the Cook County state's attorney and the Illinois attorney general had been investigating the distribution of Willow Springs police badges to outsiders.

Corbitt admitted that he owned the Swift Security Company in Willow Springs and that one of his employees also was a part-time Willow Springs policeman who carried an auxiliary badge, as did three other Swift security guards. In addition to his police work and running Swift, for about two years beginning in June 1974, Corbitt acted as assistant director of security at the Hyatt Regency Motel in downtown Chicago. A county grand jury subpoenaed both WSPD and Swift Security records, which showed that Corbitt's boss at the hotel worked as a part-time Willow Springs cop and full-time deputy chief. The hotel's resident manager also was the recipient of a Willow Springs badge. Corbitt claimed he had done nothing wrong and that the investigation was "100 percent politically motivated." The registered agent of Corbitt's security firm was a criminal defense attorney and former legal advisor to the CCSPD. As Corbitt predicted, no indictments were issued.

Corbitt had quite an entrepreneurial bent. He sold a stolen handgun to another policeman; he bragged about placing illegal wiretaps in a nearby business; he worked closely with several well-known criminals. After he caught one villain trying to burgle the Corbitt manse, the police chief kicked him in the testicles. This was the start of a beautiful working relationship. Corbitt would act as lookout in a series of thefts, including selected items at his own house. The burglar returned these to Corbitt, who claimed the insurance. This individual became nervous after Corbitt tossed him into the canal. He feared that he would be killed by Corbitt during one of their joint ventures, thus ridding Corbitt of a possible snitch while permitting him to take credit for solving the rash of burglaries.

In the fall of 1977, Corbitt fought off the first attempt by the Willow Springs Board of Trustees to fire him. In addition to Corbitt, the board wanted to dump the deputy chief, a full-time patrolman, one part-time patrolman, and two part-time matrons, one of whom happened to be Corbitt's wife. Together the Corbitt Six made up one-quarter of the department. The dismissals passed easily with a five-to-one majority, but Corbitt filed suit and was granted a restraining order.

Each of these incidents helped to increase Corbitt's natural arrogance and the feeling that he was beyond the law. Even the election of a reform-minded mayor could not put a damper on Corbitt's antics. In the spring of 1981, at the same time Corbitt was fighting Mayor Militello's efforts to fire him, a federal grand jury called for the police department's financial records. The IRS wanted to know if Corbitt had been accepting bribes and not declaring them on his tax returns. With customary braggadocio, Corbitt told associates that he had leased a safe deposit box and placed a banana inside, so that when the IRS got around to opening it, all they would find would be a piece of rotten fruit.

Corbitt enjoyed making news. Any kind of news. In September 1981, Corbitt inherited $127,500 from Joseph Testa, a Chicago businessman reported to have gang ties, who was the victim of an explosion outside his Florida home. Testa lingered for two days, during which time Corbitt flew to Fort Lauderdale to be with him. Corbitt described Testa as "a very close friend and business associate."

Besides Testa's real estate holdings in Florida, he owned Sterling Estates Mobile Home Park near Justice, a suburb just outside Summit, a restaurant in Hoffman Estates, and a home in Wooddale. All three had been damaged by bombs in 1978. Around this time, a fake bomb was found wired underneath Testa's car. Finally getting the message, Testa moved to the Sunshine State. Visiting Testa at the time of the big bang was John Hinchy, deputy chief of detectives of the Chicago Police Department. Hinchy, who had been director of the North Eastern Metropolitan Drug Enforcement Group (NEMEG), a narcotics investigative body, also received $127,500 in Testa's will.

On further questioning about his relations with Testa, Corbitt said, "The man was torn up...Just because of his Italian extraction and he ate [sic] in the same places these [gangsters] did, he was reputed to be in mob circles. Mr. Testa was a hard-working self-made man. There were no mob ties." This caused some guffawing among local mob mavens. Hard-working self-made men hardly ever are blown up. It was reported that the police were interested in talking to an explosives specialist who usually worked for Joseph "the Clown" Lombardo, a Chicago mob figure. There also were rumors that Corbitt and/or Hinchy were involved, seeing as they had a vested interest in the Testa estate. The case remains unsolved.

Once he was kicked out as chief, Corbitt's life turned deceptively quiet, although in 1985, a Willow Springs bar owner was accused of soliciting a customer to murder Corbitt. But behind the scenes, FBI Agent Dave Parker was developing the Corbitt file.

In the past, efforts to bring Corbitt to justice failed because of his cunning, his lawyers, and the reluctance of his confederates to either endanger or further incriminate themselves. Parker kept digging until he found a source who could help put Corbitt behind bars.

In reviewing the list of trucks and automobiles recovered during the canal dredging operation, Parker discovered that on December 5, 1982, a wrecked 1978 Ford pickup belonging to Raymond Gluszek of Willow Springs was retrieved. Like the other vehicles, it had been reported stolen.

When approached by Parker, Gluszek folded. He admitted he had been in an accident, and the Ford was in pretty bad shape. When WSPD Chief Mike Corbitt saw it, he suggested to Gluszek that the wreck be disposed of in the canal, reported stolen, and the insurance money claimed. Corbitt even gave Gluszek detailed instructions on the best launching site. When Gluszek expressed concern that pickup would be found and he would be caught, Corbitt reassured him. Several years before, Corbitt said, some cars had been found in the canal, but neither the law nor their insurance companies had ever pursued the owners.

Gluszek's relationship with Corbitt went beyond auto disposal. In 1977, Gluszek purchased an American Legion hall on Archer Avenue in Willow Springs, and Corbitt assisted in obtaining a liquor license for the new Livery Bar.

Trouble was not long in coming. On opening day, the neighbors began complaining about loud music and parking problems. Gluszek conferred with Corbitt, who advised hiring Alan Masters, a lawyer who could "handle" the situation. Not long afterward, the village board stopped threatening Gluszek.

Corbitt was helpful in other ways. He approached Gluszek about installing pinball machines in the bar, and when Gluszek agreed, Corbitt made the arrangements. There was to be a fifty/fifty split between Gluszek and the owners of the machines. Corbitt would be "taken care of" by the owners out of their share.

Despite all these efforts, the neighbors' complaints continued, and Gluszek was not making money. He decided to open a cabinet shop in the basement. When he asked Corbitt if this would create a zoning problem, Corbitt had a better idea: hookers. He even had a man to manage the operation for Gluszek. Gluszek expressed concern about further legal problems, but Corbitt reassured him that Alan Masters could handle anything. Despite Corbitt's optimism, even prostitutes did not improve the tavern's financial picture. What's more, the village renewed its threats to close Gluszek down. The resourceful Corbitt had another solution: arson. Corbitt asked only that he be notified a week in advance of the torching. On January 7, 1980, the Livery Tavern was leveled by fire. As the saying went in Willow Springs, "if it's too big to be shoved into the canal, burn it down."

Scorza had put many bad guys away since joining the U.S. attorney's office, and most of the time it was not personal. Corbitt and his cronies were different. Scorza despised those who abused the public trust and was delighted to find a chink in Corbitt's armor. Now that he was aware of Reed and Sabin's efforts, Scorza was convinced he could score the hat trick: Masters, Keating, and Corbitt.

Following his meeting with the county investigators, Scorza telephoned Sheriff James O'Grady to set up the ground rules for a cooperative effort between the federal government and the county police. O'Grady insisted that Reed and Sabin not be made agents of the federal grand jury, which meant that the two sheriff's detectives would not have access to grand jury testimony. It also meant that instead of going straight to Scorza, O'Grady would continue to receive copies of the detectives' reports.

Scorza was able to work out an arrangement so that Reed and Sabin would provide Scorza with all relevant information they developed. Inevitably, there were times when the investigation was hindered by O'Grady's position.

CHAPTER 2

$\mathcal{R}$eed, Sabin, and Scorza hit it off immediately. Their styles were very different but complementary in most cases. Scorza wears his brains on his sleeve and has an instinct for the jugular. As one colleague in the U. S. attorney's office put it, "Everybody has layers to their personality. Scorza's weakness is his inability to peel these layers back. A frontal assault is not always the best way to get a witness to tell what you want to know." Reed and Sabin were less ferocious, and their manner, more relaxed and accommodating. In a few instances, the wrong person conducted an interview, but for the most part, the division of labor went quite well.

Before Scorza could proceed full tilt, another county official had to be approached. At about the same time the not-quite-satisfactory arrangement was reached with the sheriff, Scorza and Anton Valukas, then U.S. attorney for the Northern District of Illinois, met with Cook County State's Attorney Richard M. Daley.

A murder charge carrying a potential death penalty was involved and took precedence should Daley want to try the case at the county level. To Scorza's relief, Daley passed. Scorza wanted Masters, Corbitt, and Keating, and he wanted them tried in some venue where there was no chance of a fix. The Criminal Court of Cook County did not fit that definition.

Having gone through channels, Scorza was free to pursue the indictments. He had just the tool he needed to get the results he

283

wanted: RICO, which stands for the Racketeer-influenced and Corrupt Organizations Act, passed by Congress in 1970. Sometimes called the mini-mafia law, RICO makes it a federal crime to conduct the affairs of an "enterprise" through a "pattern of racketeering." Legally, a pattern exists when members of the enterprise commit at least two acts of racketeering within ten years of each other. These are known as predicate acts, and they include anything illegal under state law: murder, robbery, gambling, extortion, using the phone or the mail for illegal purposes, arson and/or bombing. RICO also enables the federal government to seize money or goods realized as a result of the enterprise.

CHAPTER 3

*P*aranoia was approaching epidemic proportions among those who had been a little too close to Alan Masters. It was bad enough having Reed and Sabin on the case, but now the two sheriff's cops were working with the "G." Jim Keating was in prison as a result of Assistant U.S. Attorney David Stetler's prosecution of the cases developed from the Operation Safebet sting. Mike Corbitt seemed headed there, too, courtesy of Tom Scorza.

Still another federal investigation was headed by Assistant U.S. Attorney Sheldon Zenner. Zenner was handed a file containing information about blatant illegal behavior in the Fifth (southwest suburban) Circuit Court District and was told to "go and make something out of it." An outgrowth of another federal sting called "Operation Greylord," after the off-white horsehair wigs worn by British barristers and jurists, the file involved moles, phony cases, bugging, fixes, and bribery.

Sheldon Zenner and Tom Scorza have similarities in height and build and their reputations for legal brilliance, but in everything else, they are as different as chalk and cheese. A local lad, Zenner was thirty-four but could easily pass for a decade younger. He has an easygoing manner that impresses but does not intimidate, inspiring people to want to peel back those layers they pile on in Scorza's presence. Zenner and Scorza had another quality in common; their skill in the grand jury room.

285

Partly because they deliberate in secret, exactly what a grand jury does is obscure to most people, although it came to this country along with English common law and was incorporated into the Constitution's Fifth Amendment. A federal grand jury is composed of twenty-three people who have the power to investigate allegations of illegal behavior and vote an indictment which will lead to a trial by a petit jury. It is the prosecutor's show, but each grand juror also may question witnesses. As a check against a runaway grand jury, the federal system demands that any indictment must be signed by the prosecutor in order to be valid. Individuals subpoenaed to appear before the grand jury are not entitled to have legal representation inside the jury room, although they may excuse themselves to consult with an attorney outside the chamber before answering a question. Witnesses have no right to know whether they are targets of the investigation, to confront accusers, to examine documents produced as evidence, or to cross examine other witnesses. No members of the public, including the press, are permitted inside the grand jury room. However, once an indictment is handed down, the accused and their lawyers may see the transcripts. To some legal experts, it is an archaic and un-American institution; the British did away with it in 1933.

Sheldon Zenner quickly found that Alan Masters was a key figure in his investigation of suburban courthouse corruption. Everybody Zenner interviewed seemed truly afraid of the increasingly rotund Masters. Zenner noticed an overlap with the findings from Operation Safebet, and this led him to Jack Bachman.

Zenner's winning ways were a vital element because even someone like Bachman, a veteran cop who was trained in protecting himself, was afraid to discuss Alan Masters. After all, the feds might send you to prison if you did not do what they wanted, but informing on Alan Masters could get you killed. The choice seemed obvious. Keep your mouth shut and take what's coming. Zenner would need all the help he could get in persuading

Bachman over to the government side. When he heard that Bachman respected and trusted John Reed, Zenner asked for Reed's assistance.

"Nobody in their right mind actually investigates a case before the grand jury, so it takes a lot of preparation," according to Zenner. Part of that preparation involved spending many hours with the nervous Bachman, hours that paid off in several ways, including a direct link between Alan Masters and Jim Keating.

Already doing time on his 1986 Safebet conviction, Keating was brought back to Chicago's Metropolitan Correction Center (MCC) from his Texas prison cell to talk about his role in the courthouse crimes. By the time Zenner met him, there was no obvious trace left of the old Keating who was called "one of the three meanest assholes in Cook County" by a federal operative in a position to know. The man Zenner met was playing the role of the down-and-out, beaten cop-gone-bad, in what more than one former coworker called a really great act. Far from the threatening aspect that had intimidated so many people over the years, the new Keating had a "yessir, nosir, three bags full, sir" approach that Zenner found smarmy and tried to get Keating to stop. But Keating continued to play Uriah Heep, pleading for permission to use the men's room and weeping so copiously that during one particularly long session, Zenner worried that his office would be awash.

Much as he wanted to flip Keating over to the government side as he had Bachman, Zenner eventually decided this was not going to happen, and Keating did not appear as a witness before Zenner's grand jury. "Every sliver of truth Keating gave up was surrounded by a morass of untruth," Zenner said. "He could not bring himself to tell the story straight, and we went past him." There were those, including John Reed, who believed that Keating had been living with lies for so long, he was no longer able to recognize the truth or that he was too frightened of his associates in other illegal endeavors to do so.

The pressure from the news stories generated by Keating's 1986 trial and a county investigation that finally was on the legit combined with an veritable blizzard of federal grand jury subpoenas cannot be underestimated. Whatever the specifics of what triggered what in whom, the most reluctant witnesses started loosening up.

Diane Economou was an example. Zenner's interview with Economou provided one of the most dramatic moments of his tenure as a federal prosecutor because her breakdown was so unexpected. Zenner called Economou into his office to discuss information she might have about Masters' role in corrupting the judiciary. He tossed several "softball" questions about courthouse low jinks. She did not volunteer much, except that Alan Masters often took cash payments and that she had heard rumors that he could fix anything.

Her answers became increasingly hesitant as the session went on, and when she asked her legal counsel "Should I talk about this?" Zenner knew something big was going to break. Economou came completely unglued, crying and shaking so uncontrollably that Zenner felt sorry for her. "I know I should have told somebody," she sobbed, "I just didn't think he'd really do it."

Zenner passed her a box of tissues and waited for a bombshell. His instincts were right. Amidst her tears, Economou confirmed suspicions that Alan had confided in her on numerous occasions about his plans to rid himself of his pesky wife. She knew about the telephone tap and the bottle-in-the-vagina tape. But even more important, she knew about specific murder-planning sessions with Jim Keating, who was in Masters' office on a daily basis during the last few weeks of Dianne Masters' life.

Economou also damaged Masters' attempts to portray himself as a loving, faithful spouse. Throughout the fall of 1981, he asked Economou to cover for him on several occasions when he was supposed to be at business gatherings but actually was out with Sheila Mikel. Economou told Zenner about Alan's request that

Alan Masters on his way to the Dirksen Federal Building during his 1989 trial. *Photo credit: Daily Southtown*

Former Cook County Sheriff's Police Lt. James Keating, being interviewed during his first trial in 1986. *Photo credit: Daily Southtown*

Former Cook County Sheriff's Police Sgt. Clarke Buckendahl, who testified under a grant of immunity that he owned a house of prostitution with Alan Masters and Jack Bachman, and that he discussed with Alan who would investigate any incidents at the Masters' home. Even after the trial, then Sheriff James O'Grady left Buckendahl in place, until the media, led by columnist Phil Kadner, made it clear that this was unacceptable. Buckendahl resigned before he was scheduled to appear before the Merit Board.

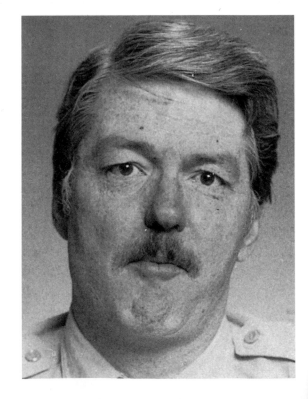

Michael Corbitt, former chief of the Willow Springs Police Department, now a three time loser in federal court. *Photo credit: Daily Southtown*

John Reed who worked the Masters' case for twenty-two months, providing continuity and hard work which led to the RICO indictments and convictions. He remains optimistic that someday he will be able to close the file on the murder charge.

Paul Sabin was an investigator for the Cook County Sheriff's Police when then Sheriff Richard Elrod assigned him to the Masters' case in the summer of 1986.

A visit with Brigitte Stark and her family in Germany helped Dianne decide to leave Alan in order to provide the warm atmosphere in which their child would thrive.

Tom Scorza, the Assistant U.S. Attorney who learned to loathe Messrs. Masters, Corbitt, and Keating, and successfully prosecuted them. *Photo credit:* Anita Krapp

Robert Colby replaced Paul Sabin as John Reed's partner on the Masters' case, spending many a messy hour going through Alan's trash.

Janet Bower Masters, Alan's third wife, who is raising Dianne's daughter under very difficult circumstances.

Patrick Tuite, Alan Masters' defense counsel. The former county prosecutor was popular in Chicago legal circles and respected for his ability to turn even the most repellent defendant into a sympathetic figure. Neither of these qualities helped him with the jury. *Photo credit:* Patrick Tuite

Bob Casey, who shared much with his friend Alan Masters, including Alan's mistress.

Economou arrange a telephone call between him and Mikel on March 20, 1982, the morning after Dianne's disappearance.

Zenner knew that Economou's "confession" would be of no small importance to Scorza's case, so he left Economou to get a grip on herself while he went directly to Scorza's office. Scorza was too busy to come over at that moment, so Zenner returned to put Economou in a holding pattern until the other prosecutor could free himself. After waiting a while, Zenner was concerned that the moment would be lost, and he revisited Scorza's office. This time, Scorza pried himself loose.

The difference in approach between the two prosecutors was never so pronounced. As he listened to Economou's tale, Scorza became visibly angry, berating her for sitting on information pertaining to a murder for five years. If his indignation was justified, it was not exactly the way to encourage a reluctant witness.

As a member of the bar and an officer of the court, Economou was duty bound to notify authorities. When he heard Economou's claim that she was too frightened to come forward, one investigator cracked, "Yeah, she was scared, and the money wasn't bad either." Her fears did not prevent her from seeking Alan's help in obtaining a judgeship after she left his employ.

Unlike most witnesses, Economou was permitted to prepare a written statement to read before the grand jury. This is sometimes done when an individual is expected to testify before several grand juries, because answers tend to vary and any inconsistencies could be used by a defense attorney to impeach the witness. But a law enforcement official familiar with federal grand juries says that professional courtesy also may have played a role.

On April 27, 1987, Economou also was questioned by John Reed and Paul Sabin, who because of O'Grady, did not know what she had told Zenner and Scorza. The lawyer had left Alan Masters' employ in 1984, but the memory clearly lingered on. She began by expressing her reluctance to discuss the case with members of the county cops because of the "strange" way in which the previous investigation had been handled. As she had in 1982, Economou told the sheriff's officers she had no information about Dianne Masters' death that would be of interest to them, going to the extent of suggesting that they check the reservation list of a Chicago luxury hotel to confirm a planned reconciliation between Alan and Dianne.

Asked for her theory of what happened, Economou said that she did not have one and that she did not want to think about the crime. To several questions she replied that she already had testi- fied to that before the grand jury, and she clearly thought it odd that Reed and Sabin were not aware of this.

A trembling Economou exclaimed, "Finally someone is coming around talking to people! It's about time you guys stopped the murders!" As the interview ended, Economou asked, "Whether people who know things should be concerned."

Sabin and Reed saved the double take inspired by Economou's last two remarks until they hit the parking lot outside her office. "Are you thinking what I'm thinking?" Sabin asked. "Yes," Reed replied. "*Murders* plural, and what does she know that she's scared to tell us?" Both men wished they could see those off limits grand jury transcripts.

CHAPTER 4

*O*ut in the suburban trenches, Sabin and Reed kept slogging along. In May 1987, Reed received a request for a lift from Ted Nykaza. Ted wanted to go to suburban Lyons where his pickup was being repaired. Nykaza just separated from the former Sheila Mikel, Alan Masters' special friend, and Ted was worried that Sheila might be working with Alan to set up Ted.

During the ride, Nykaza said Masters had told Ted to warn Reed off unless Reed had "paper," meaning a warrant. "Your own guys are reporting to Alan that your car was here," Nykaza told Reed. He also said that Alan first planned to have Dianne murdered in a home invasion, but Keating had argued convincingly against that plan on the basis it was "too obvious." Despite Nykaza's alcohol-related instability, his leads were checking out with increasing frequency. Masters had discussed the home invasion plan with others. Bit by bit, Nykaza was giving more details on Alan's reaction to the bottle tape. He claimed that in addition to Alan and himself, Joe Hein and Jim Keating had been involved, and he had been sent out of the room when the planning session began. Nykaza was prone to telling tall tales, but Reed knew from experience that "false in one doesn't mean false in all" and that people will sometimes lie about irrelevant matters for no logical reason.

Nykaza also admitted that following Dianne's disappearance, he planted a low tech bug from Radio Shack on the drapery rod in Alan's bedroom. Not long afterward, Alan had Ted sweep the Wolf Road house, and Nykaza located his own bug. This was the device Alan showed to Clarke Buckendahl.

Sgt. Joe Hein was one of Al's Pals who did not need to receive an alibi call; he was in Ireland when Dianne was killed. However, he was clearly nervous when approached by Reed or Sabin, perhaps because he worried that the Masters' home was bugged and that Hein's voice had been captured on tape during one of the get-rid-of-Dianne strategy sessions. When asked a direct question by Reed, he replied, "I really don't know if I was present when plans were discussed. Maybe I was around or maybe I stepped out of the room...would the tape show that?"

When Reed and Hein met in a fast food parking lot, Hein was concerned that a nearby van was wired. "A guy isn't much of a friend if he would involve you in something like this, is he?" Hein asked. "The only thing I heard was that Al had a violent fight with Dianne, made some calls, and had it handled....I'm finished, this is the end!" A few weeks later, Reed saw Hein again. With tears in his eyes, the sergeant said, "My police career is over. I never got a call from Al. All I want to do is protect my rights."

Because of the terms of the agreement with O'Grady, Reed did not know that Hein was interviewed by Tom Scorza on June 12, 1987. Hein admitted being present in Alan Masters' home for the repeated playing of Dianne's taped conversation with a "boyfriend," thus confirming Nykaza's story in part. Hein insisted that Alan showed very little emotion over the tapes, and Hein could not recall hearing any threats against Dianne. He reminded the feds that when Dianne disappeared, he was in Ireland with the St. Lawrence High School band. Hein did not volunteer that Alan Masters helped finance the trip by purchasing a space in an ad book.

When Dianne's body was found, Hein remembered the incident but could not accept the idea that Alan was involved. He insisted he never discussed the situation with Masters.

On July 14, 1987, Joe Hein failed an FBI polygraph test. The test administrator found his answers indicated deception when he answered "no" to the following questions: After listening to the recordings at Masters' house did you hear Masters say, "There was going to be a home invasion";...did you hear Masters say, "Dianne, the dog, and cat are going";...did you hear Masters make any threats against his wife;...prior to Dianne's disappearance, did you ever hear Alan Masters discuss any plans to kill her?

There was little flash or glamour in the plain hard work the sheriff's detectives were doing. Interviews with the people who got rid of their cars in the canal followed the same basic story: the owner had left a locked auto in a parking lot or on the street on Chicago's southwest side or in one of the southwest suburbs. Several were last seen outside one of the wateringholes in Willow Springs. When the owner was ready to depart, his or her car was missing. Upon reporting it as stolen, almost every insurance company paid the claim without question. It came as no surprise that there were many interrelationships, and several members of the Willow Springs PD were involved, especially an ex-lieutenant turned restauranteur.

Reed and Sabin studied records that gave the dates the autos were reported stolen, hoping to find someone who disposed of a car around the same time Dianne disappeared. They hit pay dirt with Edward Robert Griner, who had been convicted of mail fraud in April 1986 for filing a false insurance report.

In early 1982, Griner's sister was having trouble with her 1980 Ford Fairmont. Griner, an auto mechanic, found that the car needed major engine repair. He said he was feeling "a little lazy," so he tried to sell the parts. There were no takers.

Then Griner remembered that in the seventies he had been riding his dirt bike on the canal bank when he saw a car go into the water. This seemed a good solution to his sister's problem, so around 7:30 p.m. on March 17, 1982, Griner took the lemon to the same spot under the Wentworth Avenue bridge. After making sure no one else was present, Griner drove the car between the bridge pylons, rolled down the windows, turned off the ignition, and floored the accelerator with a hammer. After restarting the car, Griner got out, shifting into drive as he did so.

The car did not move. Ford had placed a safety device in the Fairmont to prevent just such activity. Frustrated but determined, Griner pushed. Once the car began to move, it took off very quickly, striking sparks as it crossed the ledge, whooshing at least twenty feet into the water, leaving only a few surface bubbles. He estimated that less than ten seconds elapsed from the time of takeoff to the sinking, and that the entire operation took about one minute. It was raining that night, which was helpful in keeping down his chances of being seen, but increased the messiness of the procedure. His pants and boots were covered with mud, and there were tire tracks and bootprints on the ground.

After checking a nearby bicycle path to make certain there had been no spectators, Griner walked to a tavern at the intersection of Willow Springs and Archer Roads and called a friend to pick him up.

Griner left behind a pair of large pliers, called channel locks, and a screwdriver which he thought he might need to jam the gas pedal. He was not able to return to collect the tools until about 10 a.m. on Saturday, March 20, 1982. Once again the site was empty. As he got out of his car, Griner immediately saw that not only were his tools gone, but even more important to Reed and Sabin, the ground had been raked or swept so neatly that there were no remains of the ruts or prints. Intrigued, Griner walked under the bridge where he had disposed of the Ford, right to the edge of the water. He noticed that there were scratches and gouges in the canal's rocky ledge to the left of where he had seen his sister's car disappear. On closer observation, Griner saw that someone had attempted to rub dirt over the larger chips in the rock.

Griner's description reminded John Reed of old Westerns he had seen at Saturday matinees. To hide telltale signs of their passing, Gene Autry and Pat Buttram would grab branches and swish them across the trail. Reed easily could visualize suburban cowboy Mike Corbitt doing the same thing after launching Dianne's Cadillac.

Frequently Reed and Sabin would split up so that they were able to reinterview people to resolve discrepancies or contradictions, as well as to obtain confirmation of new information. The work load was heavy, but it was rewarding. There was a sense in the community that the tide had turned against Alan Masters, and it might be safe to talk about him.

This attitude received a boost in May 1987, when Michael Corbitt was indicted in federal court for conspiring to allow an illegal betting operation to open in Willow Springs and to extort protection money, the result of his encounter with Damron; abetting arson with Raymond Gluszek in burning down the Livery Tavern; extortion of two pinball machines from Gluszek, of $7,000 from a Lemont business owner to arrange for return of heavy equipment seized by the sheriff's police, of two Smith and Wesson handguns from a suburban gun-shop owner in return for a WSPD badge, of $1,600 in carpeting and $5,000 in discounts from a Posen man, again in return for a WSPD badge; arranging to have his own home burgled so that he could collect the insurance on stolen items, including one of the guns he had just extorted; selling a police badge for $1,000.

Lawrence Camerano, an admitted car thief, was in an expansive mood when Reed and Sabin visited his Orland Park home in May 1987. Glaucoma was putting an end to Camerano's career, and he was willing to describe how, beginning in the 1970s, Alan Masters successfully represented him by fixing cases with crooked cops and corrupt judges. Alan was expensive, but effective. The thief/attorney relationship became so close that Masters once asked Camerano to steal a judge's car so the jurist could claim the insurance.

A bit of a philosopher, Camerano ruminated on the flaws in local law enforcement. "I'm a thief twenty-four hours a day," he said. "The trouble with some cops is that they want to be policemen by day and thieves at night." Camerano also had standards. He and John Reed lived in the same suburb, and Camerano assured the detective that he would never dream of fouling his nest by stealing from a neighbor.

Masters looked upon Camerano as a confidant about his troubles with Dianne. Sometimes Camerano would approach Masters for legal counsel, only to find that Alan wanted a shoulder to cry on. On one such occasion, an exhausted Alan explained that a p.i. who was following Dianne discovered she was having an affair. "She's laughing at me," Alan said, his face beet red. "I would be happy to see her dead." A couple of weeks before Dianne disappeared, Masters said the p.i. had provided him with photos of Dianne and her lover, adding, "I want to get rid of her. I won't let her get the child, I'll do something serious. I'm going to get that jewelry back that she put in a safety deposit box."

As had so many others, Camerano suggested that Jim Keating and Mike Corbitt were Alan's closest friends and most likely allies in the murder plot. When the interview ended, Camerano commented that "anyone with half a brain knows that Masters had his old lady whacked."

And anyone with half a brain knew that besides Masters, Corbitt, and Keating, there had to be a fourth, perhaps even a fifth person involved. It would have been risky for Masters to leave his young daughter alone, and it wasn't Keating's way to become physically involved. It was becoming clear that Corbitt drove Dianne's car to the canal, but there had to be another man driving Corbitt's vehicle. By now, Reed had a list of a dozen possible suspects, some of them policemen and former cops. Most of them were close associates of Mike Corbitt who were known to Alan Masters. Most frequently mentioned was Anthony Barone, a Chicago PD officer and Corbitt's brother-in-law. Also, early on, one of Reed's most reliable sources named the former Berwyn cop who had met with Charlie Bates, Corbitt, and Masters in 1980.

CHAPTER 5

*A*ugust 1987 marked the first anniversary of the no-holds-barred investigation of the Masters' case, and the sheriff's cops were optimistic that they would have their day in court. There was one setback; Paul Sabin was leaving to use his legal training as an assistant state's attorney. John Reed joked with his ex-partner that someday Sabin would head a murder prosecution against Alan Masters, et al., after the feds were through with them.

Reed would have to find a replacement, and he had just the man in mind. Robert Colby joined the sheriff's police in 1969, in the days where cops, especially Chicago area cops, were routinely spat upon. They had worked as partners before, and there was mutual liking and respect. Most cops have a second job: Bob Colby was a pilot certified to give flight lessons. During a flight over the principal sites in the case, he showed Reed how to handle a plane. "Someday you'll have to teach me how to land," Reed cracked.

In the late 1970s, Colby was assigned to the state's attorney's police detail, and he was there when Dianne Masters disappeared. Like a lot of people, at first Colby thought she might be just another runaway wife. Colby had never appeared in a court case where Masters was involved, but he knew enough about the lawyer that he could understand why a woman might want to decamp. After just a few days Colby began to suspect it was what cops call a "domestic [homicide]," and this was confirmed in Colby's mind when Dianne's jewelry was found.

299

In the summer of 1987, Colby was working in the sheriff's criminal investigations unit. One day, John Reed stopped Colby in the hallway to say, "Paul's gone, and I'm looking for someone to help me. Take some time and think about it." But Bob Colby did not have to think about it. He welcomed the chance to work with John Reed again, and the case was certainly a challenging one.

This investigation of brother officers was particularly poignant for the Colbys. Joan Colby's father was a Chicago policeman who was killed in the line of duty and whose death continues to haunt the family. In April 1969, Sgt. James R. Schaffer was assigned to a department store bombing case on Chicago's southeast side. A hapless shopper in the children's section of the store picked up a can labeled "peaches" and was blown to bits. Joan remembers her father coming home that night, exhausted and depressed by the event. A week later, Schaffer received a tip that the bomber was holed up in a neighborhood apartment. When Schaffer and his partner took the bait, they were shot to death. Frank Kulak, who had a history of leaving bombs where he hoped children would find them, was judged unfit to stand trial due to mental illness and was sent to a state institution for the criminally insane.

The comparison between her father's sacrifice and the criminal greed rampant among the police in the Masters' case was personally painful. Like the Reeds, the Colbys felt that the Masters case was like a cancerous growth that had to be removed to protect honest law enforcement officers from suffering, and if Bob could help, it would be important, even if time-consuming and unpopular.

Reed passed the increasingly weighty file to Colby, saying "Take your time." When the word got out on the sheriff's grapevine, some of Colby's coworkers expressed their envy at Colby's luck in working with a guy like John Reed. Others gave Colby a wide berth. Both men received more than the usual number of hang-up calls at home, and there were a few anonymous threats, too.

CHAPTER 6

$\mathcal{B}$eginning in October 1987, there was another good reason to avoid Reed and Colby: they were spending a good deal of time going through Alan Masters' garbage. Acting on a tip from a solid source, the men drove into the alley behind Masters' office, where they went through four uncovered, unmarked fifty-five-gallon drums filled with trash material belonging to Masters.

Some coworkers find such duty disgusting, but to Reed and Colby, it was just part of the job. "I'm very big in garbage," Reed would tell whichever bemused evidence technician he had asked for a supply of the white latex gloves used at crime scenes. Not that he needed to explain; it was just part of Reed's nature, one of the things that made him popular among the men.

Reed and Colby quickly reduced their garbage picking to a science. Three times a week, Monday, Wednesday, and Friday, the garbage truck visited the dumpster behind Masters' Summit law office, and once a week, on Friday usually, there was a pickup in front of Masters' house. When making the office run, Reed or Colby would simply drive down the public alley in an unmarked squad and grab anything behind Alan's building. Out in Palos, where alleys are declasse, they had a deal with the garbage man to take Masters' domestic detritus around the corner to Romiga Lane, where the investigators would shove it into the trunk of their car.

301

On one occasion, Bob Colby was a little late for the home garbage collection and had to chase the garbage truck through the winding lanes of Palos. When he caught up with it, the driver was able to sort out the Masters' leavings. "That's the house where the pretty lady was murdered, isn't it?" he asked Colby. On Colby's confirmation, the man looked sad. "She kept the most beautiful garden. I used to see her out on her hands and knees, taking care of her flowers. She'd stop and wave and smile at me. She was the only one who ever did that," he continued. "Say, do you want anybody else's garbage?"

Once the collection was made, Reed and Colby would be off to the nearest forest preserve, to find an empty fifty-five-gallon drum. There they would go through every piece of trash, two men dressed in suits, wearing latex gloves, falling on pieces of garbage with gladsome cries. They were the recipients of more than a few odd looks from passing nature lovers and forest preserve employees.

The gloves had been more than paying for themselves lately; the last few bags from the house had dog feces mixed in with the garbage. During his years in trash, Reed had developed certain rules. If things like excrement started appearing suddenly, chances were the generators of the garbage had become aware of the surveillance, and it was a good idea to lay back for a while, checking every now and then just to be sure the members of the household had not tired of the game. From experience they found that anything used to wrap coffee grounds merited extra scrutiny.

Arlene Reed was accustomed to having her husband arrive home wearing a slight l'air du garbage. Once she observed what she thought was rice on his shoes, until it started moving. "Do I have to sleep in the crawl space?" Reed asked jokingly. Arlene's only requirement was that he hose down immediately.

His fascination with trash as a investigatory tool began when John Reed was about six years old. In those days, the Reed family lived in Chicago, where the alleys were interesting places. Of all the characters who traveled there, the most fascinating to Jackie

Reed was the rags-old-iron man, so-called because of the distinctive cry yodeled to attract housewives who wanted to get rid of old clothes and leaky pots and pans. The rags-old-iron man had a hook-and-pan scale and paid a flat rate per pound. Reed does not recall how long he had the man under surveillance, but one day when he was at a neighbor's back door collecting worn out household goods, Jackie clambered onto the back of the truck and jumped onto the hook. He was reasonably sure how much he weighed, having just had a school physical, and he found that according to the trash collector's scale, he had recently lost a substantial number of pounds. He kept the knowledge to himself, but the experience taught him the importance of listening to gut instincts.

Reed's garbage checks had enabled him to solve more than one complicated case. But there was a downside, besides the mess, at least prior to the ruling by the U.S. Supreme Court that while a man's home might be his castle, once his garbage left it, the trash was fair game. In the course of his investigation of the murder of a biker's girlfriend by a rival gang, Reed found evidence in the trash that implicated several gang members. As a result, Reed was sued for invasion of privacy, but one of the bikers committed suicide while out on bond, and the case died with him. "Being sued for that much money doesn't look good on a mortgage application," Reed reflected.

Reed's faith in garbage again was rewarded in the case of John Annerino. Annerino was a city employee and part-time clergyman who was suspected of hiring several thugs to kill his former roommate. Good help being hard to find, these men bungled several attempts on the designated target but did manage to murder a county policeman. A police slaying is always high priority, and Reed was assigned the case. The leads were thinning out when Reed found a piece of wax with some strange printing on it in Annerino's garbage. When he held the wax up to the mirror, Reed discovered it bore the names of all the men involved in the conspiracy and murder, providing the direct link that had been missing.

Whenever Reed or Colby found anything resembling evidence in Alan Masters' garbage, they would reach for their supply of plain brown paper bags. No Ziploc plastic for them; these make a good visual in a crime movie, but in real life they stimulate fungus growths or the forming of acid compounds. By the time it was needed, what originally appeared to be important evidence could look like a child's science project. Meaningful but moist garbage was air dried by a small fan or hair drier, and then it was time for a mundane but pristine brown paper bag.

Whenever possible, copies were made of the garbage and it was logged in. Then the G-man (for garbage, not government) who made the find would write his name over the sealed bag and hand-carry it to Tom Scorza's office. Scorza would sign for it and place it in a secure place to protect the chain of evidence. Any break could make the garbage unusable if the case ever came to trial.

At first they made some valuable finds. Dianne's organ donor card was rescued from the trash behind Alan's office. Dianne was known to have carried this in her wallet because in 1982 Illinois did not have a space on an individual's driver's license for such dona-tions. On the card, Dianne had filled in her name and checked blanks indicating she wanted to donate her eyes and kidneys. By the time her body was found, her eyes were missing and her kid-neys were of no use to anyone.

There was also a list of books in Dianne's writing. One was called *Scream Quietly or the Neighbors Will Hear*; another, *Conjugal Crime: Understanding and Changing the Wifebeating Pattern*. On the same slip of paper, Alan scribbled the name of a doctor at the S & M Therapy Clinic at the University of Chicago. Both of these were interesting, but best of all, Reed found a napkin in Keating's handwriting that referred to Lary Damron. Thanks to Alan Masters, Reed did see some parts of the grand jury transcripts because Alan was making copies and throwing some of them in the garbage.

The good luck with garbage ended for a time after Tom Scorza met with Janet Bower, a young woman who was living with Alan Masters. Janet entered Alan Masters' life in June 1982. He mentioned to Janet's mother, one of his closest personal friends, that he was looking for someone to take care of Georgie. Barbara Bower suggested her seventeen-year-old daughter, who was recovering from a whiplash injury and was looking for something to do. Janet was not so sure she liked children well enough to take on the job, but Alan urged her to at least try it. Georgie's fifth birthday was just a month away. The little girl might have been unaware of the gossip about her father's responsibility for her mother's disappearance, but she was going through a difficult patch. Georgie was puzzled about Dianne's absence, remembering that the last time she saw her mother was the only time Dianne did not say goodbye.

Soon after Janet arrived on the job, she watched as Georgie played with Dear Deer, a stuffed reindeer Dianne had given her daughter. "Why did my mom with the yellow hair leave us?" Georgie asked. "She didn't leave you," Janet replied, somewhat at a loss. "Yes, she did," Georgie observed, adding with perfect logic, "She's not here." Soon after this incident, Janet began to take Georgie to a therapist for counseling.

The little girl won Janet's heart immediately. Her own mother and father had divorced when Janet was a little older than Georgie, and she knew how difficult it was for children to lose a parent that way. It was hard to imagine what it must be like to have one just disappear without explanation. It was a tough year for Georgie; during a summer trip to Florida, she was in a serious automobile accident with her father. Her injuries, including a broken jaw, kept her in the hospital for four days and slowed down her summer activities.

Originally, Janet planned to go back to school in September when Georgie was entering kindergarten, but by that time she was so fond of the child that she decided to stay on.

When Janet enrolled in classes at Moraine Valley on a part-time basis, she made no effort to hide that she was working for Alan Masters. In fact, in her speech course, she got up and gave a talk about her job, to the surprise of her instructor. This teacher, like Gen Capstaff and several others, warned Janet that she might be in over her head. They were concerned that the pretty strawberry blonde was just too young and inexperienced to understand that Alan Masters was capable of anything.

At first Janet maintained her own residence, but as the job began to look more permanent, she moved into Masters' house. Not only had her living circumstances changed; so did her relationship with Alan, which evolved into an intimate one despite the thirty-year difference in age.

By time of her fall 1987 meeting with Tom Scorza at Water Tower Place, there were rumors that Alan and Janet were married. "I will tell you how your husband killed his previous wife," Scorza began. This was not a great conversational icebreaker. Besides, Janet was surprised that with all the resources of the federal government, Scorza did not know that she was still unmarried. After twenty minutes, during which time Scorza brought up the garbage detail, Janet said, "You don't know he is responsible." Scorza replied, "We can put you in jail for withholding evidence." Soon after this exchange Janet left.

Janet rushed home to tell Alan about the trash surveillance. Masters became irate but had to admit that the authorities were on firm legal ground. So at home the couple retaliated by tossing dog feces into the garbage, and at the office, after reportedly indulging in one of his epic rages, Alan installed a shredder.

Why Masters, a lawyer who reiterated his claims to brilliance so frequently that many people believed him, a man who called himself the "master fixer," would wait five years to get rid of incriminating material, and how he could be so dumb as to just throw it into the garbage can, was a puzzler.

Reed discussed his theory with Colby. "When Dianne disappeared in 1982, everything in Alan's life went into sort of a freeze frame. He was taking Valium and plenty of it; he told anyone who would listen that you could get through anything on Valium. For years, he had been in complete control of circumstances around him. Until Dianne decided she wanted a divorce. By that time, worse luck for her, he'd been operating outside and above the law for so long without anyone laying a glove on him that her murder was the only logical answer. To him."

John Reed and Bob Colby continued to monitor garbage disposal, but for a while they retrieved little of value. They did hear that as Alan's trash tantrum approached critical mass, he referred to them in unflattering terms. "If that's all they have to do, they can get fucked in their ass," he roared.

"There's one thing you can say about Alan Masters," Reed observed. "Just one?" Colby asked. "I'm talking about his way with words," Reed replied. "Wish I could turn a phrase like that."

CHAPTER 7

*I*n response to his May indict-
ment, Mike Corbitt entered a not-guilty plea, and his trial began
on October 8, 1987. Tom Scorza opened with a bombshell: Corbitt
had forged a Florida car rental receipt that was to be used as part
of his alibi defense. Corbitt had come up with the receipt only the
previous week.

If valid, the receipt would have shown that Corbitt was in
Florida on May 27, 1982, the day he was supposed to have met with
Lary Damron and Joe Marren outside the Willow Springs PD.
Tampering with evidence was nothing new to Corbitt, but his luck
had run out. The attempt to change the date was completely
inept. Scorza demanded that Corbitt's bond be revoked and
declared he was prepared to file additional charges of obstruction
of justice.

After studying the document, Judge Prentice Marshall said, "It
is evident to the untrained eye that the date has been written, and
it is a coincidence that letters on the right hand side had been cut
off. This document is going to have to be authenticated." When
Corbitt's attorneys argued that they had no knowledge of the
forgery, Marshall reproved them, "Don't protest too much; no one
has accused you." He also spoke sharply to them about accepting a
Xerox copy as evidence. The judge then gave Corbitt until 2 p.m.
to decide whether or not he would change his plea.

Corbitt's lawyers beat the clock by an hour, informing Scorza at 1 p.m. that their client was ready to enter a guilty plea. Back before Judge Marshall, Scorza made a strong case for keeping Corbitt locked up pending sentencing. In violation of his bond, Corbitt had left Illinois twice without notifying authorities; while under federal surveillance in Florida, Corbitt was caught on film in the vicinity of airplanes used for transporting drugs and drug money; he spent $300,000 on an ocean-going yacht moored in Florida; in Illinois, he was seen in the company of known crime figures.

In revoking Corbitt's bond, Judge Marshall referred to Corbitt as a man "very apprehensive about his future, and justifiably so. He is willing to take extraordinary steps to avoid the consequences."

Then Corbitt was led away by federal marshals to the Metropolitan Correctional Center, the same Chicago holding prison where his friend Jim Keating had been kept.

Less than a week after Scorza's October surprise, Corbitt's attorneys were back in court to ask that his bond revocation be lifted. They offered his home in lieu of cash and denied that Corbitt would skip town because its resulting forfeiture would deprive his son, who has Down's syndrome, of a dwelling.

But Scorza kept up the pressure. "Why wasn't Mr. Corbitt thinking of his boy when he put twenty-five thousand dollars into a Stingray?" he blazed back. The judge found it hard to believe that given the "predicament he was in, [Corbitt] goes out and buys a twenty-five-thousand-dollar car." Terming Corbitt "an unstable member of our society," Judge Marshall added, "These are not the transactions of a man who plans to suck in his gut, do his time, and return to his wife. I'm not persuaded he does not represent a risk of flight."

As part of his argument, Scorza announced that a new federal grand jury was looking into Corbitt's possible involvement in "a 1982 murder." He did not mention Dianne Masters; he did not need to do so. The reporters and the ladies in the beauty parlor knew which unsolved case Scorza had in mind.

By November 1987, Scorza believed the odds on obtaining an indictment of Alan Masters were good. Besides hard work, there seemed to be another, more elusive factor. Serendipity is not a technique discussed in police manuals or criminal lawbooks. But Tom Scorza, not a man given to whimsy or flights of fancy, saw no other explanation for some of the twists and turns in the Masters' case. Except, perhaps, John Reed's theory of divine intervention.

That the incredibly heavy work load could be handled by five men seemed nothing short of miraculous to Scorza in his role as ringmaster. On any given weekday, Reed and Colby were interviewing sources after they sorted through Alan Masters' garbage. Harris and Griggs were also doing interviews. In addition to prosecuting Corbitt, Scorza was reading the investigative reports and talking to important potential witnesses, as well as conducting grand jury sessions. Building a case against the trifecta of sleaze definitely had the potential for consuming the lives of the law enforcement quintet, but they did not permit it to do so.

Gossip about the federal investigation was getting out to the southwest suburbs, especially the legal and the police communities. The ladies in the beauty parlors began to hope that after all the time elapsed, the men responsible for killing Dianne Masters would be brought to trial.

CHAPTER 8

*I*n early November 1987, Reed and Colby tried again to obtain access to Masters' file held in the Cook County state's attorney's office. Again, they were rebuffed, this time by Robert Forguc, head of the Organized Crime Unit. There was too much material to copy, Forgue said, and when the sheriff's detectives asked if they could just review the file, Forgue refused. Eventually a few pages were forwarded to Reed. It may have been a coincidence that Joe Hein's office was a few doors away on the same floor, and Alan Masters seemed to have almost instant knowledge of new entries in the county prosecutor's files.

With the parade of witnesses before the federal grand jury under way, the men close to Alan Masters began to show signs of stress. One of these was Howard Vanick. On November 20, 1987, at 10 p.m., Vanick arrived at Palos Country Club where John Reed was working a security detail. For the first time, Vanick admitted seeing Dianne and Jim outside the Charley Horse Restaurant where Vanick had gone to visit his waitress girlfriend. According to Vanick, the couple were "arm in arm and all chummy," leading him to think, "What a cunt," about Dianne.

In a dazzling display of the double standard, Vanick said that any cop who saw his divorce lawyer's wife out with someone else would "grab the plate." The lieutenant waffled as to whether he ran the Jim's license plate through the police computer and denied calling Alan Masters, saying he might have passed the information on to Bachman or Buckendahl.

Vanick was extremely anxious that his longtime partner be interviewed and called Ron Bennett in Reed's presence. When Bennett arrived at the country club, Vanick quickly said, "John here has some allegations that we followed Dianne Masters, which of course is not true!" Reed was intrigued by this because he never posed this question to Vanick. But Jack Bachman had told Reed that Vanick followed Dianne from the restaurant, reporting that she went directly home. Vanick had just backed up Bachman.

In front of Bennett, Vanick accused Reed of "not being candid with me. You think I'm not telling you everything. Did Scorza send you to interview me?" When Reed asked Vanick to leave the table so he could talk to Bennett in private, Vanick did so, muttering as he went. Bennett acknowledged that Vanick had pointed out Dianne Masters to him and called Jim Keating about the incident.

Before the interview could continue, Vanick returned to ask what Bennett said. Reed replied that Bennett was free to repeat his statement. When Bennett got to the part about Vanick calling Keating, Vanick became visibly disturbed, saying, "Come on, partner, that's not what happened!" Bennett replied, "Well, you called someone."

At 2:30 a.m. on the twenty-first, Arlene Reed heard her husband's car pull into the driveway. She slipped out of bed and down the stairs to take the chain lock off the door. To her surprise, an enraged Howard Vanick charged through the door behind Reed, as Arlene, clad in a sheer nightie, tried to keep to the shadows. She also plucked a gun from behind a sofa pillow in case Vanick lost control.

Reed showed Vanick a note from the Willow Springs PD stating that Vanick called Masters about the infamous lunch. "That did not happen that way," Vanick shouted. "I'm going to the FBI and tell them what happened to save my reputation. I feel used."

The next evening, Vanick phoned Reed, admitting he did run Jim's license plate through the computer but did not file a report on this when Dianne disappeared or when her body was found. He also admitted that when he heard that two Orland Park officers were suspected of watching Dianne, he knew it was a case of mistaken identity which he did nothing to correct. Vanick felt his reputation had been tarnished, and Reed was responsible.

On November 30, Vanick appeared before the federal grand jury with a slightly impaired memory. Scorza brought out the fact that Vanick paid no money to Masters regarding the divorce suit, contrary to standard practice which requires such fees to be paid up front.

Then the prosecutor moved on to the missing person's investigation beginning March 19, 1982. Vanick admitted that no detailed search was made for bloodstains or signs of a struggle. Although the police returned to the house a few days later, Vanick never obtained a search warrant.

Asked by Scorza if there was any interference in the investigation, Vanick replied, "...nobody ever told me, 'Do not investigate this case.'" The interference was more subtle.

Vanick vividly remembered his encounter with Jim Keating on Alan Masters' driveway. "There is only one way for this investigation to go...in my opinion Alan Masters was responsible for the disappearance of his wife," Vanick told Keating. Keating called Vanick "unobjective" and warned he could be replaced, adding, "...that any benefit of the doubt was to go on the side of Alan Masters." Other than being told not to try the case in the press, Vanick could come up with no other specific instances.

Then Scorza bore down on Vanick's knowledge of Dianne's affair with Jim. The lieutenant recalled writing down Jim's license plate but could not remember what he did with it. When Scorza asked if he might have given it to Buckendahl, Vanick replied, "If you ask me did I, I'd have to say there's a possibility..."

The prosecutor pressed on. "...After Dianne Masters disappeared, you understood that her having an affair with an individual would be relevant to your investigation, isn't that correct?" Vanick's reply was not to the point, although he did admit that passing the information around was something he probably would do today in similar circumstances.

Scorza was not to be hornswoggled. "What I'm asking you is, you realized, didn't you, on March 19, 1982, that piece of intelligence from a month earlier was an important piece of information in your investigation?"

"I felt that it probably had some bearing on it, that's correct, but in all honesty, I kind of minimized it. And since then I frankly still do..."

"We're not interested in you minimizing, we are interested in what you thought at the time," Scorza interjected. "You understood at the time that it would be relative, right?"

Vanick finally agreed infidelity was frequently a motive for murder.

Asked if he filed an official report on obtaining the license number of Dianne's lover, Vanick acknowledged that he had not done so. He claimed he reported it to the FBI in April 1982, while he was conducting the missing person's investigation. If he did so, no record ever surfaced. Vanick also testified that in the summer of 1982, he informed FBI Agents Pecoraro and O'Rourke about the "subtle" pressure he was under to close out the case without involving the bureau. Again, there is no record of this contact. In the memo Vanick wrote on May 20, 1982, Vanick recounted how he assured the agents that allegations of police "nonobjectivity" were unfounded.

CHAPTER 9

*J*ohn Reed never knew where he might find his next lead. One day while gassing up his county car, he was approached by evidence technician Bill Dado. A few days previously when Dado was ill, a telephone repairman came to fix Dado's phone. When the repairman learned that Dado was with the sheriff's police, he revealed that sometime in 1985, he was assigned to repair phone lines inside Alan Masters' Palos home. While troubleshooting the lines, the repairman entered a dirt-floored basement crawl space where he saw two spent shell casings. The repairman thought this information might be of help in the renewed investigation, but he but he did not know whom to call.

The next day John Reed interviewed John Hess, a veteran of thirty years with the telephone company. Hess told Reed that he picked up one of the cartridges, and because of his familiarity with ammunition, he was able to identify it as .22 caliber rimfire, although he could not say whether it was .22 long or .22 long rifle. If the latter, it would fit the bullets that had been fired into Dianne Masters' brain. Just to make sure Hess knew what he was talking about, Reed showed him another shell casing, which Hess quickly and correctly classified as a .25 caliber center fire primer. Based on Hess' recollections, Reed drew a sketch of the Masters' basement, indicating the location of the shell casings.

The information was obviously important, important enough for Scorza to obtain a federal search warrant. However, the FBI

317

agents would have to wait to execute it. On December 18, 1987, Masters left for Florida with his daughter and Janet Bower.

According to Reed's anonymous sources, Masters was anticipating an indictment any day and was not going to make it easy for the government to arraign him. After a short period in Florida, Masters and Georgie would accompany Janet to her parents' farm in Ohio, where he was convinced the government would never find him.

The sources proved inaccurate. On December 27, 1987, the bell rang at the house on Wolf Road. When she opened the door, Janet Bower was startled to find a phalanx of FBI men, headed by Ivan Harris, armed with a warrant to search the premises. Janet recovered enough to request that the agents remove their muddy shoes before tracking it through the house.

The agents found the casing where the telephone repairman had left it, but ballistics tests revealed that it did not match the cartridge found in Dianne's sleeve. That would have been too much good luck. According to Janet, the people who owned the house before Dianne and Alan used to stand on the basement stairs and fire into the crawl space for target practice, accounting for the presence of the cartridges.

Reed and Colby wished they could interview Janet, but after her session with Scorza, she was off limits. Instead, they talked to her friends. Some believed that Dianne was murdered in the basement recreation room; they claimed to have felt the presence of Dianne's restless spirit there. On one occasion, Janet and her chums tried to test spots on the carpeting to see if they were bloodstains. The carpeting had been cleaned since Dianne's death, and the test was not conclusive.

Also, soon after Janet went to work for Alan, she found a canvas tote bag behind a desk. It was filled with MVCC paperwork and matched the description of the bag Dianne had with her when she left the Village Courtyard. When Janet called it to Alan's attention, he said he would call the college and have someone pick it up. No such call was ever received.

Georgie Masters was not interviewed in 1982, although it is not uncommon for even younger children to be questioned. The girl reportedly was a very sound sleeper; one night, the burglar alarm went off, and she did not stir. On another occasion, friends said that as a test, Janet screamed at the top of her lungs, and the child did not stir. Scorza and the investigators agreed that they would not attempt to interview Georgie about what she might have heard or seen the night her mother disappeared. Georgie had suffered enough, and when the case went to trial, a jury might find it distasteful if the government involved Dianne's daughter.

Late in December, John Reed encountered Howard Vanick at the sheriff's Maybrook office. After reading case notes of an interview with Bachman, Vanick wanted to make it clear that he did not follow Dianne to the Charley Horse. When Reed asked whether Vanick followed her *from* the restaurant, he would not reply directly. "It's been six years. I can't remember. What about Rosie [a nickname for Robert Rosignal]. I don't want to read in the newspaper that I followed Dianne Masters." Vanick complained about his insomnia and accused Reed of trying to embarrass him. Before the men parted, Vanick added, "I'm willing to take a polygraph." He never did.

Just before the end of the year, Vanick phoned Reed at home at 11:30 p.m. Several colleagues asked him if he had a problem with the federal grand jury, and he demanded that Reed put a stop to the gossip. He also threatened to file a complaint with internal investigations. As he had before, Vanick warned Reed that the sergeant could find himself in a "bad spot" for investigating other policemen. He had close friends in the FBI, and they claimed Reed was responsible for "pushing" the Masters' case with Scorza.

In January 1988, Dianne's brother phoned John Reed to say that he had hired a former U. S. attorney to file a suit for custody of his niece, whom he had not seen since Dianne's memorial service five years earlier, when and if an indictment was handed down. He had also been advised to file a civil suit against the Cook County Sheriff's PD because of the department's involvement in the cover-up.

There were frequent tips that Alan was involved in child pornography, and ugly rumors were circulating about the nature of his relationship with his daughter. Alan attributed both to Dianne's brother. A social worker from the Illinois Department of Children and Family Services called to schedule an appointment to talk to Georgie. There had been a child abuse complaint, and it would have to be investigated. The social worker spent about twenty minutes with the girl but found no cause to remove her from her father's custody. Alan reacted by taking steps to make Janet Georgie's legal guardian in his absence.

Mike Corbitt was to have been sentenced in December 1987, but when he was brought before Judge Marshall, Corbitt denied his part in the torching of the Livery Tavern, saying, "I never had any pre-information on this fire." Corbitt also denied extorting the pinball machines.

A furious Scorza informed the court of Raymond Gluszek's grand jury testimony that he had sought and obtained Corbitt's approval before the fire and that Gluszek acted on Corbitt's advice when he dumped his clunker in the canal. Referring to the launching of unwanted cars, Scorza observed, "it seems half of Willow Springs did [this]." He cited the example of WSPD Lt. James Bonello, who was in charge of the arson investigation at the Livery bar. Bonello was connected personally to three of the cars dredged from the canal, and it came as no surprise that he was unsuccessful in investigating the fire loss of the police chief's pal.

Under the judge's questioning, Corbitt admitted that he met with Lary Damron to set up an illegal gambling establishment in

Willow Springs and that he obtained permission to do so from local crime bosses Carmen and Sal Bastone, as well as Jim Keating and other members of the CCSPD Vice Control Unit. Sal Bastone owned Rent All Amusements of Chicago, the company which provided the pinball machines and pool tables to the burned-out Livery Tavern. Corbitt's lawyer also represented the Bastone brothers. On January 11, 1988, Corbitt, characterized by Scorza as a "prostitute wearing a badge," was sentenced to four years out of a maximum of sixty. Dressed in federal prison blues, Corbitt wept, probably in relief at the short sentence. "I don't have any excuse for what I've done. It was wrong. It was illegal. I would like to apologize to my family, to my mother, to the court, to my community."

But the community was not buying Corbitt's crocodile tears. Back in Willow Springs, there was outrage over what many in the community saw as little more than a rap on Corbitt's knuckles. At a meeting of the Willow Springs Board of Trustees, a shouting match erupted between those who were Corbitt partisans and those who felt Corbitt had ruined the name of Willow Springs forever.

It was particularly upsetting to the residents that in his sentencing remarks, Judge Marshall made reference to the many favorable letters sent to him by elected and appointed public officials from Willow Springs as a considerable factor in the sentencing. The village board had not authorized any letter-writing campaign, and it immediately passed a resolution that any such communications with the judge were unauthorized. The village attorney was instructed to request copies of the letters from Judge Marshall. The kindest view was that Judge Marshall had been conned. "Never trust a guy with two last names," one Willow resident observed. In any event, respect for the justice system took another heavy hit.

The *Southtown Economist* newspaper chain sued under the Freedom of Information Act and made the letters public. Former mayor Frank Militello observed, "It's a miscarriage of justice that he didn't get twenty years. You try to clean up a town and despite your efforts, it goes back to being the way it was...He could be out of jail in a year or so, and he'll still have all the bribe money he extorted from taxpayers. I'm the guy who threw him out of office, but it took me sixteen months and a lot of time in court and a lot of money. When something like this happens, you wonder if it pays to be honest. But at least I can still look at myself in the mirror every morning."

Behind the headlines, Mike Corbitt was playing let's make a deal with the federal government. He disliked Chicago's noisy, crowded Metropolitan Correction Center. As an ex-cop, he was kept in protective custody, which meant he spent very little time out of his cell, and it was driving him crazy. On at least one occasion, he got into a fight with a member of the El Rukns, formerly the Blackstone Ranger street gang.

After some preliminary negotiating, Corbitt and his attorney met with Tom Scorza, Ivan Harris, and Roger Griggs on two occasions in January 1988. The arrangement was that they would listen to Corbitt's "proffer," a legal term for the body of information Corbitt was willing to provide. If the feds accepted Corbitt's proffer, he might get a short sentence, or even immunity from prosecution in the Masters case.

Corbitt admitted receiving kickbacks on cases he referred to Masters, to listening to the bottle-in-the-vagina tape in Masters' office, and to being solicited to murder Dianne on several occasions. At one point, Alan gave Corbitt the key to the Masters' home, which Corbitt returned after several days. Corbitt claimed he refused to be drawn into the home invasion plan, suggesting Masters obtain a divorce. According to Corbitt, Alan refused to do so because he was afraid he would lose Georgie.

Corbitt also admitted that he followed Dianne from Moraine Valley to Artie G's restaurant but claimed he left before Dianne. It was clear to Corbitt that Alan had others tailing Dianne because he seemed to know every move she made. According to Corbitt, he was in Masters' office when Howard Vanick called with Jim Church's license number.

In March 1982, Corbitt saw Masters at the Fifth District courthouse. Alan claimed a reconciliation with Dianne. To celebrate, he wanted to buy her a new car. But first he wanted Corbitt to dump her Cadillac in the canal so that an insurance claim could be filed. Corbitt agreed to do so on one day's notice.

A couple of days before Dianne disappeared, the two men met at one of their favorite restaurants. Corbitt told Alan to leave the car in back of the Blue Front Tavern on Archer Avenue in Willow Springs. The key would be under the mat. Masters agreed to have it there around midnight on Thursday.

Corbitt overslept, waking up around 2:20 a.m. He hurried to the saloon, to find Dianne's car waiting. Parked nearby was a Jeep and Corbitt noted down the plate number. As he was launching the Cadillac into the canal, Corbitt heard a noise in the rear which he associated with a flat tire. When he walked back to the Blue Front, the Jeep was gone.

The following day, Corbitt received a telephone call telling him that Alan Masters had reported Dianne missing. When he dialed Masters from a pay phone, Alan said they would talk later. Corbitt went to Masters' office a few days later, asking what had become of Dianne. At this, Masters laughed out loud, saying, "You know where she is, she was in the car,' adding that Corbitt should not worry because Keating and the sheriff's police were handling the case.

According to Corbitt, Masters claimed Dianne was having four or five affairs, and he did not want to lose everything. Someone named Bobby shot Dianne when she got out of her car. When she continued to make noises, Masters shot her a second time. Corbitt suggested that "Bobby" might be Robert Rosignal. Eventually, Corbitt collected eight thousand dollars in cash as payment for getting rid of the car.

Scorza concluded that Corbitt was not being truthful, and no deal was struck.

CHAPTER 10

Colby and Reed made a point of constantly reviewing the old files in light of new information. In mid-January 1988, Bob Colby pulled the MUDS for Alan Masters' office phones for the month Dianne disappeared. He was looking for a record of calls placed to the men who claimed to have received alibi warnings from Masters. Colby confirmed that calls were placed to Bachman and Nykaza, as well as to the sheriff's vice and criminal investigation units at the appropriate times. Several of the numbers were unlisted, but Colby recognized one of them as Clarke Buckendahl's. When he was giving Buckendahl flying lessons, Buckendahl provided Colby with a private number not listed in the sheriff's personnel file. Records were not available for Alan Masters' car phone or Jim Keating's mobile phone. What's more, Howard Vanick failed to preserve the tapes of transmissions over the sheriff's band, which are kept for a month and recycled unless they are needed as evidence.

Vanick's failure to cooperate was a continuing source of frustration. He claimed he provided Major Thomas Newman, a high-ranking sheriff's police officer, with confidential memoranda and reports, but Newman had no recollection of this. Bob Colby searched the 1982 files, which were stored in the county warehouse, but could find only two memos listing Dianne as a missing person.

Reed and Colby wanted to talk to Beat Officer Robert Rosignal because he was a friend of Alan and Dianne Masters and because he was mentioned by several sources as a possible participant in the conspiracy. In February, the three men had a confrontation. A furious Rosignal blamed his problems on Howard Vanick. "Investigate all you want. I do my job. I know him [referring to Alan Masters]. I know you. Is that a crime?" Rosignal refused to discuss the Masters' case further but added, "At least I didn't give somebody's plate to anyone! Are you doing anything about that?" Reed was curious how Rosignal found out about Vanick and the license plate, but Rosignal refused to reveal his source.

Clearly, not all the leaks had been plugged. Sometimes this worked to the investigators' advantage. They were receiving more and more anonymous tips from men who clearly had to be police officers. Some tips were not germane to the Masters' case, but added to the picture that was rapidly developing of long-standing, widespread corruption.

CHAPTER 11

$\mathcal{J}$ack Bachman was no longer a source for John Reed; Bachman had legal problems himself and was talking only to the federal government. In March, he had several sessions with Roger Griggs and Ivan Harris at the FBI's Orland Park office. He admitted on the record that he and Clarke Buckendahl owned two houses of prostitution in the 1970s, and Buckendahl negotiated the purchase of a third in 1977. Buckendahl owned the building, and Bachman, Buckendahl, and Alan Masters each put up fifteen thousand dollars to convert the Isle of Capri into the Astrology Club. The three men set up a bank account in the name of Alan Masters' secretary, who was the owner of record.

In addition to his knowledge of the circumstances surrounding Dianne Masters' death, Bachman also described how the bribes from Ciccro gamblers were funneled through Alan Masters. Initially, one-third of the monthly payments went to Jim Keating, one-third to Bachman, with one-third going to Bachman's immediate superior, either Bruce Frasch, Clarke Buckendahl, or another officer. One day when he picked up the envelope, Bachman found a note from Alan Masters saying that henceforth the attorney was going to take $100 off the top. The arrangement continued until the FBI visited Keating.

In April, Clarke Buckendahl received a federal grand jury subpoena and a request for an interview with the FBI, which he declined. Following negotiations with his lawyer, the U.S. attorney

327

agreed that if Buckendahl would testify voluntarily about "matters relating to the disappearance and murder of Dianne Masters," the questioning would be confined to that subject.

When confronted with the telephone records, Buckendahl could not remember hearing from Alan Masters shortly before Dianne disappeared and flatly denied receiving any alibi warnings. The only explanation he could give for the phone records was that Alan was handling a personal injury suit against his parents around that time.

Although they were cut out of the federal investigation loop, Reed and Colby were being kept abreast of developments by anonymous informants. At the end of March, Jim Keating was moved from his Texas prison back to the MCC, the assumption being that he was talking to authorities. It was a solid tip.

In the spring of 1988, Jim Keating and his lawyer met with Scorza, Harris, and Griggs. After discussing his twenty-five year friendship with Alan as well as Alan's earlier problems with Dianne, Keating cut to the period just prior to her disappearance.

Alan knew of the planned divorce, Keating said, and was in a very bad humor. Keating was so worried about his friend that he discussed his concern with Barbara Klimek, Alan's longtime secretary, explaining his frequent visits to the law office.

Keating admitted soliciting Jack Bachman to murder Masters' wife but only because he wanted to see Bachman's reaction. On another occasion, he told Bachman that Masters had found somebody else to do it and that Bachman should have an alibi that night. There were a couple of additional conversations with Alan about killing Dianne, but Keating claimed he refused to become involved.

The next thing Keating remembered was a phone call from Masters at 7 a.m. on March 19, 1982, saying that Dianne had not come home all night—again. Keating counseled Masters to wait before calling the police, as Dianne had done this before. When

Masters called again around noon, Keating advised him to call the sheriff's police. Masters said a car was on its way, and Keating told his pal that he would come to Masters' house as well.

Keating described events at Dianne's home that day, including his discussion with Howie Vanick, and the subsequent ransom demand. Finally, Keating confronted Masters, who admitted hiring someone to kill his wife. This man, who needed money to support his children, waited until Dianne returned home after her board meeting, and hit her on the head before placing her body in the trunk. After Dianne was dead, Mike Corbitt put the car in the canal. All this cost Masters $30,000: $20,000 for the murder and another $10,000 to get rid of the Cadillac.

Scorza & Co. were no more impressed with Keating's proffer than they had been with Corbitt's. There would be no deal.

For the past year, John Reed made regular appearances before the grand jury, describing the conduct of the various investigations and reading reports into the record. Sometimes Scorza asked him to escort a witness. Occasionally, as a tactic, he assigned Reed just to sit outside the grand jury room.

While the agreement forced by Sheriff O'Grady kept Reed and Colby from having access to the grand jury testimony, the sheriff could not put a spoke in the rumor mill, and the detectives heard plenty. Some grand jury witnesses began giving Reed and Colby details they had previously omitted. For example, in May, they heard from Clarke Buckendahl about his 1981 conversation with Alan, where Masters asked who in the sheriff's office would respond to a call from his home. Buckendahl claimed it did not set off any alarm bells in his head when Dianne disappeared, but he admitted that the Sheriff's PD should never have investigated the case and had no explanation as to why he never filed an official report about what he knew and when he knew it.

CHAPTER 12

On Monday, June 13, 1988, more than six years after Dianne Masters disappeared, U.S. Attorney Anton Valukas held a press conference to announce that the indictments of Alan Masters, Michael Corbitt, and James Keating. Flanked by Tom Scorza, Sheldon Zenner, and State's Attorney Richard M. Daley, Valukas detailed the federal racketeering offenses against the three men.

Alan Masters was accused of planning, soliciting, aiding, and abetting Dianne's murder and of mail fraud related to her life insurance; James Keating, of aiding, abetting, and soliciting; and Michael Corbitt, of aiding and abetting the murder and of dumping the Cadillac with Dianne's body in it. All three men also were charged with concealment of the murder and impeding the investigation of Dianne's disappearance and death. In addition, the trio were indicted on unrelated counts of bribery and corruption.

If found guilty on all counts, Masters faced a maximum of 50 years in prison and a $277,000 fine; Corbitt, a maximum of 20 years and $250,000; and Keating, a maximum of 40 years and $275,000.

No one was charged with the actual murder, a fact that was to elude not only most of the reporters who would cover the trial, but some of the defense attorneys as well.

Valukas acknowledged the efforts of Tom Scorza, the FBI, two unnamed detectives from the Cook County Sheriff's Police, and apparently for political reasons, the state's attorney's office which had for six years shown very little interest in the case.

The original plan was for Scorza and Zenner to prosecute the case together, but the two men were incompatible, so Zenner stepped aside. His spot was filled by Patrick Foley. Foley, who came from a family of Chicago restauranteurs, had the appearance of an overgrown altar boy and a courtroom manner to match.

In anticipation of the indictment, Alan Masters took Georgie out of school and flew to Florida with her and Janet. The media could not locate Masters, but Tom Scorza assured reporters that the government knew Masters' whereabouts, and he was being given a chance to turn himself in.

Unaware of the pending federal announcement, Reed and Colby received a tip that Alan was flying back to Chicago and might be met by someone of interest to the detectives. They went to Chicago's Midway Airport to observe Masters' touchdown, and as they were crossing the access road, a car roared up, striking Bob Colby and flipping him over the hood. Two things went through Colby's mind during the seemingly endless flight: that he had survived Vietnam only to be felled by an automobile and that more cops are killed by cars than by gunshots. A horrified John Reed called for an ambulance, and though badly bruised, Colby was back on his feet in short order. The driver, who had no insurance, also had no connection to Alan Masters.

On Tuesday, June 14, 1982, Alan appeared before U.S. District Judge James Zagel to enter a "not guilty" plea. He was released on $200,000 bond and given one week to raise the ten percent, or $20,000, that had to be posted as security, either in cash or in kind. Corbitt and Keating also pleaded not guilty but continued to be entertained by the government at the MCC.

Reacting to the news, State's Attorney Richard M. Daley and Sheriff James O'Grady announced that the county's investigation into the homicide case would continue. This was not the case.

In September 1988, articles appeared about Reed and Colby's treasure hunt through Alan Masters' trash, although the search was attributed to federal agents rather than to the two sheriff's policemen. This and all pertinent information was provided to the defendants' attorneys under rules governing discovery, but might have gone unnoticed by the media if a source "close" to the federal investigation had not brought it to their attention. Although he refused to comment for the record, the source was widely believed to be Tom Scorza. As one Scorza watcher said, "Tommy doesn't just leak. He RELIEVES himself."

On September 23, 1988, Judge Zagel set the case for trial in January 1989, despite the government's wish to go to court as early as October. Then he denied defense motions to dismiss charges.

In October 1988, Janet Bower and Alan Masters slipped over the Indiana state line and were married in the county courthouse in Crown Point, thus avoiding the expensive AIDS screening test required by Illinois at the time. It was not exactly the ceremony every girl dreams of, and it was kept secret until the trial.

Unaware that he was mentioned as a possible hitman in Corbitt's proffer, Robert Rosignal recognized that some people were treating him differently. In February 1988, he retained a lawyer who notified Scorza that if Rosignal were to be called before the grand jury, he would exercise his Fifth Amendment rights. Rosignal later regretted taking this advice, because while such action was perfectly legal, it furthered the notion that he had something to hide. And he learned that many people do not believe a policeman should take the Fifth.

Because the lawyer also was representing Anthony Barone and there was a possibile conflict of interest, he advised Rosignal to retain other counsel. In the meantime, John Reed presented Rosignal with an invitation to visit Tom Scorza as soon as possible. Except for denying that he killed Dianne or concealed evidence, Rosignal again refused to answer Reed's questions, blaming his problems on Vanick and FBI Agent Pecoraro. He also mentioned previous run-ins with Corbitt. The officers parted on unfriendly terms. Reed felt Rosignal was carrying loyalty to Alan Masters to extremes, and Rosignal felt he was being abused.

On November 4, 1988, Rosignal and his new lawyer, Jed Stone, met with Tom Scorza, Ivan Harris, and an assistant state's attorney. Rosignal, who is prone to be emotional, was extremely nervous and remembered Harris as "Irving the Terrible, the big FBI guy." Scorza provided Rosignal with a proffer letter, which Rosignal signed, and a grand jury subpoena. Then the questioning began with Scorza threatening to indict Rosignal for murder that very day. To emphasize the point, Scorza slid a toothbrush across the table.

Rosignal denied any knowledge of Masters' marital woes or Dianne's divorce plans. "I was home with my wife the night Dianne disappeared. I took a medical leave to study for college exams." He did not learn of Dianne's disappearance until he read about it in the newspapers, and shortly afterward he did visit Alan to see how he was doing.

In November 1988, an FBI agent went to an Orland Park restaurant to meet a woman who married one of Alan Masters' clients in 1980. Her husband signed his house and car over to his new wife because his son from a previous marriage was seriously ill, and he wanted to prevent creditors from seizing his property. By 1981, the marriage was breaking up, and the couple went to Alan Masters' office, ostensibly to discuss a divorce. The woman discovered that the real purpose was to force her to sign away her property rights. When she refused, Alan Masters told her, "You are going to leave this marriage with no more than the clothes on your back. [Your husband] can blow your head off with a shotgun, or you could end up in a canal, and there would be no witnesses."

At this, the woman became frightened and decided not to press the matter. Subsequently, whenever the couple would be driving in the area, the husband would point out the S&S Canal, remarking that there were many autos sunk there and adding that no matter what trouble he got into, Alan Masters could fix it. Although they had no knowledge of Charlie Bates' encounters with Masters and Corbitt between 1979 and 1981, Scorza, Reed, Colby, and the FBI agents believed that Dianne's murder was not the conspirators' maiden voyage into mayhem.

Just before the trial was to begin in January 1989, defense attorneys requested a lengthy continuance. "If you stacked up the statements of witnesses and the grand jury testimony, it would reach two feet high," one lawyer said. "We've got thirty-five hundred pages of discovery documents. There may be more than fifty witnesses...a number...have made statements to the government and their statements have to be checked out, and their credibility and reliability as witnesses must be determined." Over Scorza's objection, Judge Zagel rescheduled the trial until May.

PART IV

The Trial

The only place you can find justice
in Cook County is at 76th and Archer
(the village hall of a suburb named Justice)

—saying prevalent among the
Cook County Sheriff's PD

CHAPTER 1

*T*he law is one thing. Justice is another. The two should not be confused. Sometimes, through happy coincidence, they collide. In May 1989, the people who loved Dianne Masters hoped that such a collision would occur in Room 1919 of the Everett McKinley Dirksen Federal Building on Dearborn Street in downtown Chicago.

On the outside, the Dirksen Building is just another glass-and-steel high-rise Mies van der Rohe clone. Inside, there are security guards and deputy marshalls controlling access to courtroom floors by airport-style magnomomcters.

Room 1919, the domain of Judge James S. Zagel, is large, wood paneled, high ceilinged, and rather plain. The judge sits on a dais, just below a large white-on-black seal of the Northern District of Illinois. Below him is a tier with space for his clerk, Donald Walker, and his court reporter, Wanda Barnes. The witness stand is on a level between the judge and his staff. In front of the railing known as the bar is a lectern used by the attorneys. The set is static and unchanging; the drama is provided by the lawyers and witnesses.

Appointed by a Republican administration, Zagel has a reputation for being conservative and unemotional, firm but fair, and scrupulously honest. Something of a scholar, Zagel has published legal textbooks. The defense attorneys repeatedly demanded that Zagel recuse himself, or step aside, because he was director of the Illinois Department of Law Enforcement when the state police

339

conducted their 1983 investigation into Dianne's murder. The judge denied these motions immediately, saying that he had not participated in the investigation in any way.

The courtroom atmosphere in large part is determined by the presiding judge's demeanor and approach. Zagel maintains tight control of proceedings, expecting attorneys to stick to the rules and observe professional courtesy. He does this in a low-key but firm manner, never raising his voice. Speaking softly but carrying a big stick works.

On Tuesday, May 16, 1989, the real action in Case No. 88 CR 500 began when a panel of forty prospective jurors was escorted by federal marshals into Room 1919. Four at a time they were ushered past five double rows of hard-wood spectator benches, through a little gate, and into the jury box to the spectator's right.

James Zagel, a middle-aged gray-haired white man wearing wire-rim spectacles and clad in a government-issue black robe showed so little outward emotion that he could be posing for Mount Rushmore, that his hobby as an actor seems somewhat out of character. It was Zagel who would conduct the *voir dire*. Literally translated from the French, it means to speak truly, but in legal jargon it is an examination of jurors to determine their fitness to serve.

As the prospective jurors perched on black leather swivel chairs, Judge Zagel asked for their vital statistics and then posed a series of questions, which had been agreed to in advance by both the prosecution and the defense. Several had to do with attitudes toward lawyers and the police, but others were an intriguing preview of pending testimony.

These teasers included, "Have you ever given money to a TV evangelist?" and "What is your favorite TV program?" When the tape of Alan Masters joking with Lary Damron about TV evangelists was played, Alan Masters' lawyer did not want anyone on the jury who might be offended by it.

As is customary, Judge Zagel also asked if the jurors had heard or read about the case. In itself, this is not an automatic disqualifier. Having formed an opinion is. A south suburban man who believed Masters, Corbitt, and Keating were guilty of betraying the public trust was an immediate out. A woman on the panel knew one of the defendants. He handled her divorce, and she was satisfied with his work. "You've changed a lot in twenty years, Mr. Masters," she said. She was excused.

After two days, twelve jurors and two alternates were seated. For the rest of the trial, the jurors remain mute, although like grand jurors, members of petit juries may questions witnesses. Jurors usually are not aware of this, and attorneys and judges do not encourage the practice. The courtroom is *their* stage, and they do not appreciate even cameo appearances by people who do not hold the legal equivalent of an equity card.

On Thursday, May 18, 1989, the courthouse buffs, retirees who make a serious hobby out of trial watching, arrived. More than one lawyer has been known to consult the buffs to ask, "How am I doing?"

The prosecution team, consisting of Tom Scorza, Pat Foley, and Ivan Harris, took up their places at a long table on the right, nearest the jury box.

On the left are three tables, one for each defendant. Alan Masters chose Chicago native Patrick Tuite to represent him. Born in 1937, the son of an Irish immigrant electrician, Tuite was the first member of his family to receive a college degree. He worked his way up in the Cook County state's attorney's office, finishing as chief of the criminal division before going into private practice. Tall, graying, and personable, Tuite was regarded as one of Chicago's leading defense attorneys, a man well liked by the press.

William Murphy was Jim Keating's court-appointed lawyer. Another Chicago native, Murphy started his legal career as a public defender and took pride in never having worked the other (prosecution) side of the courtroom. Corbitt retained Dennis Berkson, a former assistant U. S. attorney.

Behind the defense tables, on the wall opposite the jury box, are two doors. One is an emergency exit, while the other is the entrance to a holding room where Keating and Corbitt were kept when the trial was not in session. Because Alan Masters obtained bond, he remained at home and retained freedom of movement within a proscribed area.

Finally, the clerk called, "All rise," and as Judge Zagel entered, everybody stood out of respect for the abstract concept of justice he represented. The spectator benches were filled with press, the buffs, and friends and family members of major figures in the trial.

As usual, the attorneys for both sides requested that prospective witnesses be excluded from proceedings except when testifying. As usual, the motion was granted, frustrating some people who had been waiting more than seven years for this moment. The only exempt witness is case agent Ivan Harris. To John Reed, who worked longer on this case than anybody else, it meant sitting outside where Scorza could easily reach him.

Tom Scorza was on his feet almost before the judge recognized him. "May it please the court?" he began. "Mr. Scorza," nodded Judge Zagel. The overture was over, and the curtain was up.

"Defense counsel," Scorza nodded dryly at the opposition. Then, with more brio, "Good morning, ladies and gentlemen of the jury." Scorza introduced himself, his cocounsel, Patrick Foley, and FBI Agent Harris.

The opening statement for the government was particularly important in this complicated case. Scorza used his time to give the jury an outline, a sort of verbal *Cliff Notes*, for the trial.

After pointing out the defendants, Scorza described what the government expected to prove. The case is "about a criminal association that operated in the ordinary ways, that is to say bribery, shakedowns, fixing of cases...which reached its height or maybe its depth in...the murder of Dianne G. Masters...This case is about the corrupt association between three defendants and how the defendants conspired to commit that murder, solicited the murder, aided and abetted the murder, and then after committing the murder, covered it up...It's a case about an unholy trinity of greed, corruption, and murder."

Scorza outlined the case. FBI undercover agent Lary Damron would provide the structure of the criminal association, its goals, and how each defendant operated to achieve them. Scorza explained, "...the whole story of Lary Damron is to show you this corrupt association in action from the inside, how what Corbitt does has to fit into the scheme of his actions with Keating, and how what both of them do are within the scheme of the general actions with the master fixer, the guy with the connections to all of the top cops, all of the judges: Alan Masters.

"Plus it shows you how these defendants slide so easily from the ordinary corrupt activities to the extraordinary corrupt activity..." that was Dianne's murder.

The jury would not only hear Damron's testimony, they would listen to the tapes the agent made of meetings and phone calls with Keating and Masters. Damron's overview would be followed by a procession of individuals who would testify to specific examples of the "ordinary corrupt" activities—taking bribes, fixing cases, extortion—and then by witnesses who would testify to the "extraordinary corrupt" activities, the slaying of Dianne Masters. There would be some overlap, as several individuals had knowledge of both areas of activity.

It quickly became clear that Scorza's strategy was to first bring on the witnesses who could connect the threesome to bribery, shakedowns, referring and fixing cases as well as fee splitting. Some of these people would also be able to give evidence about the Masters' marital difficulties and his plans to solve it by getting rid of Dianne. It was essential to prove two racketeering counts to convict under RICO, but to the jury, the evidence surrounding

Dianne's murder was most compelling. That is why it would be presented closest to their deliberations.

Whenever Scorza mentioned Dianne or her murder, the jury, media, and spectators seemed almost to snap to attention, hanging on the prosecutor's words. The other acts—stolen cars, chop shops, kickbacks, payoffs, extortion—all were business as usual in Chicagoland. But murder, especially of a pretty woman believed to have led a wild sex life, that was more like it.

Scorza portrayed Dianne as a late bloomer, desirous of making a contribution to her community, politically active, a battered woman who tried to help others in the same situation, a wife afraid of her husband, determined to escape a disastrous marriage and build a better life for herself and her beloved daughter. As she prepared to sue for divorce, her friendship with Jim Church deepened into a sexual affair.

But Dianne's infidelity was not the basis for the murder plot. At least six months before the affair began, Alan Masters spoke to Clarke Buckendahl, asking what would happen if a crime were committed at the Masters' home. Witnesses would testify to Alan's threatening Dianne, to hearing different plans for eliminating her, to stalking Dianne and bugging her phones, and to being solicited to kill her.

When Scorza began to describe Dianne and Jim's meeting on February 24, 1982, he had the entire courtroom hanging on every word. "I get to probably what you will find the most memorable part of the evidence...It involved some very, very sensitive and graphic sexual matters. I apologize to you if I need to...probably ten years ago I would not be able to tell you this in open court. These are the kinds of things we see more and more on television and in the movies, so I am going to go through it with you."

The specifics were important, Scorza explained, because knowledge of the details "is one of the keys of figuring out who is in the know in the murder plot. The story begins in the Bible, believe it or not." Then Scorza described the *Song of Solomon* article, how Dianne and Jim experimented as a result of reading it, and how they discussed the results over the tapped telephone the next day.

Listening to the tape of this conversation triggered a violent reaction in Alan, Scorza told the jury, and combined with the imminent filing of divorce papers to give Masters a sense of urgency about the murder plot. The first two attempts misfired, "maybe by premonition, maybe by luck, maybe...you will even suspect divine intervention." On the third try, Dianne Masters' luck ran out. Still, Dianne's known pattern varied the night of March 18-19, 1982, and while it was not enough to save her, this deviation eventually would trip up her murderers.

After Gen Capstaff saw Dianne within seconds of her home, "...a curtain falls across the stage. It's a peculiar kind of curtain. It's not one of those thick red ones you see in downtown theaters that you can't see through at all. Unfortunately, it's not one of those transparent curtains you sometimes see on a shower stall, at least where people are not too fastidious. It is a curtain which you can see through partially, as Saint Paul says, as through a glass, darkly." However, thanks to strong circumstantial evidence, Scorza promised the jurors, they would be able to see things very clearly, although there would be certainties and uncertainties.

The certainties include proof beyond a reasonable doubt that shortly after 1 a.m. on Friday, March 19, 1982, Dianne Masters arrived home, that her skull was shattered by a blunt instrument, that later that same morning Michael Corbitt and an accomplice drove the Cadillac with a comatose or dead Dianne in the trunk to the bank of the canal in Willow Springs. Before launching the Cadillac into the water, two bullets were fired into Dianne's brain. Horrible as the crime was, it was compounded by the fact that the murderers left Dianne no dignity in death. Her skirt and underwear were pulled up so that her body was naked from the waist down.

The uncertainties centered around precisely whether the bludgeoning occurred on the driveway or inside the house, and whether she was alive when shot. The coconspirators took "precautions against being found out...There were some very special actions taken to cover it up," so that the curtain never could be lifted.

"In all secretive conspiracies, the defendants take precautions against being found out. That's why there is a curtain in most murders. Look at the defendants." The jury complied. "One is a criminal lawyer. He knows the system. The other two are cops. They know what policemen look for. They know how to arrange things.

"Now it sounds odd for a prosecutor to talk so openly about the uncertainties. We're the guys that have to prove things beyond a reasonable doubt. But you will notice that the indictment in this case does not actually charge the murder, doesn't say exactly who did it, exactly the cause of death, and this is why, because there is uncertainty there," Scorza continued.

"The indictment charges who conspired, who solicited, who aided and abetted, who covered up, because on those matters, there is no doubt. That's what we have to prove. That's what we're gonna prove...I have no trouble talking about the uncertainty is that I think in the end when you look at all the evidence, you are going to be able to make a pretty good estimate about what exactly happened.

"You're going to be able to tell from the evidence what happened, not from my argument, but from the evidence. And you know why? Because you're going to know not only what happened before the curtain dropped, you're going to know what happened after. And in light of common sense and common experience, I think you're going to be able to conclude what happened, even though for this case and this indictment, some of those things we just don't have to prove."

The jury caught on. Scorza would present them with a jigsaw puzzle. Some of the pieces would be missing, but if they put the others together correctly, they could determine the picture. That is, they would solve the murder. It was an irresistible idea. Scorza might not be a fun guy to his colleagues, but he was great with juries.

After a ten-minute recess, the defense lawyers took their turns. William Murphy had defended many unpopular figures over the years but came to feel real affection for Jim Keating. Like Scorza, Murphy appealed to the jury's sense of importance, sympathizing with them over the difficult job facing them and for being taken away from their homes and their work. Nobody in the jury box looked terribly oppressed.

Middle-aged, pleasant-looking, slightly taller than average, Murphy is so relaxed that he frequently appeared on the verge of yawning. His courtroom demeanor is from the aw, shucks school of lawyering. "I know I'm not a particularly eloquent person, and I know that a lot of times I appear a little nervous; and if I do that, I apologize...I'm not a real polished person."

Having established himself as just folks, Murphy launched into his plea for Keating. "He was an excellent cop, a leader at times, afraid at times. He made mistakes. He let himself down." These were references to Keating's previous conviction. Lary Damron was a stumbling block to Keating's defense, but the most damaging witness would be Jack Bachman. Murphy depicted Bachman as conniving, cunning, and desperate, a man who played into the prosecution's hands by helping the government decide who killed Dianne and by bending the facts to fit the theory.

The spectators scurried off for a quick lunch; fireworks were expected from Tuite in the afternoon.

At 2 p.m., Dennis Berkson, Corbitt's lawyer, stepped to the lectern. First, he provided the jury with some background on Corbitt and introduced Corbitt's wife Sherry sitting in the first row with Corbitt's retarded son. Bringing little children into court is a risky business.

When Berkson described Corbitt as "a hands-on police chief," there was sniggering among the spectators. Berkson may have heard it because he elaborated. Corbitt "wasn't the kind of person who sat behind and did just administrative [sic]. It wasn't a nine-to-five job...he protected the people at all hours of the day or night."

Characterizing Scorza's opening statement as a myth or fairy tale, Berkson insisted that, "The murder is the real reason we are here...a fantasy of the prosecution."

If it was not already clear that this would be yet another trial where the victim was going to get the blame, Berkson eliminated all doubt. "Now, you know, I hate to say these kind [sic] of things, but this woman was not true to her husband...not true to her marriage vows. This woman was known to get around."

In addition to Dianne's bad character, Corbitt's defense would rest on the time shown on the car clock and Dianne's watch, making it appear she was placed in the canal shortly after she was last seen by Gen Capstaff, "this nosy neighbor [sic] who followed her because she wanted to see who Dianne Masters was shacking up with."

It would be necessary to discredit the testimony of Robert Olson, who encountered Corbitt on the canal after hearing shots fired, and Jack Bachman. "You're going to love him," Berkson assured the jury sarcastically. Bachman could have been tried on charges that would have brought him 100 years in jail, Berkson continued, but Bachman cut a deal, and almost a year after his trial, still had not been sentenced for a simple reason: "Jackie has got to satisfy the government."

The judge sustained Scorza's objection, but Berkson continued in the same vein. Bachman "knows exactly what the government wants because they're telling him." This resulted in another sustained objection.

The jury is not supposed to keep track of how many objections are made and how many are sustained, as in baseball box scores, but lawyers know that they tend to do so. Sometimes attorneys figure it is worth it to make a statement or ask a question that the judge will tell the jury to disregard.

The defense attorneys coordinated their arguments to some extent. However, without the Masters connection, it would be hard to make a case against Corbitt and Keating on these particular charges. As a result, the heaviest burden fell upon Patrick Tuite. Tuite's reputation was always solid, but it and his fees soared with his successful defense of a judge during the Operation Greylord prosecutions. The buffs had great expectations of Tuite's opening.

Patrick Tuite had just finished defending unsuccessfully a minister accused of child molestation, and to many of the spectators, he appeared tired and dispirited. He denounced Scorza's presentation as a scary fantasy, "phony as a three dollar bill." So fictive was the prosecution case that Tuite expected to see Alan Funt of "Candid Camera" and Angela Lansbury of "Murder, She Wrote."

According to Tuite, Alan Masters knew nothing about what became of Dianne from the time she left for the MVCC board meeting until her body was found nine months later. As to the other racketeering charges, Tuite reemphasized a point already made by Berkson: that for a policeman to refer cases to an attorney for a fee was not illegal, although it may have been unethical. The mail fraud charge was based on Alan's filing a false statement on Dianne's life insurance claim, because the coverage ceased once she arrived home. Tuite promised to prove Dianne never made it to her driveway, let alone into her house. What's more, Tuite claimed that the government ignored any evidence contrary to its theory and would not call witnesses who would so testify. This brought objections that were sustained by the judge. There was some whispering on the benches; this was more like it.

Tuite's strength as a defense attorney is said to be his ability to make even the most sleazy client seem human, but he definitely was off his game. To begin with, it was clear that such suburbs as Summit, where Alan had his law office, were terra incognita to him. A resident of a trendy city neighborhood, Tuite could place Summit only in reference to a popular dinner theatre. Alan was "like the old general practitioner." A little divorce work, a little personal injury work, a little traffic court work, a little real estate work. The jurors turned gazed at Alan. At each "little," Masters seemed to shrink before their very eyes. Good old Alan Masters, your cracker-barrel lawyer.

Dianne Masters was another matter. She lived with Alan before his divorce. She even took his name. "In fact, they had their child out of wedlock." At this, some juror chins went up. This reflected poorly on Alan Masters. Tuite rushed on. Dianne slept around. "There's times he's been angered by that, he's been hurt by that. A little overweight, has a hairpiece." Masters adopted a hangdog look. Probably every juror at one time or another has tried to diet and failed, but it would take more to persuade them to identify with Alan.

Now that Dianne was put in her properly oversexed place, it was time for the kinky stuff. After belaboring Ted Nykaza's drinking problem, Tuite segued into Nykaza's interest in ladies' scanties. Nykaza "used to go to shopping centers with a laser light and shine it on ladies to see through their dresses so he could look at them because this laser light sort of somehow made the outer clothing invisible, and you could see through to the underwear." The women in on the spectator benches reflected on the condition of their own undies, remembering mother's admonition to always wear respectable panties in case of accidents. Mother never said anything about lasers in malls.

But the most tantalizing bit came at the end of Tuite's opening argument. "We don't have to produce anything, but we are. We are going to produce some very important evidence that will establish that Alan Masters didn't have anything to do with his wife's death, nor did Mr. Corbitt, nor Mr. Keating." The culprit, it was clear, was Ted Nykaza.

"Perry Mason is alive and well and in Judge Zagel's court," muttered one onlooker.

Once the opening statements were out of the way, Lary Damron took the stand to describe the pattern of corrupt interrelationships he observed as an undercover agent. Damron's testimony was lengthy and it would go into the next day.

As the day ended, Tom Scorza joined John Reed in the hallway. "Do you think Masters will take the stand?" he asked Scorza as the two men were returning to Scorza's office. The prosecutor shook his head from side to side, adding, "The baloney is always afraid of the grinder."

CHAPTER 2

"$\mathcal{S}$ex tape alleged to have triggered Masters' slaying," read the headline in Friday morning's *Chicago Sun-Times*. "Scenario given in Masters' death," was the more sedate lead in the *Chicago Tribune*. The *Sun-Times*'s Adrienne Drell picked up on Tuite's promise to prove that someone other than the three defendants killed Dianne.

The courtroom was even more crowded the second day of the trial. After a legal wrangle over admissibility of evidence, the jury was back in its box, listening to Lary Damron. Damron produced two cocktail napkins. They bore Alan Masters' office telephone number and a "safe" number in Michigan in Keating's handwriting. As the tapes of the conversations were played, the jurors gripped printed transcripts. They listened as Keating explained Masters' reluctance to work with Damron after Dianne's body was found. The lawyer was just being cautious.

Following the lunch break, the cross examination began with Dennis Berkson on behalf of Corbitt. Berkson needed to diminish the importance of Damron's meeting with Corbitt outside the Willow Springs police station. He emphasized Keating's description of Corbitt as a "bullshitter, someone who is kidding," in the hope that the jury would believe that Corbitt was merely a braggart and not corrupt.

Bill Murphy also wanted to take the sting out of Damron's testimony. When Murphy brought up Keating's previous conviction

353

and fifteen-year sentence, Tom Scorza objected. This resulted in a sidebar, a discussion among the lawyers and the judge which cannot be heard by the jurors and spectators but the content of which is taken down by the court reporter.

Scorza told the judge he was flabbergasted by Murphy's question, saying, "I thought he was going to say, 'Did you know that he left the police force?'" Asked by the judge for his specific objection, Scorza said he was concerned that Murphy was laying the groundwork for a mistrial. "It's his client," the judge replied.

But there was another matter Scorza wanted to go into on the sidebar. During his cross-examination of Lary Damron, Berkson pressed the agent about Corbitt's talk of obtaining "approval" for the new whorehouse. As a result, when it was time for redirect examination, Scorza told the judge he would ask Damron if Corbitt asked about other approvals, including the mob.

"We kept out the matter of organized crime from the tapes. We kept it out from this man's testimony," Scorza said, but now Corbitt's own attorney had brought it into the open.

Indeed, it was puzzling to the press and spectators that the specter of the mob did not come up during the trial. The conventional wisdom is that no illegal business can operate for more than a few minutes in Cook County without the permission of the outfit.

The judge postponed his ruling until the cross examination was completed and the jury was excused. Then Wanda Barnes was asked to read Berkson's questions. Scorza pointed out that after asking about the county's permission, Berkson inquired about the Bastone brothers, who were allegedly organized crime figures operating in Alan Masters' sphere.

"Are you going to argue that this reference to the county might very well have meant filing under the assumed names act or something like that?" the judge asked Berkson. Corbitt's lawyer denied such intention. "On behalf of Mr. Masters we would object to any interjection of organized crime in this case," Tuite jumped in, also mentioning that he represented the Bastones.

In the judge's opinion, Scorza was correct in asserting that Berkson had opened the door when he started asking about legal filings, "leaving the jury with the impression that the 'county' is an innocent term." However, based on the assurances of Corbitt's attorney, the judge ruled that Scorza could not go into an organized crime connection.

Tom Scorza scheduled some weekend R&R. Trying a case like this was an intense experience. Sometimes it led to burnout. Scorza had perfected a regimen to prevent this. Once he arrived at the office early in the morning, he was completely focused on the trial. He took lunch breaks to go over reports or talk to scheduled witnesses. If he felt low in energy, he had candy bars ready. But when he left the Dirksen Building, that was his time to spend with his family, dine out, go a baseball games, and the like. He approached the trial like an athlete in training for competition.

CHAPTER 3

*T*he trial did not resume until Tuesday because Pat Tuite was ill. The buffs took the opportunity to rate the performances of the principal players to date. A major criminal trial is an unfolding drama. The leads are usually the attorneys for both sides, with cameo appearances by witnesses; the defendants often remain mute figures, and the victim is invisible. In commenting on the similarities between lawyers and actors, distinguished British actor Sean Arnold observed that while they share childish ways, actors are nicer on the whole, as they lack the lawyer's unpleasant detachment from the sheer ugliness of crime and violence.

Scorza's courtroom demeanor was almost professorial, although he did give off the impression of a barely grounded live wire. He used words to skewer balky witnesses and the defense, rocking slightly back and forth, one hand to his chin, the other bracing it.

Tuite's style, on the other hand, was much more flamboyant and theatrical, lunging here, parrying there, shaking his long, wavy locks. He seemed to be playing to the gallery of media rather than the jury. In attire, Tuite was something of a dandy, favoring those expensive Italian-style suits that always fit as if they were tailored for somebody else.

John Reed took the witness stand on Tuesday, but his testimony did not reveal the depth of his involvement in solving the

357

case. Scorza took Reed through his garbage-picking exploits. Reed was asked to identify a couple of items plucked from Masters' coffee grounds, one of which was another cocktail napkin bearing the legend "I've got rhythm" and a handwritten note reading, "Larry Wright [Damron's undercover name] looking for tavern biz in Summit/McCook area."

On cross examination, Tuite asked, "When was the last time that you had been in the Masters' garbage at his office?" He seemed startled when Reed responded, "The sixteenth of May, this year." Just one week before he testified, Reed found a note in Alan Masters' handwriting that read "should we attempt to find an expert who can say that the blows to wife's head were the cause of death and the shots that were fired were not the cause of death plus more P R." Reed was struck by the use of the word "say" rather than "prove" as well as the reference to public relations.

Caught off guard, Tuite switched gears, asking Reed if "someone" had told the sergeant that "they" were going to put something in the garbage for Reed to find. When Reed denied this, Tuite wanted to know if Ted Nykaza was Reed's source. Reed said no.

Tuite's demand that Reed identify the frightened tipster resulted in another sidebar. Scorza offered to reveal the name of the source in private should the judge desire it but said the individual was not a government witness. Tuite wanted to know if the source was working for the government and had stolen Alan Masters' property from the office and placed it in the trash where it would be legal for Reed to find. The judge sustained Scorza's objection. Reed would not have to give up his source.

Scorza proceeded to bring on the witnesses to the kickback, referral, case-fixing, and extortion schemes. When Tim Ayres was arrested for drunk driving, Corbitt told him to hire Alan Masters. When Ayres' father learned the fee would be $3,500, he hired another attorney who charged only $750. Roger Griggs read into the record the statement of the late Richard McCarville, who retained Masters after receiving similar advice. It cost him $2,500. Herman Pastori told how he received kickbacks from Masters for referring cases.

The McCarville statement sparked one of several discussions over the introduction of hearsay testimony. When a witness testifies about what another person has said, that is hearsay. There is an enormous amount of disagreement in the courts as to when hearsay is proper and when it is not, but generally when a person has died, as in the case of Dianne Masters or McCarville, it is admissible, and Judge Zagel so ruled.

After the lunch break, Robert Vanerka, who had resigned from the Bridgeview PD, also testified to receiving kickbacks from Masters for skimping on the evidence against a Masters' client in court.

Larry Camerano was a pivotal witness; he could describe Masters' ability to corrupt the law enforcement process after Camerano's garage filled with stolen auto parts was raided by Jim Keating and Robert "Ice" Neapolitan. It cost Camerano seventeen thousand dollars for Masters' fee, which included payoffs to the judge and arresting officers. Like Pastori, Camerano was on the receiving end of Masters' confidences about his problems with Dianne and his plans to get rid of her before she could get a divorce.

All three defendants were linked together by the testimony of Fred and Lorna Kuhnke, who owned a towing business in Willow Springs. Because the Kuhnkes refused to pay a bribe for local towing referrals and because Mrs. Kuhnke confronted Corbitt about his malfeasance in office, Corbitt set up a raid through Keating. The Kuhnkes were arrested for having stolen auto parts, and Corbitt told them to hire Alan Masters. It cost them eighteen thousand dollars in cash to have the case dismissed.

In another raid, on a Lemont boatyard owned by Dennis Egan, Keating's men seized heavy equipment. Some of it was stolen, but the rest was Egan's property. For a percentage, Corbitt set up the payoff to the sheriff's cops. When CCSPD Officer Robert Borowski went to Keating on Egan's behalf, Keating threatened to hit him in the head with a lug wrench. The jury was indirectly reminded that Dianne Masters had been bludgeoned, too.

Patrick Tuite moved for a mistrial and the severance of Alan Masters from the other defendants because of potential harm done by Borowski's testimony about Keating's threat. The judge replied that he believed the jury capable of sorting this out, and the motion was denied.

Helene Maignon was the first member of Dianne's immediate circle to testify about Alan's threats and physical abuse and Dianne's fears that her husband would not stop at murder. Maignon was questioned by Patrick Foley, Scorza's cocounsel, who handled most of the female witnesses.

Her graphic description of what happened when she tried to intervene when Alan was dragging Dianne by her hair and her recollection of Dianne's reaction to Alan's telephone threat to destroy Dianne caught the attention of both the jury and the media. There were only so many ways that cops and attorneys could corrupt the law, and because of the sheer volume of such trials in recent years, unfortunately these methods had become familiar. It was the juicy details of the Masters' private life and Dianne's murder that separated this trial from so many others.

Next, Brigitte Stark was called to the stand. After describing the tempestuous and often violent nature of the Masters' relationship, Brigitte was asked about the last time she spoke to her friend over the phone. A few days before Dianne disappeared, she told Brigitte that the divorce papers would be filed shortly. Dianne knew she was being followed, and she had collected some license numbers that she was having checked out.

Brigitte also related the results of her visit to the house on Wolf Road after Dianne vanished. As Brigitte arrived, Georgie left with some friends. When Alan was on the phone, she discovered that all Dianne's things had been removed, and Alan's clothes were hanging there instead. Dianne's valuable jewelry also was missing, as were her fur coats from the front hall closet. She did not like the idea of snooping, but she was sure Dianne was dead and Alan was involved.

Pat Tuite's cross examination centered around Dianne's ex-husband. Brigitte replied she never met the man, that Dianne seldom mentioned him and never with reference to abuse. The only beatings Brigitte knew about were administered by Alan.

When Tuite inquired if Brigitte knew that Dianne had an affair while her first husband was on military duty, Scorza objected. In a sidebar, Tuite told the judge that he expected to produce evidence that Dianne had been seen in a car with her first husband on the canal bank one week before her disappearance, and somehow a twelve-year-old extramarital affair, if there had been one, would tie in. The judge upheld Scorza's objection.

Pat Casey followed Brigitte, confirming Dianne's fright over her deteriorating marriage as well as Brigitte's discovery that Dianne's clothes had been put away or disposed of soon after she disappeared. Even Dianne's needlepoint refrigerator magnets were gone. "It was like she never existed," Pat told a hushed courtroom.

Pat also testified about Alan's offer to get rid of one of the Casey autos and an outing to Alan's whorehouse. Bob Casey was entertaining business contacts, and Alan thought they might enjoy visiting a bordello. When the group arrived, Alan had to phone someone to send over the "dancers." These women were light years away from the delectable *belles du jour* portrayed in films. Indeed, they were so homely and awkward that Pat felt terribly sorry for them.

It was a grueling experience for both women. Brigitte was in the midst of cancer treatment, and Pat dreaded returning to Chicago from her new home in Florida. However, more than anything they wanted justice for Dianne, and testifying was one last service they could do for their friend. They were still trying to come to grips with the fact that they had spent time socializing with a murderer. It was something that happened to other people, and now it was their nightmare.

Dianne's hairdresser revealed that Dianne visited his salon on Thursday, March 18, 1982, telling him she was very worried about her pending divorce because Alan was "acting very irrational." The hairdresser suggested Dianne take her daughter and go to Florida until the divorce was filed.

Dr. Cullen Schwemer, Dianne's psychiatrist, concerned about physician/patient privilege, requested guidance from the judge. In murder trials, the confidentiality privilege usually does not apply. In this case, however, the doctor was going to be questioned only about his conversations with Alan Masters, who was not his patient and thus not covered by the privilege.

Dr. Schwemer was free to tell the jury how Alan had tricked him into a tacit admission that Dianne was seeing another man in the 1970s, as well as Masters' threat that someone would be hurt. He described Dianne's bruised condition when next he saw her. The note Schwemer wrote after inadvertently disclosing private information about Dianne was introduced into evidence.

The trial was adjourned for the day after Maureen McGann-Ryan gave evidence about her consultations over the planned divorce and about the calls she received from judges asking that she intercede with Dianne. In front of the grand jury, Dianne's lawyer had related a conversation with Alan during which he said, "You know that bloodbaths take place in divorce court, but you have never seen the kind of bloodbath that will take place in this case." Alan was threatening and out of control during this conversation, but it was not brought out before the petit jury.

On Thursday, May 25, 1989, John Reed picked up Ted Nykaza at his home near the Will County line. It was early and Ted was sober, which was unusual. He also had an acute case of nerves over having to go to court and was understandably shaky. As Nykaza entered the federal courthouse, he collapsed in an epileptic seizure, and Reed called paramedics to take Ted to the nearest hospital.

Tom Scorza's training paid off. With the jury out, he explained to the judge why the prosecution's first witness of the day was unavailable. Instead, Joe Hein was substituted.

Scorza questioned Hein about his and Nykaza's afternoon visit to Alan Masters' house to listen to a tape recording of an "intimate" conversation between Dianne and Jim talking about a wine bottle—by now, everyone knew it was not a Coke—in Dianne's vagina. Contrary to Nykaza's recollection, Hein believed the recording had been played in the basement. Hein asserted that he had not heard Alan make any threats on Dianne's life, but that he might have been in the bathroom when it happened. At this, a spectator muttered, "Now pull the other leg."

On redirect, Scorza homed in on one of Hein's answers during cross examination. "Is it your testimony that the mere listening to that tape was not relevant to a murder investigation?" Hein tried to say that it was relevant, but based on his personal knowledge of Alan Masters, he did not think there was any connection. Results of his polygraph were not admissible.

Scorza would not let him off lightly. Hein had to agree that someone with his background knew that the tape would be important to the murder investigation. "And you feel guilty about that, don't you?" Scorza asked. "I don't feel good that I permitted personal knowledge to shade how I would look at something," Hein replied. Scorza snapped back, "And wouldn't you agree that it's even worse if you heard a threat and did not report that?" Hein had no choice but to agree.

After the lunch break, Pat Foley questioned Diane Economou. Economou never heard what the press was now calling the "sex tape," but Masters and Nykaza both told her about it, she said. It caused a rustle in the courtroom when Economou admitted Masters had talked to her on several occasions about having his wife killed and making it look like an accident with the help of Jim

Keating, who was at Masters' office almost every day around the time of Dianne's disappearance. Fear was her excuse for waiting until 1988 to tell authorities.

When it was Tuite's turn, he asked, "Did [Alan] tell you his wife complained about his being overweight and the fact that he had wore [sic] a hairpiece?" Economou replied that Dianne Masters said she did not like her husband's rug. But once again, Tuite did not see trouble coming. "And she demeaned his appearance at times in his presence?" "He said that," Economou answered. "She never did it in my presence."

Howard Vanick's recollection of turning over Jim Church's license plate was still a little feeble. He "could have" given it to Jack Bachman. Keating's reference to Masters as the "client" during his confrontation with Vanick on March 19, 1982, was not part of Foley's direct examination, and Keating's lawyer danced around it when it was his turn to cross examine the lieutenant. Murphy seemed to know about rumors that Vanick had sent invoices to Alan, billing him for Dianne's surveillance.

The last witness of the day was someone spectators had been waiting to see. Jim Church, looking like the guy next door rather than the other man, told the jury about meeting Dianne, becoming her friend, and eventually her lover. He was calm when details of their affair were brought out, handling a sticky situation with as much delicacy as was possible under the circumstances, especially when it came to the wine-bottle incident.

Church also revealed that following the March 2, 1982, board meeting, the MVCC gang went to Artie G's as usual. The service was slow, so Church went to the bar for a couple of glasses of Chablis for himself and Dianne. A man sitting at the bar asked Jim if he was with the college. "Yes," Jim answered, and he noticed the man "squishing out a big cigar." After answering the man's questions about his name and what he taught, Jim took the drinks back to the table. He did not realize the man was Jim Keating until years later when he saw Keating's photo in the *Chicago Sun-Times*.

Time ran out before Church could be cross examined; he would have preferred not to come back another day. For one thing, the publicity was disturbing to his daughter, Emily. As he was walking to the elevator with Tom Scorza, Patrick Tuite popped up to taunt them. "Want to throw in the towel now?" he asked. "We look forward to tomorrow," Scorza snapped, placing his document cart in front of the elevator door so that Tuite would have no further opportunity to apply stress techniques to Church.

Despite the Nykaza setback, the trial continued to go well for the prosecution. Alan Masters, with the self-confidence born of running riot over the justice system for decades, did not appear to realize this. Instead, he tried to provoke John Reed, whose involvement Masters seemed to be taking personally.

One day Masters came up to Reed outside the courtroom and asked, "Have you seen *Time* magazine this week?" When Reed answered, "no," Masters continued. "Well, it seems cancer researchers have decided to switch from laboratory rats to police sergeants in their experiments. There's a shortage of lab rats, but there's an inexhaustible supply of police sergeants. People become attached to lab rats, but they don't have to worry about that with police sergeants. And there are some things lab rats just won't do." In fact, the joke in the magazine applied to lawyers.

While delivering what he obviously hoped was a crushing insult, Masters was sweating profusely, his eyes were bulging out of his head, and his tongue and hands were wagging back and forth like a Maori warrior trying to intimidate the foe. "I wonder if that's the last sight Dianne saw," Reed thought to himself. Down the hall, Patrick Tuite peeked around a corner. "Maybe he hopes I'll pop Alan one," Reed mused.

On another occasion, Alan walked by, saying to Reed, "If your feet get any bigger, you'll have to wear boxes." Apparently Reed was supposed to shrivel up and blow away because Masters cast aspersions on Reed's extremities.

CHAPTER 4

*P*eople were squeezed together like sardines on the spectator benches to watch Jim Church complete his testimony. That Tuite was going to try to embarrass him was obvious by the lawyer's tone when he addressed him as "Mr. Witness" and commented on Church's tendency to answer a question before it was fully asked. Tuite suggested that Church had been rehearsed so many times by the prosecution that he knew precisely what was coming next. Jim fluffed that off, explaining it was a habit he acquired during his teaching career.

This gave Tuite the opportunity to point out to the jury that Church was a molder of young minds. "They're all adults, I think," Jim replied.

"I take it from your testimony you weren't teaching morals?" Tuite asked rhetorically. Scorza objected before Jim could answer, and the judge sustained the objection. "Teaching ethics?" asked Tuite. Another objection. Sustained. "...teaching sex education?" Still another objection. Sustained. "Was that only things you did in motel rooms [sic]?" Scorza was on his feet again. "Judge, he's badgering this witness." "I'm not," Tuite replied. Another sustained objection.

After that, Tuite stayed pretty much within the acceptable boundaries for giving a prosecution witness a hard time, referring to Dianne as "your girlfriend," and bringing up the article about the *Song of Solomon* from which the couple had obtained the idea for wine incident. Church explained that they usually shared some wine when they went to a motel and sometimes crackers and cheese as well.

Tuite jumped on this. "Just like the opening of an art gallery, right? A little wine and cheese and adultery always goes good, right? Tell me, sir, does white wine or red wine go better with adultery?" Tuite's cross examination of Church had about as many objections as it did answers. The lawyer was taking a chance that the jury would ignore this, remembering only Tuite's insinuations about Jim and Dianne's character and behavior.

As had Brigitte, Helene, and Pat Casey, Jim testified that Dianne always wore underwear, including both panties and panty hose, but he could not remember the texture or fabric when he was pressed to do so.

Bill Murphy wanted to cast doubt on the reasons for Jim's recollection of his encounter with Keating at Artie G's. Murphy asked about all the occasions when Jim had been questioned by various investigators without mentioning seeing Keating on March 2. Jim replied that it was only after he saw a photo of Keating accompanying a June 1988 newspaper article that he recognized Keating as the man who approached him back in March of 1982.

Murphy tried to blame Jim's recent recollection on Church's desire to help the prosecution, but like all the efforts to discredit Church, it went over like a pregnant pole-vaulter. Church was so normal, so average, that was hard to visualize him as a cad trying to fornicate his way into a tenured position. Church was the kind of fellow you would ask to take in your mail while you were on vacation and who could be trusted to return your garden tools.

When Church's ordeal was over, Scorza introduced evidence, stipulated, or agreed, to by defense attorneys, of motel records, a calendar for 1982, and the weather reports for February and March of that year.

While Church was finishing up, John Reed tried to calm an edgy Jack Bachman. Bachman had already pleaded guilty to racketeering and tax evasion before another federal court judge and knew that his cooperation in the Masters' case would help in his sentencing. He had a lot riding on his testimony, and he knew he would be a prime target for the defense attorneys.

Scorza believed in using preemptive strikes with witnesses who had bad records or shady backgrounds, beating defense counsel to the punch. He would strip such witnesses bare and then rehabilitate them. Bachman was the first big test of this strategem in this trial.

Bachman's job history, his resignation from the Sheriff's PD, and his guilty plea were laid out. Then Scorza asked, "Do you want to go to jail, Mr. Bachman?" When Bachman gave the obvious answer, Scorza inquired as to whether the government promised Bachman any other benefits than telling the judge about Bachman's cooperation. Again, Bachman answered "no." He also told the court that after detailing the penalty for perjury, Sheldon Zenner warned him that "if I lied on the stand either to help or hurt the case, [the government would] come down on me like a ton of bricks."

Bachman testified that he met Jim Keating and Michael Corbitt almost immediately on joining the CCSPD in 1966 and encountered Alan Masters circa 1971. In 1972, when Bachman was working on the vice squad, he asked Masters if Alan was giving money to Jim Keating not to arrest Cicero bookmakers. Alan said yes, but that he thought Bachman was collecting some of it. Bachman told Masters he was not. The next day, Bachman was in Keating's office, saying, "Somebody told me that you are getting money from Alan Masters not to hit the bookmakers in Cicero." At first, Keating denied this. About a month later, Keating told Bachman that he did indeed have a deal with Masters and from that time on Bachman was part of it.   In 1973, Keating was sent to a special traffic school run by Northwestern University, and he asked Bachman to pick up the bribe money. Around the first of each month, Bachman went to Masters' Summit law office. If

Masters was not present to hand it to Bachman personally, it was waiting for him in a mail slot or pigeonhole.

Bachman explained that eventually Alan Masters cut himself into the deal. The transactions continued until the summer of 1984 when Bachman told Keating he did not want to be involved anymore; the feds were investigating the sheriff's office. The bribes were a good investment for the bookies because over the years they paid off, they were never raided. A year or so later, Alan Masters phoned Bachman, asking if the Cicero deal could be resumed, but Bachman refused.

Bachman maintained that he only took bribes in vice cases involving gambling or prostitution. However, he was involved in the raid on Dennis Egan's construction yard and received approximately one thousand dollars from Mike Corbitt, which money he shared with Jim Keating.

By the Friday lunch break, Scorza had just begun to question Bachman about the ex-cop's coownership of the whorehouse with Alan Masters and Clarke Buckendahl. Tuite's objection led to a sidebar where Scorza successfully argued that Masters' partnership in the Astrology Club was relevant because in questioning Lary Damron, Tuite tried to say that Alan had no intention of helping the undercover agent open a whorehouse. Alan's ownership of a bordello would provide another link.

If Jim Church spent a long time on the stand, Bachman's stint seemed like an eternity. When the trial resumed, Bachman told how he once received a $5,000 referral fee from Masters, and how Masters handled Bachman's divorce, for which the cop paid only $140 for filing costs. He described his growing personal friendship with Alan and his knowledge of the tempestuous relationship between Alan and Dianne. Gradually, Scorza led Bachman through Howard Vanick's phone call about Jim Church's license number and Keating's offer of $25,000 to kill Dianne.

Because Bachman's testimony was especially damaging to Jim Keating, it was agreed among the defense counsel that Bill Murphy would take the major responsibility for cross examination. What his colleagues did not know was that in addition to the pressures of a high-profile trial where he spent days without opening his mouth, Murphy was in the midst of a personal emergency. The stress on Murphy was so great that he came down with an acute case of psoriasis.

Murphy confronted Bachman with several seemingly contradictory statements the ex-cop made before other grand and petit juries and to various prosecutors. Scorza objected that they were being taken out of context, and the judge ruled that they had to be read in full. Whatever point Murphy was trying to make was lost in the shuffle.

In fact, Murphy probably gained some sympathy for Bachman by getting him to admit that prison was not the best place for an ex- cop to be. Murphy asked if Bachman knew that policemen were beaten up, raped, and in general not nicely treated in the big house. Bachman said he did not know that, but he certainly would like to avoid going to jail. Turning to John Reed's numerous reports of interviews with Bachman, Murphy tried to discredit Bachman's testimony because he did not immediately tell Reed everything.

Bachman was relatively untouched during the long hours of cross examinationby both Bill Murphy and Dennis Berkson, Corbitt's counsel. The jury heard the most damning testimony against Masters, Corbitt, and Keating, and attempts to make Bachman look like a lying lapdog of the federal government were lost amidst legal verbiage and arguments about the decor in Alan Masters' law office.

Bachman was not the only one who heaved a sign of relief when the trial was adjourned for the long Memorial Day weekend. Bill Murphy went home haunted by the realization that he had failed to discredit Bachman.

The Chicago Sunday newspapers had a field day with the week's testimony, especially about the wine bottle and the tape recording.

"Sex-spiced Masters trial packs 'em in" ran the headline in the *Chicago Sun-Times*. The article by Adrienne Drell stated that, "The trial has featured evidence that judges were fixing cases, prosecutors were dismissing charges and crooked cops were getting payoffs from bookies or running whorehouses. But official graft is not what's luring the huge crowds of onlookers. 'It's sex' admitted one elderly court buff. "I want to hear THE tape." Drell did explain that the tape "is believed to have disappeared," but many people believe that it was played in court; some even claim to have heard it there. A suburban housewife is depicted as laughing out loud at some of the testimony and then declaring, "This is so much fun. I had the idea that court stuff could be fun from 'L.A. Law.' This sure proves it."

The trial was living up to expectations as to its entertainment value. Except that "L.A. Law" is fiction. The murder of Dianne Masters was real.

CHAPTER 5

$\mathcal{T}$he trial resumed Tuesday
morning with FBI agent Ivan Harris. Harris confirmed the chain of
custody of some of the physical evidence, such as the Cadillac's
clock, Dianne's jewelry, including her watch; and the shell casing
and bullets found in and on her body on December 11, 1982. Harris
also pointed out the locations of the various landmarks on a large
map that had been blown up for the purpose.

Harris was followed by a procession of people who had
attended the MVCC board meeting and the gathering at the
Village Courtyard with Dianne on March 18/19, 1982. They agreed
that she gave every indication that she was going straight to her
house.

After the jury was excused, Tom Scorza told the judge that
"Barring another epileptic seizure," Ted Nykaza was ready to testify. But first, Scorza had a few comments about Tuite's intention
of laying Dianne's murder at Nykaza's feet. "I'm going to be
blunt," the prosecutor said, as several people who knew him
cringed at the thought of what this might mean. "We know of no
evidence tying Mr. Nykaza to the murder of Dianne Masters."

Scorza wanted to remind the court that Nykaza was a witness,
not a defendant, and he wanted guidelines established about Ted's
cross examination. Scorza said he was expecting Nykaza to be
asked if he killed Dianne Masters in order to steal her underwear.

373

The judge reserved his ruling, the jury returned, and Ted began to answer questions.

Initially, Nykaza looked like an easy target for the defense. He showed the ravages of his longtime alcoholism, and he did not have the most stable background, despite all his commendations from the Chicago PD. He was the veteran of three failed marriages, willing to sail a little close to the legal wind in his p.i. work, with an unseemly interest in ladies undergarments. However, Nykaza came across as too unstable and unpredictable to both plan and conceal a murder.

As with Bachman, Scorza immediately let the skeletons out of Nykaza's closet. He was disciplined for tardiness and once for being intoxicated while he was a Chicago cop, but received many commendations as well. He injured himself while drunk and sometimes ran afoul of the law. He tried to shoot the chain off a driveway to a monastery because he wanted to investigate reports of ghost sightings there. Scorza established that Nykaza had not been granted immunity by the federal government nor had he been paid an informant's fee.

Summing it all up, Scorza asked, "It would be fair to say that all of these problems indicate that in ordinary language you're a drunk?" "That's correct," Ted replied.

Ted testified to his long-standing relationship with Alan, including the arrangement that permitted Ted to use space in Alan's law office, for which he paid in kind. Their offices were close enough that Nykaza frequently overheard Masters' conversations. In mid-1981, Ted heard a quivery-voiced Alan saying, "Dianne, why are you doing this to me?" Toward the end of 1981, in front of Diane Economou, Masters complained about Dianne, turning aside Ted's suggestion that Alan's infidelity might have something to do with his marital problems.

Scorza established that Nykaza knew Masters' request for a telephone tap was illegal and then produced invoices for the equipment Nykaza purchased in early 1982 for that purpose. Ted described the afternoon he spent with Masters and Joe Hein, playing the tape of Dianne's phone call with Jim Church. The two were whispering, Ted said, and to the best of his recollection, Jim asked, "Are you okay?" "There's just a little bit of spotting," Dianne replied. Jim seemed concerned about this. "Well, maybe we won't use the bottle next time."

Ted told the jury how he replayed the tape for Alan many times and how Alan shouted, "I'll kill that motherfucker." At Scorza's next question, "Anything besides that?" Ted had to take some time to compose himself. Apologizing to the court, Nykaza described Alan's swearing that he would stage a home invasion, where everything alive in the house would be killed. Those two phrases stuck in his mind, and Nykaza would never forget them. He also remembered vividly that Joe Hein was present throughout.

Ted took the tape recordings with him when he left the house on Wolf Road, and the next day, while he was in bed with his wife, he played them for her. At Alan's request, Ted played the tapes several more times, using a decibel meter to try to discover what telephone number Dianne dialed before the intimate conversation took place. But Alan did not want to spend much money, the taping equipment was bottom of the line, and as a result the attempt was unsuccessful. A few weeks later, around the beginning of March, Alan Masters phoned Nykaza and told him to destroy the tapes, and Nykaza did so.

On two occasions in March 1982, Nykaza received telephone instructions from Masters to "make sure you have an alibi" for a specific day, but Ted could not remember the exact dates. Questioned further, Nykaza admitted that he did not go to authorities after hearing Alan's threats in February 1982, after Dianne disappeared in March, or after her body was found in December. He also continued to work for Alan during this time and up till the summer of 1987. After receiving a handwritten note from Masters telling Ted he would have to "shape up or ship out," Nykaza opted for the latter.

Ted admitted lying to State Policeman Charles Kitchen when asked if he placed recording devices on Dianne's phones and in saying he had no information that would be of interest to the police. He also testified that when John Reed began questioning him in October 1986, Ted did not immediately tell the sergeant the truth about his knowledge.

Patrick Tuite's cross-examination would have to wait for the next morning, and it was expected to be rugged. After all, Tuite promised in his opening statement to prove who killed Dianne, and it was clear that Ted Nykaza was the designated hitter.

Tuite confronted Ted about setting his car on fire in 1987 and attempting to defraud the insurance company. Another Nykaza auto met a fiery end in 1983, but Ted denied torching that car, although he admitted spray painting "You'll be next" on the garage door of his home during that period. At the time, Ted's second marriage was on the rocks, and he was trying to scare his wife by indicating she might share Dianne Masters' fate.

Tuite ran Ted through a litany of other examples of strange behavior, including boasts that he killed several people while on the Chicago PD. Ted insisted that he had made all these stories up while inebriated.

When Tuite asked if Nykaza had ever said, "I can't kill again" while talking to himself at home, Scorza objected and the judge called for a sidebar. Before the judge, Tuite said, "It is our theory that [Nykaza] was responsible for the death of Dianne Masters..." The "can't kill again statement" was relevant "as to whether or not he had anything to do with her death."

Scorza repeated a point he raised before, emphasizing that Nykaza was a witness in the case, not a defendant. The fact that Nykaza made false statements in the past had already been brought out. But Tuite argued that one way to raise doubt as to a defendant's guilt was to show someone else could have done it.

Judge Zagel ruled that Nykaza could answer Tuite's question, but he was not going to permit Tuite to argue that "there is any showing" that Ted was responsible for Dianne's death.

Back in front of the jury, Ted said he did not recall such a statement, but he might have said something to that effect while drunk. "Have you ever either in a drunken or sober state told anyone that little voices tell you to kill?" Tuite asked, pushing the judge's ruling. "No, that's ridiculous," Ted responded before Scorza could raise an objection. The question and answer were ordered stricken from the record, and the jury told to disregard both. Lawyers for both sides know that this is a difficult thing for juries to do, however much they may try, and sometimes the risk of judicial sanctions make it worthwhile to get the question out front.

Then Tuite turned to Ted's personal knowledge of Alan and Dianne. "When you saw Alan with Dianne, you realized that he was very devoted to her?" Tuite asked. "Well, I had my own opinion. If you want to buy somebody, sure," Ted replied. This was not exactly the answer Tuite wanted, so he switched tactics.

"Where were you about 1:15 in the morning hours of March 19, 1982?" Tuite demanded. Ted said he could not tell; he did not remember where he was last week. When he found out that Dianne disappeared on that date, he had no reason to think about what he had been doing that night because he was not involved. On the two occasions when Alan told Ted to have an alibi, Ted believed it was "just another irate husband mouthing off."

Tuite switched between accusing Ted of murdering Dianne and nit-picking questions about invoices and shipments of tape recording devices, so that a good deal of the cross examination was really quite boring. Tuite seemed to sense that he was not making a convincing case against Ted as Dianne's murderer, so he tried again.

"Nykaza, that evening March 19, as a favor to a friend, did you stop and abduct Dianne Masters?" Tuite almost shouted.

"Are you serious?" Ted replied in wonderment.

But Tuite was playing to the gallery. "Yes, I am serious, sir. This is not a joke, sir. Maybe it is to you..."

"It's not a joke," Nykaza interrupted.

At Scorza's objection that the question had no good faith basis, the judge called for a sidebar. "Maybe I don't understand this," Zagel said to Tuite. "Is the implication of your question that the government's RICO charge is basically wrong because your client hired Nykaza?"

Tuite tried to explain his theory. "No, [Alan] didn't hire him. That [Ted] did [Alan] a favor without telling him because of his despondency and because he was upset..."

Scorza pointed out that in his opening statement and other comments, Tuite claimed to the jury that it would be proven that Dianne voluntarily met Nykaza in some previously arranged interlude. As a result, Scorza had inquired of other witnesses whether Dianne appeared to have an appointment that evening. Then in another sidebar, Tuite asserted that Dianne met her first husband, and that man killed her. Now he was trying to say that Nykaza kidnapped Dianne and murdered her as favor. "Judge, it's being made up as we go along."

Judge Zagel turned to Tuite. "Well, what's the basis for the abduction question?"

Tuite backed down a little. "Maybe abduction's a bad word...We think he saw her, that he did something with her, that he killed her. I think that's reasonable because we have a witness who says...that this man was sitting in this room saying: I can't kill again. He has guns. He shoots at people...if he were on trial, this would go to the government, and the government would establish those facts. We have definite strong evidence that this man wears and collects women's underwear..."

"The objection to the question as phrased is sustained. If you want to ask this individual whether or not he killed Dianne Masters, you can do that," Judge Zagel ordered.

Back before the jury, Tuite said, "Mr. Nykaza, on the early morning hours of March 19, 1982, did you beat, shoot, and kill Dianne Masters?"

"No, sir," Nykaza declared.

When Tuite asked if Ted removed Dianne's underwear, Scorza objected, and the judge refused to permit Ted's answer.

But Tuite would not quit. "Isn't it a fact that in March of 1982 that you wore women's underwear as a regular matter?" Another sidebar was called. The judge pointed out that if Tuite could offer direct evidence that Nykaza killed Dianne, that would be fine. But on cross examination, once Ted denied the murder, that was as far as Tuite could take it.

Tuite insisted he planned to prove that Nykaza was involved, but it was necessary to bring out Ted's predilection for ladies' underwear because when Dianne was found, hers was missing.

"Indicative of her getting home," Scorza interjected.

"You can ask him if he wore women's underwear. You can ask him if he saw her that night, and then let's stop the show," Judge Zagel continued.

"Judge, we are going to object to anything about his wearing habits," Scorza added.

The jury and court watchers did not have long to ponder the subject of the heated discussion. Tuite asked if Nykaza saw Dianne Masters in the early morning hours on March 18/19, 1982, and Ted denied it.

"Did you in March of 1982 sometime before and sometime after that wear women's underwear?"

"In sexual games my wife and I played, it's very possible I did at that time," Ted tried to explain.

"Did you...have on you or in your collection —"

"Objection," Scorza called.

"—shiny—"

Another objection.

"—lacy, feminine women's underwear?"

When the judge sustained the prosecutor's third objection. Tuite declared he had nothing further. Neither Murphy nor Berkson had any questions, but Scorza had a few on redirect examination.

He brought out what he termed the "scary scenario" constructed for Jude Fogerty at Alan Masters' request. Scorza produced a note in Alan's handwriting. At this point, the judge called for a break for the jury, and the attorneys discussed the note which read: "Ted, re: Fogerty,...have Brenda [one of Nykaza's operatives] call me so I can tell her what I want her to do. Number two, I thought putting a grave type flower wreath to Jude Fogerty on her doorstep one night would shake her up." Scorza's point was that Tuite was trying to prove that Nykaza planned Dianne's elimination to help Alan, and Ted had a habit of developing little plots. However, the Fogerty episode would "rehabilitate" Ted because it proved that Alan was capable of formulating nasty little plans on his own. The judged ruled that the Fogerty episode showed that Alan did have confidence in Ted, and it could be admitted.

"Don't these people ever throw anything away?" one of the spectators asked another.

Finally, just before lunch, Ted Nykaza's two days in court were over.

Alan Masters still seemed supremely confident. Approaching John Reed who was on duty outside the courtroom, Masters said, "I know you've got a sense of humor, and that's why I am telling you how to slap someone." As Reed listened in disgust, Masters continued. "You're an asshole, a son of bitch, a pedophile, a child molester, a motherfucker. Now your line is, 'You called me everything but a cocksucker,' and I say, 'I knew you were trying to quit.'" Throughout this recital, Masters was sweating heavily and making slapping gestures.

Scorza's keen eye for staging was evident when Genevieve Capstaff was called as the next witness. Replacing the shaky, seedy Nykaza with the white-haired retired humanities professor was a nice touch. Gen related how she left the gathering at the Village Courtyard, got into her maroon station wagon, and pulled out of her parking space, but did not leave the restaurant lot because she was inquisitive. Instead, she pulled alongside the building. Scorza provided photos of the restaurant and had Gen point out the two locations of her car. Sometime after 1 a.m., when the rest of the college party left the bar, Gen saw Dianne speak to Mary Nelson for a brief time, then get into her car and drive west onto 123rd Street. Gen also saw Mary Nelson turn east, as did the cars driven by the remaining members of the MVCC group. Finally, Gen left the lot, turning west. She was about one block behind Dianne. Capstaff saw no other automobiles going in either direction on the road, and noticed nothing odd about Dianne's driving. The last she saw of her friend was when Dianne made the turn on Wolf Road, which Gen knew from experience was only about twenty seconds from Dianne's front door.

Patrick Tuite was well aware that some of the Moraine Valley group did not believe Gen was waiting in the parking lot, and he went after her like a terrier, looking for discrepancies in various statements she had given to investigators over the years about the exact time she had last seen Dianne.

Tuite read from a number of documents made available by the prosecution on discovery, and Scorza rose to ask that it be established whether Gen had ever read any of them. She had not. Asked about the fifteen or so minutes difference in times she had given, Gen replied that she did not know exactly, that all times had been approximate.

At one point, after throwing out several different sets of numbers, Tuite asked, "You follow me?" "No, Gen replied, "I am completely confused." So was everybody else in the courtroom. Before Scorza could say "objection," the judge called, "stop." Scorza said, "It's very confusing and in fact badgering." The judge sustained the objection.

Spectators thought Tuite's handling of the seventy-two-year-old woman was not sitting well with the jurors. In any event, proving she was off by fifteen or twenty minutes would not make much difference. Anyone could understand that over the years a person might lose a few minutes here or there. Besides, a guilty verdict did not require split-second timing.

Pat Tuite was not having a nice day. If Ted Nykaza had proved to be a convincing witness, Capstaff was as solid as the Rock of Gibraltar.

The rest of the day was comparatively unexciting. Two of the Masters' neighbors testified they had heard no shots or altercation during the early morning of March 19; CCSPD Investigator Mark Baldwin relayed his observations about Alan Masters during the beginning of the missing person's investigation; the defense stipulated to Scorza's admission of Alan Masters' telephone records for March 1982, including the fact that at that time Illinois Bell provided an unlimited service option known as Call-Pak, and because of this, the company could not provide an itemized list of calls made from Wolf Road to surrounding communities. However, the phone company did show long-distance calls to Alan Masters' sons in Washington D.C. at 8:52 p.m. and Ithaca, New York, at 8:54 p.m. on March 18, 1982. One was attending Georgetown University Law and the other, Cornell.

Joseph LaRocca, a former Willow Springs PD radio operator, testified about entries he made in the Willow Springs police log for the third shift, running from 4 p.m. to midnight on March 19, 1982. Scorza took LaRocca through an explanation of the codes used by the WSPD and the twenty-four hour clock, and then he got down to the important entries. At 2235, or 10:35 p.m., on March 19, LaRocca received a transmission from car 50, a number given to whatever vehicle Chief Corbitt happened to be driving. Corbitt radioed that he had arrived at a bar named In First Place where there was a lockout, police jargon for those occasions when a citizen locks the keys in a car and needs assistance.

At 2241, or 10:41 p.m, LaRocca heard that car 52 was at a traffic stop, and four minutes later, car 52 reported he was available again. At 2247, or 10:47, car 52 reported that he had arrived at In First Place, and one minute later he was back in service. Car 52 was driven by George Witzel.

At 11 p.m., the Willow Springs PD shift changed. At 2303, or 11:03 p.m., LaRocca entered a report of "shot fired west of station." Six police cars, including Corbitt's number 50, reported that they were investigating the shots. LaRocca also identified the time cards of George Witzel, who worked the shift ending at 11 p.m., Robert Olson, who drove car 52 between 11 p.m. and 7 a.m., and Mike Corbitt, who was on injury leave.

When Dennis Berkson cross-examined LaRocca about these details, eyelids began to droop all over the courtroom. Throughout the trial, Berkson spent so much time in a seated position that when he did rise he had to twitch at his clothes to keep them from strangling him.

Having gone through the events leading up to Dianne's disappearance, Scorza was proceeding in an orderly fashion through the events in Willow Springs the following night. At 10:35 p.m. on March 19, George Witzel testified he heard Mike Corbitt's voice reporting the lockout. At 10:47, Witzel drove to In First Place, after handling a traffic stop. As Witzel was pulling up outside the establishment, which included a garage, he saw Mike Corbitt driving toward him, and the two cars stopped driver-window to driver-window in a signal eight. Witzel remembered that Corbitt had a passenger, but the lighting was poor and Witzel could only say that he was a man of medium build wearing a leather jacket, who was gazing out the passenger window.

When Witzel asked Corbitt if everything was okay, Corbitt said, "Yes. Before you go off duty, I want you to go there and clear out the canal." Replying that he would check it out, Witzel drove directly under the bridge, illuminating the area with his spotlight. There were no automobiles and no people present at the time. At

10:51 p.m. Witzel radioed in his mileage because he was going off duty. At 11:03 he was inside the police station taking care of paper work when he heard LaRocca's transmissions about shots fired. Witzel also testified that when Alan Masters represented recipients of drunk-driving tickets, the paper work seemed to disappear.

Having placed Corbitt on Willow Springs' main drag, with an interest in an empty canal bank, the scene was set for Robert Olson to testify to finding Corbitt at the canal when Olson responded to hearing shots in that vicinity. An attempt to make the most of some discrepancies in Olson's testimony and the FBI 302 completed by Dave Parker failed when Scorza objected that Olson had not been given an opportunity to review or sign the document. Judge Zagel once again told Patrick Tuite to quit waving a piece of paper lest it give the jury a false impression.

Jack Lynn was another member of the Willow Springs police force. After Dianne disappeared, Lynn asked Corbitt, "Do you think they will ever find her?" Corbitt replied, "They got about as much chance of finding her as they do Jimmy Hoffa's little pinky." As he was saying this, a laughing Corbitt raised his hand and wiggled his little finger.

CCSPD Sergeant Clarke Buckendahl testified under a grant of immunity from prosecution. After admitting he owned a whorehouse with Bachman and Masters, Buckendahl was questioned about Masters' concern over who would handle a report of trouble at Masters' home in 1981. Buckendahl also told the jury about Masters' behavior on the day the investigation began.

The forensic evidence began with former Willow Springs Chief Jim Ross and the evidence technicians who processed Dianne's Cadillac after it was pulled from the canal. FBI Agent William Tobin, a specialist in forensic metallurgy, examined Dianne's watch and the clock from her Cadillac timepiece which read 1:50. The car clock was an electromechanical mechanism powered by a twelve-volt system operating off the car's main battery. If it was working when the car went into the water, it would have stopped within a few seconds. Based on all the factors involved, Tobin believed that it was not possible to rely on the car clock for an accurate reading of the time of the immersion.

Dianne's expensive Baume Mercier watch was a conventional timepiece with two hands, powered by a mainspring. Once wound, it could stay in working order for as long as thirty-six hours. The watch stopped because it wound down, not because of water damage. When found, it read 1:54.

Tobin's expert opinion was that it would be statistically improbable for the clock and the watch to have stopped within four minutes of each other. Instead, the most likely explanation for the similarity was that both timepieces were altered.

It was inescapable that the most likely candidate for time alteration was Mike Corbitt. After all, in the arson trial, Scorza caught him changing a car rental form. Tampering with evidence was no big deal to Big Mike.

The second week of the trial was over, and Tom Scorza felt good about it. His two riskiest witnesses, Jack Bachman and Ted Nykaza, had been believable. Crooked and strange, but believable. As the rest of the prosecution personnel packed up exhibits, Scorza shot past them to his office. Struggling with a bulky exhibit, one man worried out loud to another member of the team that he would not get the package through the office door. "Don't worry," the other man replied, "the only thing that won't make it through the door is Scorza's head."

CHAPTER 6

*R*obert J. Stein, a crusty gentlemen with impeccable credentials, became Cook County's first medical examiner in 1976 when the elective office of coroner was abolished. On Monday, Dr. Stein told the hushed courtroom about being called to Willow Springs on December 11, 1982, to examine Dianne's body in the trunk and how it was then removed to the old morgue building. He described the autopsy, during which he extracted two bullets from the softened tissue of Dianne Masters' brain and determined that her skull had been shattered in two places by a blunt instrument. As a result, he called in Dr. Clyde Snow to reconstruct Dianne's skull. Stein agreed with Snow's conclusion that Dianne was bludgeoned first and then shot. It was impossible to be certain because of the degree of decomposition, which also precluded any finding as to whether the blows had broken the skin.

When Stein's testimony ended, Patrick Tuite called for a sidebar. Alan Masters left the courtroom during Stein's presentation because he was weeping, and he wanted to waive his appearance during Dr. Snow's testimony. "I think we will have to hear it from him," Judge Zagel said. The jury was excused, and Masters assured the judge that it was his wish not to be present. Courtroom functionaries stared as Masters exited, and a buff murmured, "That man does not know shame."

387

Clyde Snow, a specialist in the reconstruction of skeletal remains, related how at Dr. Stein's request, he applied his skill to rebuilding Dianne's skull, using the forty-nine available fragments. Slides of the reconstruction were shown as Snow explained that Dianne was hit twice "with considerable force." One blow caught her horizontally across her forehead; the other, across the back of the head. Such damage could not have been inflicted as Dianne lay in the Cadillac trunk. Snow was firm about his conclusion that Dianne was beaten first, placed in the trunk, and then shot. Again, the decomposition prevented him from determining whether she was still alive when shot, but he believed it was possible; one portion of her skull bore what looked like bloodstains, and dead bodies do not bleed.

State Trooper Charles Kitchen followed with details of the state police investigation. He was succeeded by Alan Masters' divorce lawyer, who testified how he helped fill in the life insurance claim; by an insurance claims manager for the Hartford; and by a trust officer at Masters' bank. The prosecution case was in the homestretch.

On June 6, 1989, after entering into the record the laws of the State of Illinois which the defendants were accused of breaking, Tom Scorza rested the prosecution case. Patrick Tuite, Dennis Berkson, and Bill Murphy presented the customary motions for a directed verdict of not guilty, which Judge Zagel denied.

There was a rustling among the spectators when Pat Tuite rose to begin his defense of Alan Masters. Thus far, as one observer put it, Scorza went around Tuite's head like a haircut. Perhaps that was about to change.

The first defense witness was an emergency-room nurse from Palos Community Hospital. Tuite began asking the woman if she had been on duty on December 11, 1988, but she barely answered when Scorza objected, asking for a sidebar.

Tuite told Judge Zagel that the nurse would testify that when Ted Nykaza was brought in after an accident, he was found to be wearing women's panties. After legal wrangling between Tuite and Scorza, the judge ruled that Tuite did not have enough to connect Nykaza's fetish to Dianne's murder. "I am generally willing to let the defense cobble whatever theory together they can...But that is a different question from permitting into evidence something whose relevance at best is highly marginal...and in my view not advance the search of truth."

Back before the jury, Tuite told the witness, "...the government has objected to your testimony, so we can't..." Before he could complete the sentence, Scorza objected. Telling the judge he was excusing the witness, Tuite did manage to ask if the nurse had examined Nykaza at the hospital, but when he followed up with, "Did you have occasion to undress him," Scorza had enough. Tuite was flirting with violation of the judge's ruling, and he had to let the nurse go.

It was not an auspicious beginning for the defense.

The second defense witness was Donna Davis, the woman who kept house for the Masters in 1982. She testified that there was no sign of a struggle or bloodstains the morning after Dianne disappeared. A locksmith told how he rekeyed the locks on the Masters' house on March 25, 1982. The owner of a security service testified that Masters upgraded his alarm system in April 1982, although when Reed and Colby visited the company in 1987, there was no record in the ledger of any work done at the house on Wolf Road.

To bolster the defense case against Ted Nykaza, Tuite called Sheila Mikel, Alan's onetime receptionist/mistress and Nykaza's ex-wife, to the stand. Mikel told the jury she did not know Ted had a drinking problem when they were wed, which seemed incredible in light of the fact that the two had known each other for years.

Tom Scorza requested a sidebar, and the judge asked Tuite, "Other than the underwear, which I already ruled on, what are you going to get in with her?" Tuite wanted Mikel to tell the jury that while the couple were married, she found Ted crying and telling an empty chair, "I can't kill again." When the marriage was breaking up and she was packing, Mikel also found a bag of women's underwear which did not belong to her.

"Let me see if I understand your theory about the relevance of Nykaza as an alternative suggested killer," the judge said. "One, he works for Masters. Two, he knows Masters is upset about Dianne's infidelity. Three, he knows that Masters wants something done about her infidelity. And, four, because he works for Masters and he knows Dianne Masters, he knows where [she] lives, and he has some idea of [her] movement...And, five, he never killed anybody and makes the statement I can't kill again, thereby implying that he has in fact killed in the past. And the person that he might have killed is Dianne Masters. That's your theory."

"Um-hum," Tuite replied.

Because it looked like the sidebar argument over Mikel's hearsay would be lengthy, the judge excused the jury. Finally, the judge ruled the statement inadmissible because the "excited utterance" and other precedents did not apply. Before the jury was brought back, Tuite asked that the judge exclude evidence of Mikel's sexual relationship with Alan Masters. Scorza wanted it in as evidence of Mikel's bias, and the judge said he would allow it.

Then Tuite raised the underwear question again. This time, he said that Mikel could testify that Ted had stolen her underwear. Scorza observed, "The last time we walked away from here with a ruling, I thought that we weren't going to go into the underwear at all, and then we had a surreptitious question about it. Mr. Tuite went out there and asked the lady on the stand if she undressed Mr. Nykaza."

"Mr. Tuite perhaps gets carried away in the passion of the moment," Judge Zagel replied.

"It's the subject matter that inflames him, the underwear," Scorza observed.

"Mr. Tuite, I'm sure, will not do that again," the judge replied.

On cross examination, Mikel admitted that in 1978, Masters loaned her five thousand dollars for a home down payment, which she never repaid. He also gave her presents, although she thought that stopped in 1981. She also was a little hazy as to how often she and Alan saw each other. And although she lived with Ted for two months before their wedding, and saw him drunk, she did not realize he had emotional problems resulting from his drinking. Scorza also established that on the day she moved out of Nykaza's home, John Reed was present, but Mikel did not tell him of her suspicions that Ted had killed Dianne Masters nor did she express any fears for her own safety.

Scorza pressed Mikel as to whether she told anyone that she received an alibi warning from Alan, but she denied it. She did admit seeing Alan for "advice" several times after Dianne disappeared and during her marriage to Ted, as well as arriving at court as part of Alan's entourage on that very day.

The defense staggered on with the owner of the towing company that handled the 1982 canal dredging in Willow Springs. Alan Masters was his lawyer, and Tuite tried to make much of the fact that although Alan knew about this job, he never tried to direct the car recovery operation away from the area where Dianne's car was eventually found. A woman Dianne befriended when both were working in real estate sales testified that she continued to visit Georgie and that Dianne's clothes and possessions had a prominent place in the Masters home.

Tuite called both Charles Kitchen and John Reed as defense witnesses in hopes of throwing some doubt on Jim Church's evidence, and FBI Agent Dave Parker was questioned about his interviews with Church and Robert Olson.

Paul Sabin was summoned by Corbitt's attorney in the continuing effort to dispute Olson's testimony. Like John Reed, his testimony did not reveal the role he played in solving the case. Corbitt's next witness was Willow Springs policeman Sonny Fisher, who testified that two weeks before she disappeared, he saw Dianne Masters in her Cadillac on the canal bank. A man with a Southern drawl was in the driver's seat.

John Reed and Ivan Harris were called by the government as rebuttal witnesses, and then suddenly, it was all over but the closing arguments. The buffs shook their heads; if this was the best the high-priced talent could do, send in the paralegals!

The rules provide that government sums up first, followed by the defense attorneys, and then the government has an opportunity to answer their arguments. Slowly, calmly, Patrick Foley went over the evidence. As he did so, Foley became increasingly indignant. He began talking faster and faster, and his face reddened. Even the drowsiest juror was alert.

"Amidst all of this corrupt, despicable behavior, Alan Masters, Michael Corbitt, and James Keating plan and solicit the murder of Dianne Masters...This is not a lark...not a frivolous detour in the association's activity. The mere fact that these men did this, the mere fact that Alan Masters goes to Michael Corbitt, a chief of police, James Keating, a lieutenant in the Cook County Sheriff's Police Department, is evidence of the association because it clearly shows their prior corrupt relationship."

Foley asked the jurors if they could imagine going to their local police officer and asking for his help in killing someone. "No, you couldn't," Foley answered his own question. "But Masters can because he is the master fixer. He's the man who pays the judges, who pays the cops, who has the corrupt relationship. And the trust that developed. Oh, what trust."

Then Foley reminded the jury about the human being that had been Dianne Masters. "She would have been forty-three this month. She comes into our case in 1970 as a bridesmaid." The jurors could visualize the pretty young woman in wedding finery. "She has some marital problems...Alan Masters represents her in the divorce. She's young. She's impressionable. She's vulnerable." Alan is the married man who lavishes her with gifts and pays her bills.

"Mr. Tuite will tell you that this is a generous and kind man, Alan Masters. What he is, is a man who knows nothing but paying bribes, a man who knows nothing but graft, corruption, a man who buys things that suit and serve his purposes.

"While there may have been some love...some affection, Alan Masters had a pretty woman on his arm, the man who bought the judges, the man who bought the cops, the man who bought Dianne. Dianne obviously enjoyed it. He didn't drag her into it. He sucked her into it, but she liked it. But there was a big price to pay. And it started early on."

Foley described the beatings, the abuse, the birth of Georgie, the long-awaited marriage, followed by marital problems which became general knowledge beginning in the fall of 1980. Alan begins to think of murder in 1981 and looks for a killer for hire before she can file for divorce.

Finally, Foley arrived at the last night of Dianne's life. "We know that Dianne went to the board meeting on March 18, 1982. She had a satchel with all the papers they have to discuss at the meeting. She wore stockings and a brown suit." When the meeting ended, at Dianne's suggestion, they went to the Village Courtyard. Around 1 a.m., Dianne left, driving toward her home. "Whatever they want to make out of Genevieve Capstaff, the seventy-two-year-old woman with bronchitis, she followed Dianne Masters to Wolf and McCarthy, and you know it. I know it. And they know it."

Foley explained that the three men were not charged with the actual murder "because there is some gray area on that matter...I think we all know what happened...Everything points to the fact that Alan was home with the best alibi in town, his four-year-old daughter, and that [Dianne] got in the home, and Alan, the man who cannot handle his rage, the man who knew what was at stake, the man who knew he was going to lose his daughter and lose the woman he bought...it's likely she got whacked right in the home."

A very wired Foley finished, "Ladies and gentlemen, when you look at each defendant in this courtroom, you know the government has proved the case beyond a doubt. These men have committed horrendous acts, and they should be found guilty of them."

After a thirty-minute lunch break, Bill Murphy spoke in behalf of Jim Keating. After telling the jury that there were times during the trial where he had so little to do that he felt lonesome, Murphy belittled the prosecution's case, claiming that the government had thrown all the "muck" it could find against a wall in the hope that some of it would stick.

On Friday, June 9, 1989, the crowded courtroom included Dianne's daughter Georgie, now almost twelve years old. Subjecting the child to hearing her dead mother dragged through the mud and her father described as an evil, corrupt murderer made a bad impression on the jury. It was a monumental error in judgment.

Berkson repeated his argument that the case was a work of fiction cooked up by the federal government. In his attack on Dianne's character, Berkson observed, "I guess you could say she probably saw more ceilings than Sears latex paint." Then he likened the government's behavior to the way the Nazis eliminated dissent in Germany.

Patrick Tuite told the jurors that as logical, reasonable people, they could only arrive at a not guilty verdict. He quoted from Murphy's closing statement, adding, "for a moment...I thought my God, they're throwing in everything but the kitchen sink, but then we heard from Kitchen. I was waiting for Sink." The effort at cuteness failed. Making fun of somebody's name was a bad idea. There probably were some jury members who had difficulty over their names. "A guy who is lucky to be called Two-wit ought to know better," one buff said.

After attacking prosecution witnesses, especially Bachman and Nykaza, Tuite returned to his theory of who murdered Dianne. In the beginning it was obviously Ted Nykaza. Now that Ted had testified, Tuite was not so sure. "I'm not saying it was Church. I'm not saying it was Nykaza. It could have been someone else." Tuite suggested that Dianne went willingly to the canal to have "an interlude in the front seat of the car." During the "interlude," her underwear was taken off. This did not explain the absence of her shoes, purse, and tote bag. There might have been an argument, and Dianne might have left the car. Whoever the man was picked up a weapon. "Boom." Dianne is placed in the trunk. "Bang, bang, into the water."

"They'd have you believe that she got home and that Alan Masters with a two-by-four, baseball bat, clubbed his wife to death in the house." Then the lawyer stopped to apologize to Georgie. The jurors glanced toward the child and back at Alan Masters. They did not look happy.

In closing, Tuite brought up the American depiction of justice as a woman with a blindfold holding scales and a sword. "Let's hope she doesn't have to cry under that blindfold, because justice cries out for not guilty."

Then it was Tom Scorza's turn. "Look at Tommy," whispered one hip buff, "he's really ready to rock and roll." It seemed as if Scorza might have heard him, because after he explained to the jury why the government has an additional opportunity to summarize the evidence, the prosecutor said, "I will get rolling here in a minute." Scorza delivered, playing the jury like an electric guitar.

He understood that they might feel the diverse testimony overwhelming, but he was confident they could sort it out. Although they had been silent for the past few weeks, the truth was that they were the main actors. The jurors represented "the common sense of the community." Scorza quoted from one of John Reed's favorites, Ralph Waldo Emerson, "Common sense is genius in its working clothes." Once the jurors applied their everyday genius to the evidence, they could arrive at only one verdict in all three cases: guilty.

Scorza defended all the government witnesses, even those he described as problematic. "The reason that Ted Nykaza and Jack Bachman have so many fleas is they spent so many years laying down with dogs. And everything you want to think badly of them before they came over to us, go right ahead. We cheer you on. Jack Bachman was a crooked cop. Nykaza was a drunk...He's a weird guy...We put him up with all his blemishes, and the same thing with Jack Bachman." Scorza compared the two men unfavorably to Saint Paul, who "had the terrific advantage of being knocked off his horse by God" and was immediately redeemed. Nykaza and Bachman, unlike Saint Paul, "got knocked off their horse by us."

Scorza took up the defense attorneys' allegations that the government had taken a collection of separate crimes and tried to weave them into a corrupt association to fit the RICO law. The government repeatedly demonstrated how the three defendants operated together, how they could depend upon one another. The problem with their plan to murder Dianne is that it did not go according to plan.

Alan's original scheme for killing Dianne was abandoned because his police confederates felt there were too many points where things could go wrong. The objective was to kill her away from the house, after a board meeting. If Jim Church was killed too and their bodies were never found, it would look as if they had run away. What the defendants did not anticipate were Dianne's changes in her usual pattern of behavior.

Scorza compared what happened to Dianne that night to an old black-and-white movie short of Charlie Chaplin as the Little Tramp. Chaplin walks down the street, narrowly missing being hit by a safe, a ladder, and so on. Eventually he got where he was going. "That's what happened in a very serious manner to Dianne Masters...She went to where she was going...She was going home." Except unlike the Little Tramp, Dianne Masters did not emerge unscathed.

As Scorza told the jury in his opening remarks, the curtain fell after Gen Capstaff last saw Dianne. But the jurors would know what happened: she made it home. While preparing for the trial, Scorza watched a movie called *Broadcast News*. Actress Holly

Hunter went into her hotel room and began undressing by taking off her shoes and pulling off her panty hose. "I'm sitting in the movie theater and saying: Holy mackerel. She's dressed, right there on the screen, right now, the way Dianne Masters was found. I took a poll of women that I knew," Scorza told the jury. "Excuse me, do you ever take off your panty hose first? I'm glad Mr. Tuite didn't hear about it. He'd be in here telling you I did the murder."

"You didn't collect them," Tuite interjected. Scorza ignored him, continuing, "It also explains where all the papers in a big satchel are...why was there no satchel in that car, not one soggy piece of paper." It was consistent with the evidence, though not proven, that Dianne took that satchel with those papers inside the house, Scorza asserted.

"This is a very special case," Scorza said near his closing. "When you find these defendants guilty, you will have rendered a true verdict...you're going to be proud of what you did in this case. Because of all the people in the world, you're the ones who are going to determine whether justice is done in the case of Dianne Masters."

If the jurors returned to the Dirksen building in six months or a year, they would not see their names on a monument. Instead, "the monument's going to be your own memory, that when the work of justice became your work, you didn't flinch...I think you are going to tell your loved ones, your children, and, if God's good to you, your children's children that when Dianne Masters could not point to those who plotted and carried out and covered up her murder, you pointed for her. That when she couldn't speak, you spoke for her. And you will beg your loved ones to understand that although you could not bring Dianne Masters back to life, you're the ones who breathed new life into the principle that in the end, right makes might...It is my job to stand here and to urge you on behalf of the United States to find these defendants guilty because the evidence demands it. But beyond my job, in light of the evidence in this case, I'm ready to stand in front of you as a fellow citizen, as a fellow human being, and I want to implore you, good God Almighty, don't let these crimes pass as if they happened in a dream."

It was powerful and moving, only the presence of federal marshals kept some in the spectator seats from cheering or clapping. Following a ten-minute break, the lawyers agreed as to which exhibits would be given to the jurors, who were called back into the courtroom to listen to Judge Zagel's instructions. After deliberating for approximately one hour, the jury was sent home until Monday.

A crowd milled around outside the courtroom. Reporters and the buffs placed bets on a quick conviction. Scorza refused to be drawn out on the subject, but he looked pleased.

That weekend, Janet and Alan Masters joined Patrick Tuite and his wife for dinner at Jack Gibbons Gardens, a roadhouse in Palos Township. Champagne was ordered, and a waitress noticed that everyone but Janet seemed in a celebratory mood.

CHAPTER 7

On Monday, June 12, 1989, the jurors resumed their deliberations. After four additional hours, the foreman sent a message to the judge that they had reached a verdict. People who observed Alan Masters believe it was not until that moment that it dawned on him that he could be convicted.

At 3 p.m. Monday afternoon, the defendants, lawyers, media, and spectators were back in Room 1919 to hear the verdict. Masters, Keating, and Corbitt were convicted of bribery, taking payoffs, case fixing, conspiring to murder Dianne Masters, and aiding, abetting and soliciting her death. On the verdict form, the jury did not check off the racketeering activities that would convict them of concealing Dianne's murder or the mail fraud charge against Masters, which was tantamount to acquittal.

The jury was not quite finished. Under RICO, the guilty parties would have to forfeit any proceeds realized from racketeering activity. This included approximately forty-two thousand dollars in bribe money plus Dianne's property, including her home and jewelry.

For once, Pat Tuite seemed to have his fingers on the jury's pulse. "I guess the last thing you wanted today was to hear from us." An atmosphere of "we've done our bit, and it's been interesting, but let's get out of here" hung over the jury box. If Dianne's jewelry and the house were forfeited to the government, Tuite argued, Georgie would lose the home in which she had been reared, as well as her mother's mementos.

While the jury was out deciding the forfeiture issue, Scorza and Tuite presented the case for and against the revocation of Alan Masters' bond. Judge Zagel accepted Scorza's argument that the risk of flight was now different than it had been. "The government's case was built out of a set of tiles to make a mosaic as a whole," Zagel continued. "An objective lawyer could have looked at the evidence in this case and concluded that the defendant had some chance, however slight, of acquittal." The judge believed the chance of flight was substantial.

Zagel also found that based on the evidence, when angered or feeling betrayed, Alan "at the very least contemplated violence, intended to do violence, and took substantial steps toward the completion of acts of significant violence."

Then Zagel ordered that Alan be detained pending sentencing.

The spectators seemed relieved that Alan Masters finally would be off the streets. Janet Masters sobbed. No one had warned her that her husband would probably would be locked up immediately if found guilty.

Meanwhile, the jury finished its deliberations on the forfeiture question. Masters, Corbitt, and Keating each were socked with a forty-two thousand dollar fine, the amount of the bribes documented by the government, but Dianne's home and jewelry need not be surrendered. Pat Tuite finally won an argument. Judge Zagel dismissed the jury with thanks and set an August sentencing date.

In front of the television cameras in the federal building lobby, Patrick Tuite discussed the "victory" he had just won because his client was not convicted of murder. Tuite criticized the government for bringing federal charges. "If this was tried where it should have been in state court at Twenty-sixth and California [the Cook County Criminal Court building], it would never have gotten past a directed verdict."

Asked for his response, Tom Scorza pointed out, not for the first or last time, that murder had not been one of the charges, at least in part because there of "problems with the evidence" as to who delivered the blows or shots that killed Dianne. This made the use of RICO particularly attractive. There were other reasons for staying out of the state system. "We are dealing with fixers, and we wanted them in a venue where nothing could be fixed." Scorza added, "I wonder if Alan Masters finds the verdict such a victory now that he's behind bars at the MCC, facing a possible forty-year prison term."

Even the jurors seemed confused; one ambled out of the courtroom to say they didn't really have enough to convict the three men of murder, but they got them for everything else.

The media were grateful that the jury had done its work in a timely fashion; items about the convictions led the news at five, six, and ten o'clock.

A reporter and photographer for the *Southtown Economist* caught Janet Masters as she pulled into her driveway the following day. Under pressure and quick to weep, Janet told the reporter, "I don't think they [the jury] were right. I don't consider my husband an animal, or dangerous, or anything that has been said about him for the last seven years."

She did recover her equanimity sufficiently to refuse to answer questions about when her relationship with Alan changed from employer/employee and to deny that the couple's marriage was a cynical gesture toward retaining custody of Georgie. Throughout the trial, Dianne's brother told reporters that he was planning to sue for after or the right to visit his niece. Janet was apprehensive about this threat, and she was leaning heavily on her father. It seemed especially cruel when Harold Bower was killed in a tractor accident on his Iowa farm in mid-July, just before Georgie's twelfth birthday.

Once the trial wrap-ups were over, the media turned to the revelations about police corruption. Clarke Buckendahl, Howie Vanick, and Joe Hein were still working as sheriff's policemen. The *Southtown Economist* headlined Phil Kadner's column about the situation, "Masters' former brothel partner remains a cop." Sheriff James O'Grady, elected as a reformer, seemed disinterested in taking action. Indeed, O'Grady became the invisible man. The story would not die down, and on August 19, 1989, the three officers were suspended for violating department regulations.

CHAPTER 5

$\mathcal{A}$t 2:15 p.m. on Thursday, August 24, 1989, there was a reunion of sorts in Judge Zagel's courtroom. Before proceedings could begin, Bill Murphy asked to speak to the judge about a series of articles which had been running in the *Chicago Tribune*. Keating appeared as a major figure in the series, and Murphy was concerned about the impact on Zagel. Before Murphy could get any further, Judge Zagel interjected, "It's very difficult to imagine what effect it would have since I didn't read them...I hate to admit this for the record, but I am not a devout reader of newspapers...particularly not a devout reader of newspaper articles about crime, the police, prosecution, or law-related issues..."

Murphy was incredulous. "It's been all over. It was on TV. It was also alluded to in the *Sun-Times*."

"It is all a complete mystery, Mr. Murphy. I don't know what you are talking about." The judge added that if he had read the series, he would give Murphy a separate chance to comment on it. The only item he did see was a short piece about the suspension of Vanick, Buckendahl, and Hein.

Then Keating rose to address the judge, the first and only time he spoke in sentences. "Your Honor, I don't mean to be disrespectful. Somebody saw fit to cut a small article and put it on your desk, but nobody left pages and pages of information, headlines with pictures of me, full page articles, nobody saw fit to cut that out and put it on your desk but one small article?"

"No," was the curt reply. "Are we ready?" Then he proceeded to deny defense motions for a new trial and the other motions that were presented as a matter of form.

In arriving at the sentences, it was permissible for Judge Zagel to have access to evidence not presented before the jury, including the Keating and Corbitt proffers. "Facts in aggravation and mitigation do not have to be proved beyond a reasonable doubt," Zagel explained, "may not actually have to be proved by a preponderance of the evidence."

Tom Scorza was concerned about letters written on behalf of Alan Masters that depicted the convicted lawyer Masters as ethical and honest. Scorza was prepared to present evidence from the investigation of corruption in the Fifth Circuit Court District that would set the record straight.

But if Judge Zagel did not read newspapers, neither did he put much faith in presentencing letters. He was aware that letter writers are usually selected because of their positive attitude toward the defendant and observed that he had never seen a letter with negative information. Zagel indicated to Scorza that the court's time could be better used on other points. No slouch on picking up signals, Scorza said, "I will be guided by the Court."

The attorneys for defendants Keating and Corbitt presented similar arguments. Both men had been previously convicted on the same evidence, the jury did not convict on the insurance fraud or concealment of a homicide, so in essence both men were found not guilty of Dianne's murder. Both men were devoted to their families; Corbitt has a mentally retarded child, and Keating two children and an ex-wife who needed him.

Patrick Tuite informed the court that Alan Masters did not feel he had received a fair trial, but a light sentence would help his attitude. Then Tuite zinged the judge for refusing to step down. "Your Honor said you did [not] read anything about it, and we don't doubt that. But there is the feeling that you were involved...So going into this trial Mr. Masters has felt the deck has been stacked against him."

Masters was responsible for many good works, including visiting "old people's homes," taking ice cream along with him. This prompted one of the elderly courtroom buffs to remark, "It isn't bad enough to get old. It isn't bad enough to get stuck in a nursing home. It isn't bad enough that every four years you provide a captive audience for presidential candidates. Now on top of all that, you've got to put up with having Alan Masters bring you dessert. I hope they lock him up forever."

But Tuite was not finished. Masters' clout extended even to the Mayo Clinic, and he helped people beat the long lines to get in. He would be willing to help Judge Zagel or Tom Scorza, as well as members of their families, should they need a fast admission.

At this point, there was a rustling noise in the spectator seats as onlookers shifted their weight. Heads twisted to see if Scorza's expression had changed. It had not. The prosecuting attorney still looked as if he were smelling something very bad indeed.

As Tuite waved a videocassette of Georgie's plea to the judge, he confirmed rumors that someone had notified the State of Illinois that Georgie was being physically and/or sexually abused. When a caseworker called, Alan responded in "his own inimitable fashion," according to Tuite. The caseworker could have all the time with Georgie that was necessary, but if she found the complaint unfounded, Alan would be rewarded with caseworker's children. When the interview was over, the caseworker supposedly asked, "When do you want me to bring my kids over?"

When it was Scorza's turn, he was contemptuous. "I am somewhat surprised by the comments...suggesting that the Court has not been fair. But...there is no question whatsoever why...Alan Masters cannot recognize an honest and a fair judge."

Then Scorza related an experience he had while watching television coverage about the suppression of student activities in

China, including the government line that no one had been shot. One of Scorza's children expressed disbelief that anyone could write a news story while knowing it was false. Scorza replied, "you have to understand that [these] people are not really lying in the sense that we mean it. They have reconstructed reality so as to take away what really happened out of their mind."

To which the prosecutor's child replied, "I can't believe that somebody can reconstruct reality like that."

"Well, that's because you've never met a defense attorney," Scorza explained.

Describing the defense's presentation on behalf of Masters as obscene, Scorza said, "Alan Masters was the most notoriously corrupt attorney in the south suburbs. He defiled every courtroom that he ever slithered into."

With regard to Dianne, Scorza observed that "some of the remarks about Dianne Masters were so offensive that I just let them stand in front of the jury. I had planned to defend her. I didn't have to. But I will defend her here. I don't think Dianne Masters for her mortal sins was all that bad of a human being. She wanted love, and she had none at home, and she found it elsewhere. I don't believe that is the greatest sin of a woman...I can't believe that a just and merciful God turns his back on Dianne Masters, and although I'm not a pious man, I see a lot of things that make me think that this case turned out the way it did as a way of signaling to us that Dianne Masters was not the human being portrayed by the defense at trial."

Scorza also addressed a question on the minds of many people who never thought they would find themselves in the middle of a murder case. "Judge, there is a big mystery in this case for me, and the mystery is how a just God allows people like Masters and Corbitt and Keating to crawl on the face of the earth. I think it's to test our mettle. I think it's to test to see what we will do when faced with them, to see if we will flinch."

Finally, Scorza gave credit to the men who had worked to put the case together: Paul Sabin, John Reed, Robert Colby, Ivan Harris, and Roger Griggs, as well as the grand and petit jurors.

Judge Zagel began by observing that the sentences requested by the government could mean a life sentence for the three middle-aged men before him. Zagel acknowledged that all of the defendants had demonstrated a level of devotion to their children, adding, "I do have some concern with the degree to which Mr. Masters' daughter participated in these proceedings."

The positions the three men had held permitted them to commit crimes beyond the reach of ordinary citizens. "The crimes and the people who commit them do damage beyond the immediate damage to the criminal justice system which they serve. In the case of defendants Corbitt and Keating, they damage police officers...somewhere, somehow, some innocent police officer pays that price of not being believed, not being listened to, and not being obeyed. And society suffers as a result. The damage done to lawyers and to courts by the kinds of actions found in this case are similarly great...defendant Masters..has damaged the image of all lawyers."

Judge Zagel accepted the proffers in which both Keating and Corbitt said that Alan Masters admitted murdering Dianne. Even if Alan made these statements falsely, "they display a callous immoral sensibility in personality that the Court cannot disregard in imposing sentence." The judge repeated that it was unnecessary that he determine whether Alan actually committed the murder, because the evidence that he planned and solicited it was bad enough. The judge also found on the basis of the evidence that Michael Corbitt aided in the concealment of the homicide. Michael Corbitt was sentenced to twenty years, without fine, to run concurrent with his previous sentence of four years.

James Keating was sentenced to twenty years on Count 1, and to fifteen years on Count 2, the two sentences to run consecutive to each other, but concurrent with Keating's previous sentence of fifteen years.

Alan Masters was sentenced to twenty years on Count 1 and to a consecutive twenty years on Count 2. He was also fined.

Beginning on September 1, 1989, a rash of articles and an editorial praising Howard Vanick appeared in Chicago papers. The prime mover was FBI Agent Robert Scigalski, who claimed Vanick was "an unsung hero...I would compare this guy to Serpico, but I think Vanick was better than Serpico." The bashful Vanick was quoted as not wanting to reveal his undercover role even when he was suspended.

Vanick's role was apparently under such deep cover that Tom Scorza never heard about it. On September 10, 1989, The *Sun-Times* carried a story headlined, "Did 'hero' cop in Masters case Inspire Killing?" Questioned about his role in revealing Dianne's affair to Alan, Vanick said, "I told others about it and it apparently got back to Masters. I wish I hadn't taken lunch that day."

When the *Chicago Sun-Times* sued under the Freedom of Information Act, the proffers and presentencing letters were made public. In anticipation of this, a lawyer for Robert Rosignal tried to have the cop's name expunged from Corbitt's statement but did not move swiftly enough. On September 8, 1989, Rosignal made the headlines. In his case, O'Grady moved quickly. Internal investigations personnel went to Rosignal's home, asking for his gun, badge, and squad car. He spent the next month in a locker room, then was placed on restricted duty.

Buckendahl and Hein resigned before their suspension hearing; Vanick was hailed as a hero and promoted.

On February 6, 1991, the United States Court of Appeals for the Seventh Circuit upheld the convictions of Masters, Keating, and Corbitt. Scorza, Murphy, and Tuite argued that new sentencing guidelines might apply to Count 2. That Scorza joined the defense counsel on the question did not give defense counsel pause, but it should have. He figured that under the new guidelines, Keating and Masters would serve more time.

The case was returned to Judge Zagel to make that determination and if the trial judge found that the guidelines did apply, to impose new sentences. Corbitt's lawyer did not ask for the guidelines, so he was not included. Judge Zagel also was called upon to enter a finding as to whether the $250,000 fine would impose a hardship on Masters' family.

On July 12, 1991, Alan Masters reappeared in Judge Zagel's courtroom. Dressed in a federal prison blue jump suit, Masters waddled out of the holding cell, to the accompaniment of a toilet flushing.

Judge Zagel decided that the new guidelines applied, and he would later sentence Alan Masters to the maximum twenty years, but this time without parole.

Although there had been ample time to prepare them, not all the financial documents that would enable the judge to rule on whether or not the fine was a hardship were not available. The defense was given three weeks to come up with the paperwork.

When Patrick Tuite argued for a lenient sentence, since the jury had found his client not guilty of murder, Scorza interjected, "Judge, I wrote the indictment and I will eat the indictment if Mr. Tuite can show me...that it charges murder. It deliberately did not." When Tuite continued the same line of argument, Scorza repeated his promise to devour the indictment, adding, "...and I'll do it publicly."

When Judge Zagel added additional time because a firearm was used in Dianne's murder, Tuite tried to argue that the government proved "quite effectively that the lady was dead when the firearm was used...There is no criminal act to punish someone for shooting a dead body." Scorza replied that there was uncertainty as to whether Dianne was dead or dying when she was shot, but that it did not matter. Some legal wrangling over precedents followed, but in Illinois law, a person is not dead, no matter how decomposed, until the medical examiner or a physician declares death as occurred.

When all the lawyers and the judge finished thumbing through heavy binders containing the new guidelines, Zagel was ready to pronounce his decision, because of "...my basic finding that the defendant's actions were such that he is liable for the death of his wife." Legal jargon calls this "the preponderance of the evidence" and may be used by the judiciary, although not by juries who must find guilt beyond a reasonable doubt. Further action was postponed for three weeks so that the defense could come up with the required financial documents. It was clear that Masters would not get off lightly.

However, on August 2, 1991, Patrick Tuite explained he had been trying another case which included an instruction conference the previous evening ending at 7:30 p.m.

"He was in an instruction conference that was all in Chinese," Tom Scorza observed, referring to Tuite's participation in a gambling case involving members of Chicago's Chinatown.

Tuite continued to describe Alan's impoverishment, stating his net worth at a mere $1,740. There were snorts from the spectator benches at that.

Tom Scorza observed that his office had knowledge of various holdings and trusts, some of which were not included in the statements. "...if there is something improper about the affidavit, there is the possibility of a criminal investigation...the matter of the fine could be reopened on the theory that fraud was committed on the Court." With that admonition, Scorza was willing to proceed.

The judge agreed, so long as both the Masters' provided affidavits "consistent with the representations." Then he warned that if these documents were found to be "materially untrue," the government had the power and the ability to request the court to impose substantial sanctions.

Then Zagel announced that Masters would have to serve the two sentences consecutively. Alan would be eligible for parole on Count 1 after approximately seven years, and if parole were granted, he would immediately begin serving his sentence on Count 2. If he received the maximum time off for good behavior, he would serve a minimum of twenty-four to thirty years.

Outside the courtroom, an ebullient Tom Scorza made the point that seldom does a defendant appeal and receive a longer term. The usually amiable Patrick Tuite dashed past the assembled reporters, snorting, "Great country, America."

Although he swore that his only asset was a fund balance slightly over $1,700, Alan Masters was able to raise funds to appeal his sentence. In the fall of 1992, the Court of Appeals for the Seventh Circuit upheld Judge Zagel's resentencing.

Writing in behalf of the panel, Judge Easterbrook observed that, "Judges and genies have this in common: by granting supplicants exactly what they wish for, they may produce misery and regret. Alan Masters, sentenced to forty years in prison for racketeering activities that ran the gamut from protecting bookies to soliciting the murder of his wife, asked to be resentenced under the guidelines...Masters now rues his request and appeals again. So does his henchman James Keating, who on the first appeal adopted Masters' arguments but now disclaims any desire for a guideline sentence."

In other words, be careful what you ask for, because you might get it.

EPILOGUE

I cannot rest, I cannot rest
In straight and shiny wood
My woven hands upon my breast—
The dead are all so good!
The earth is cool across their eyes
They lie there quietly.
But I am neither old nor wise;
They do not welcome me.

—Dorothy Parker

*I*t would be satisfying to write that the widespread corruption and criminal activity revealed during the Masters trial resulted in a cleanup of the system, but it would be untrue. Some of Alan Masters' corrupt coterie have been indicted, and their trials are pending; others have died or been retired by the voters. But hustlers and fixers still ply their trade in the courthouses, and ugly secrets lurk behind otherwise wholesome appearing suburban facades. Many of the law enforcement officials who knew what was going on are still holding down the same or better jobs, while the talents of cops like John Reed are not being fully used.

Alan Masters originally was sent to the Federal Correctional Institution (FCI) in Oxford, Wisconsin but was moved for security reasons. As of spring 1993, he is doing his time in the FCI in Memphis, Tennessee. In May 1993, the U.S. Supreme Court refused his latest appeal on the guidelines resentencing, so that he will serve a minimum of twenty-four to thirty years.

In June 1990, Michael Corbitt was prosecuted for the third time by Tom Scorza, receiving a four-year sentence for tampering with evidence related to his first conviction. Although Corbitt did not appeal his sentence on the guidelines issue as did Messrs. Masters and Keating, Scorza swore to find a way to do so. In November 1992, he made good on that promise. Judge Zagel changed Corbitt's sentence, assuring that he will serve at least seventeen years before parole. In May 1993, Corbitt's lawyers filed an appeal of the resentencing.

Corbitt was imprisoned at Latuna, Texas, until February 1993, when he was moved to a minimum security institution (known in the prison business as Club Fed), at Tallahassee, Florida. According to Corbitt, this was due to his "outstanding record" as an inmate. He has dropped about forty pounds, lowered his cholesterol, and no longer has to take high-blood-pressure medication. His wife and son live in Fort Lauderdale.

James Keating resides at the FCI in Oakland, Louisiana. Keating is employed by Unicor, a prison industry, which pays him two hundred dollars per month, big money in the big house.

Jack Bachman was sentenced to four years at the FCI in Yankton, South Dakota. This was considered a harsh sentence given the extent of Bachman's cooperation and the fact that without him, there might not have been a case. When Bachman's lawyer neglected to file an appeal within the statutory thirty days, Tom Scorza intervened with federal prison authorities. Bachman was released but must perform public service at a local hospital when his schedule as an over-the-road truck driver and construction worker permits.

Janet Masters still lives with her stepdaughter in the house on Wolf Road. She works part time as a point-of-purchase product demonstrator and has a seasonal tax business. Around the anniversaries of Dianne's murder and the discovery of her body, there are strange occurrences, and she frequently has called the Palos Park Police, who now have jurisdiction, about prowlers, minor vandalism, and on one occasion, finding a skinned cat in the backyard.

Georgie Masters, who bears a striking resemblance to her mother, was graduated from grammar school in June 1991. Other children have not always been kind about her predicament, but she has found a measure of security at a private school in Chicago.

Dianne's friends hope that someday she will want to talk to them about the mother she can scarcely remember.

The former Mrs. James Keating has lost her home in Michigan and declared personal bankruptcy. The Keatings' son is in college and their daughter repeatedly has entered drug and alcohol abuse treatment programs.

John Reed received a commendation from then U.S. Attorney General Richard Thornburgh and a much belated one from his own department. He still believes every case is solvable, and there are several he would like to tackle. For example, there are allegations that Alan Masters wanted to have a circuit court judge murdered, and Reed would like to know why.

Arlene Reed continues to teach in a southwest suburban school system. Nicole Reed is a freshman at DePaul University in Chicago, and young John Reed is a high school freshman.

Robert Colby likewise received a commendation from Thornburgh. In June 1992, Colby passed a rigorous FAA examination and was certified as a flight examiner. He has yet to teach John Reed how to land a plane.

The Colbys' older son Jim, named after his murdered grandfather, became an Eagle Scout in 1990 and attends Moraine Valley Community College. Robert, the younger son, is a high school student.

In February 1993, after twenty-three years on the force, Colby was promoted to sergeant.

Paul Sabin is a supervisor in the Felony Review Section of the State's Attorney's Office.

The FBI has yet to explain why it provided the media with erroneous information about Howard Vanick's "heroic" contribution to the Masters' case. Their motto seems to be, "Never apologize, never explain, and if we are wrong, we will hid behind the need for confidentiality in our operations." Observers and sources close to the investigation believe Vanick's matriculation at the FBI's pooch academy is not a sufficient reason for several agents to "pimp for Howie." Instead, the theory is that Vanick is aware that Dianne Masters went to the FBI and knows to whom she spoke. The agency does not want to be "embarrassed" should this get out, and so it suits both sides to protect the other.

Despite his unprofessional behavior in the Masters' case, Vanick's name is on the certified list for captain, and he is awaiting further promotion. He may have regretted "taking lunch" at the Charley Horse and informing on Dianne, but he remains a regular at the bar, where he can be seen reading *Police Chief* magazine.

Anthony Barone, the only person on the list of suspected accomplices named in the trial after he was picked out of a photo lineup, may have left the Chicago PD. In May 1992 he was indicted for evading more than one million dollars in fuel taxes on three personal businesses.

The former cop named by several people as Corbitt's partner in crime, who shall be called Berwyn Man for convenience, lives in the far west suburbs. Documents filed in divorce court reveal that under other people's names, Berwyn Man owned a plane, two large boats, a pricey home complete with bomb shelter, approximately $100,000 in silver, and several high-priced cars. During the trial, Judge Daniel Ryan, the same jurist who tried to intervene on Alan's behalf when Dianne was seeking a divorce, asked Mrs. Berwyn Man to describe what happened to the contents of a basement safe after a flood. The couple used hair driers to blow dry $500,000 in U.S. currency. When Judge Ryan asked where the money came from, the wife's attorney said his client had been kept in the dark on the subject.

Another man frequently mentioned as a potential conspirator was arrested by federal agents in June 1992 with $500,000 in counterfeit bills and plates outside a suburban printshop. This individual purchased Mike Corbitt's home and drives a Corvette with the vanity plate "It Pays." No one believes this refers to hard work.

Yet another man on the short list for accomplices is a retired state policeman with a record of wife- and child-abuse complaints. Despite his background and his close connection with Alan Masters, he was recently hired by the sheriff's office to work in internal investigations, indicating that higher-ups still have not read the Masters' file—or they do not care.

The officer named by Jack Bachman as the recipient of bribe money from Cicero bookmakers has been promoted to deputy chief of patrol.

Besides the open murder charge and the identity of accomplices, there is another loose end: the mysterious "accidental" death of Annie Turner, which has yet to be looked into by the Cook County Sheriff's Police, the agency having jurisdiction at the time.

Ted Nykaza is bitter about the way he was portrayed in trial and because the government never paid for his emergency room treatment. He lost his home, and now lives in a trailer in downstate Iroquois County, where he continues to struggle with his drinking problem.

James O'Grady lost a particularly brutal reelection campaign to Democrat Michael Sheahan in November 1990, but not before he used his muscle to have Danny Davis, his stand-in at Special Operations Associates, presented with the Lambert Tree Award for "solving" the Masters case. Because this award customarily is given to police or firemen for spectacular acts of courage, it enraged the public safety professions. In August 1991, Tom Scorza announced Davis' indictment on charges of obstruction of justice in the investigation of SOA. As politicians go, O'Grady should receive has done the best disappearing act since Judge Crater.

James Dvorak, who served as O'Grady's second in command, faces prosecution in federal court on charges he took kickbacks for jail contracts, as well as bribes from bookmakers, and used political funds on gambling junkets to the Bahamas, Atlantic City, and Las Vegas. The long-expected indictment forced Dvorak's resignation as chairman of the Cook County Republican Party.

Sources in the U.S. attorney's office believe it is unlikely that O'Grady will be indicted, but say he will be "embarrassed" by forthcoming revelations.

Two of Alan Masters' close friends, former Judge Alan Stillo and his lawyer nephew Joseph, were convicted of corruption in federal court in July 1993.

Although Mike Sheahan received solid campaign support from members of the sheriff's PD, most of the men who presided over the CCSPD while Alan Masters and his pals ran amok are still there. Sheahan is about as invisible as his predecessor, except when he appears on the football field as a referee in professional games.

In response to the outcry from the media and the public, Sheahan created the position of inspector general and hired former FBI Agent Richard Stilling to fill it. Regarded as an "empty suit" by some of his more capable colleagues at the Bureau, Stilling has become known as Stallings among the sheriff's rank and file because of his slowness to act on department problems.

As one source close to the sheriff's office puts it, "Same toilet, different sheriff."

Robert Rosignal, named in Mike Corbitt's proffer, was stuck on restricted duty for three and one-half years, even after paying for a private polygraph examination which cleared him of involvement in the murder of Dianne Masters. He finally was returned to patrol in February 1993.

In a surprise victory, Republican Jack O'Malley was elected to fill out Richard M. Daley's term as state's attorney. He won a full term in November 1992, but seems no more inclined to pursue murder charges in the Masters' case than his predecessor.

Former sheriff Richard Elrod continues to serve as a circuit court judge and possesses the respect of his peers.

Patrick Foley is in private practice with the politically connected firm of Pope & John.

Sheldon Zenner is head of litigation for the firm of Katten, Munschen & Zavis. His representation of Lawrencia Bembenek, known as "Bambi" in the tabloids, won the former Milwaukee policewoman her freedom.

James S. Zagel presides from the bench in Room 1919. For light relief, he acts under the name J. S. Block and has appeared in two movies. In *The Music Box* (1989), he was typecast as a judge; in *Homicide* (1991) he played a doctor. He also presided over the trial of Walter Kozubowski, whom Scorza was supposed to succeed as city clerk after Kozubowski's conviction for hiring ghost pay-rollers.

In March 1993, Dr. Robert Stein retired as medical examiner of Cook County.

Mary Nelson left MVCC in June 1982 to become director of public relations at Oak Lawn Library. She currently is a consultant there.

Jim Church teaches economics at Moraine Valley.

Gen Capstaff is professor emeritus at MVCC.

Brigitte Stark made an excellent recovery from cancer, and manages a retail store in a northwest suburb. It was not until June 1990 that Brigitte was told that Dianne was buried at Saint Adalbert's. Since then, she and her husband Dan have maintained Dianne's hitherto neglected grave.

Before the trial, Pat Casey relocated to Florida to prepare for her and Bob Casey's retirement. Unknown to Pat until Bob filed for divorce, he has been living in unwedded bliss with Alan Masters' former mistress and Ted Nykaza's ex-wife, Sheila Mikel, who gave birth to their first child in the winter of 1993. They received $60,000 in a brown paper bag from Jan Masters to build the model home in which they live. In May 1993, the FBI obtained the divorce case file, and two FBI agents called on Casey and Mikel, reportedly asking why "the corrupt circle is still in place." Good question.

Rusty, Dianne's last surviving pet, stopped having nightmares after Alan's conviction, according to Ted Nykaza.

Red Gate Woods on the outskirts of Willow Springs has been closed to the public while environmental groups and government agencies argue over the danger from radioactive contamination. The U.S. Department of Energy, initially reluctant to admit anything could be amiss, has allocated $3.4 million to investigate.

In 1992, the Willow Springs PD conducted another auto-dredging operation in the canal. No bodies were found, but not all the cars have been pulled up.

Shaggy, Corbitt's associate in terrorizing hitchhikers, runs the Kankakee Count (IL) auto speedway.

Like most states, Illinois has an Attorneys Regulatory and Disciplinary Committee to police the profession. And also like most states, the Illinois ARDC seems more inclined to protect lawyers than the public. In the various courthouse scandals that erupted in the 1980s, the ARDC let juries do their job, and it was no different in the Masters case. They did order the transcript of the testimony of Diane Economou, the attorney who worked for Alan and heard him talk about killing his wife on various occasions, but who did not come forward with this information until years later, when Sheldon Zenner was interviewing her. As an officer of the court, it was her duty to inform authorities; her explanation that she was too afraid of Alan to do so seems particularly lame in view of the fact that she continued to work for him after Dianne's body was found. Further, after leaving his employ, she was not too afraid to solicit his support in her attempt to be nominated for a judgeship. She continues to practice law in the Palos area.

But even more galling to Dianne Masters' friends is the fact that Economou became active in the Crisis Center for South Suburbia, the shelter for battered women which Dianne helped found and nurture. Economou was president of the board at the time of the trial, and although she stepped aside briefly, she returned in this capacity.

The Crisis Center went through a rough patch when in 1989 the MVCC board decided to pull down the cottage housing it to make way for a parking lot. In order to build a new facility, the Crisis Center had to secure the approval of the Palos Hills City Council. During the the public meetings which followed, the good burghers of Palos Hills successfully fought against any new construction in their town. One person went so far as to pontificate, "If a woman gets hit by her husband, she probably deserves it." Just when it seemed the only shelter in the south suburbs would disappear, State Sen. William Mahar secured a new location on state property in nearby Tinley Park, with the full support of the mayor of the village. After a fund-raising drive brought in $3.3 million, the new edifice was opened in July 1991.

In November 1992, NBC aired "Deadly Matrimony," a four-hour miniseries "inspired" by this book. Starring Treat Williams as Alan Masters (see illustrations for the accuracy in casting) and Brian Dennehy as John Reed, the average percentage of verisimilitude never made it into double digits. It did provoke some reactions, however.

Mike Corbitt's suit to stop the telecast failed, but he is contemplating further litigation to prevent reruns.. He particularly resents being portrayed as a prosecution witness, since snitching is unpopular with fellow inmates.

In a fit of pique after hearing that Alan described her sexual talents as including the ability "to suck the chrome off an auto bumper," one of Alan's former doxies offered to go to the Masters' home and reenact how Dianne got hit in the master bath.

Another pal of Alan's revealed that the morning after Dianne's death, Alan was excited, almost frenzied, about ridding himself of his wife with Corbitt's help. "Mike's not such a macho guy," Alan chortled. According to Alan, Corbitt became so spooked by the sight of Dianne writhing in her death throes in the trunk, he shot her to speed the process along. This confirms the opinion of the forensic experts that Dianne was still breathing when shot. The only comfort to her friends is that the experts do not believe she could have regained consciousness during the twenty-plus hours between the bludgeoning and being sent to a watery grave.

Around the time the miniseries was scheduled, John Reed was taken off homicide investigations and bumped around to various outlying sheriff's substations, finally fetching up at the Criminal Court Building where, in a dazzling display of bureaucratic expertise at wasting talent, he has been assigned to serving writs and paper shuffling. By chance Reed met Stilling in the criminal court parking lot, but when he asked the inspector general about the hiring of the former state cop, Stilling was incensed. In the manner of a marine drill instructor, Stilling leaned into Reed's space, shouting that the sergeant should forget about the case and the file. In any event, the new IID man had a brief career with the sheriff's office, and reportedly was fired for incompetence.

On May 18, 1993, the same day the U. S. Supreme Court turned down Alan Masters' appeal, Chicago Mayor Richard M. Daley announced the nomination of Tom Scorza to the office of city clerk, a job vacated when the incumbent was found guilty of felony charges resulting from his hiring ghost payrollers.

Scorza met Daley when both men had children attending the same school, and Scorza contributed several thousand dollars to Daley's campaign. Daley turned to Scorza once beforoe when the mayor found himself in a tight spot. In October 1992, there was an uproar over Daley's perceived lack of reaction to the murder of yet another child at one of Chicago's housing projects. Amid much fanfare, the mayor announced that Scorza would head an anti-gang task force, but since the press conference, little change has been noticed.

Naming Scorza interim clerk would provide Daley with a two-year grace period during which he can decide which ethnic groups he will offend by not choosing one of their number for his mayoral ticket. A Polish-American has held the job for almost forty years, but African-Americans and Hispanics also want it.

Described in the *Chicago Sun-Times* as having "a squeaky clean image and a reputation for abrasiveness," Scorza promised not to run in 1995. Local pundits were puzzled as to Scorza's motives for accepting Daley's offer; making sure the folks who sell license stickers show up on time does not compare with the power he held in the U.S. Attorney's Office. There was speculation that would become Daley's new *eminence grise*, now that the old one has taken a job in Washington D.C. Scorza was considered a shoo-in by observers, but this was short lived.

On May 28, 1989, the *Chicago Tribune* ran a story headlined, "Rukn Whistle Blower Is Masters (sic) Pal," identifying Mike Corbitt as the "John Doe" who claimed he saw members of the vicious El Rukn gang who were helping the federal case have sex with female visitors to the MCC "openly and routinely." He also reported watching El Rukns swallow drug-filled condoms and balloons which had been smuggled into the sixth floor of the prison, and then obtain large quantitites of laxatives to speed the drugs through the g.i. tract. In response to demands from El Rukn defense attorneys, a federal investigation into activities by assistant U. S. attorneys is being conducted by the judges who heard the cases, and reportedly by the U.S. Justice Department's Office of Professional Review. Tom Scorza was the supervisor of these prosecutions, and the question became "what did he know and when did he know it?"

A couple of aldermen were dissatisfied with his response, and as a result, the confirmatio was delayed. By the end of June, six convictions were overturned, and more are expected.

On June 28, 1993, a tan and fit Mike Corbitt made yet another appearance in federal court, this time to recite what he knew about the special treatment afforded some of the cooperating witnesses in the El Rukn cases. On the same day, a former El Rukn general testified that he was permitted to have sex with his wife and another woman in a federal office building, and that he celebrated a couple of birthdays in the U. S. Attorney's Office, during which time he was given such gifts as Bugle Boy jeans, in the presence of Tom Scorza.

Scorza denied ever attending such an event, and Mayor Daley declared his continuing support. Alderman report receiving information from present and former associates of Scorza's office indicating that Scorza was aware of the misconduct. It was believed that Daley could push Scorza's nomination through the Council as a test of personal loyalty, but the situation began to run rapidly downhill.

When the nomination was announced, Scorza said he would take time off to prosecute O'Grady crony Jim Dvorak, but later announced that the Justice Department would not permit this. Scorza's explanation was that this would be seen as political because Scorza is a Democrat and Dvorak, a Republican.

On July 12, 1993, only two weeks after he announced, "I'll be damned if I'll withdraw." Scorza did just that, surprising everyone who knows his feisty nature. He appeared before the City Council Rules Committee, but not to present his case and make his explanations as expected. "I was taught by my parents and by the Roman Catholic sisters and brothers who pointed me in the right direction that there are things worth fighting for at whatever cost. Unfortunately, a twenty month stint as city clerk is not one of them." The eleven page statement giving his reasons for bailing out was paraphrased by the *Chicago Sun-Times* as a version of the country song, "Take This Job and Shove It."

On July 9, 1993, there was a major shake up in the sheriff's office. John Reed was taken off the shelf and promoted to lieutenant and is now working as a watch commander in the Sixth District, where he is Bob Colby's boss. He replaced Howard Vanick, who was moved to Skokie, the Cook County equivalent of Siberia for a man who lives in the southwest suburbs.

In addition to the El Rukn revelations, Corbitt allegedly is talking to authorities about his mob-related activities. In a story that was clearly leaked to the *Tribune*, it was reported that it is "much too early" to know if Corbitt's cooperation will result in any new charges in Dianne's murder. According to the news story, Corbitt was inspired to help the government after his resentencing. According to his lawyer, Corbitt is much upset by the article.

In fictional crime stories, all the loose ends are tied up, and the guilty are punished, which probably explains their long-term popularity, because it is not like real life. The murder of Dianne Masters is an open file, but no one is pursuing it, especially now that Reed and Colby have been promoted to other duties.

There is some consolation that in the past, every time the case seemed to hit a blank wall, something else popped up. Perhaps John Reed is right: Someone wants this one solved.